The Shanghai Maths Project

For the English National Curriculum

Series Editor: Professor Lianghuo Fan
UK Curriculum Consultant: Paul Broadbent

Practice Book 5

William Collins' dream of knowledge for all began with the publication of his first book in 1819. A self-educated mill worker, he not only enriched millions of lives, but also founded a flourishing publishing house. Today, staying true to this spirit, Collins books are packed with inspiration, innovation and practical expertise. They place you at the centre of a world of possibility and give you exactly what you need to explore it.

Collins. Freedom to teach.

Published by Collins
An imprint of HarperCollins*Publishers* Ltd.
The News Building
1 London Bridge Street
London SE 1 9GF

Browse the complete Collins catalogue at
www.collins.co.uk

© HarperCollins*Publishers* Limited 2016
© Professor Lianghuo Fan 2016
© East China Normal University Press Ltd. 2016

10 9 8 7 6 5 4 3 2 1

ISBN: 978-0-00-814466-1

The Shanghai Maths Project (for the English National Curriculum) is a collaborative effort between HarperCollins, East China Normal University Press Ltd. and Professor Lianghuo Fan and his team. Based on the latest edition of the award-wining series of learning resource books, *One Lesson One Exercise*, by East China Normal University Press Ltd. in Chinese, the series of Practice Books is published by HarperCollins after adaptation following the English National Curriculum.

Practice book Year 5 is translated and developed by Professor Lianghuo Fan with assistance of Ellen Chen, Ming Ni, Huiping Xu and Dr. Yan Zhu, with Paul Broadbent as UK curriculum consultant.

All rights reserved. No part of this book may be reproduced, stored in a retrieval system, or transmitted in any form or by any means, electronic, mechanical, photocopying, recording or otherwise, without the prior permission in writing of the publisher. This book is sold subject to the conditions that it shall not, by way of trade or otherwise, be lent, re-sold, hired out or otherwise circulated without the publisher's prior consent in any form of binding or cover other than that in which it is published and without a similar condition including this condition being imposed on the subsequent purchaser.

British Library Cataloguing in Publication Data
A Catalogue record for this publication is available from the British Library.

Series Editor: Professor Lianghuo Fan
UK Curriculum Consultant: Paul Broadbent
Commissioned by Lee Newman
Project Managed by Fiona McGlade and Kate Ellis
Design by Kevin Robbins and East China Normal University Press Ltd.
Typesetting by East China Normal University Press Ltd.
Cover illustration by Daniela Geremia
Production by Rachel Weaver
Printed by Grafica Veneta S. p. A

Contents

Chapter 1　Revising and improving
1.1　Multiplication and division / 1
1.2　Addition and subtraction of fractions / 3
1.3　Decimals (1) / 5
1.4　Decimals (2) / 7
1.5　Mathematics plaza — which area is larger? / 9
Unit test 1 / 11

Chapter 2　Large numbers and measures
2.1　Knowing large numbers (1) / 14
2.2　Knowing large numbers (2) / 17
2.3　Knowing large numbers (3) / 19
2.4　Rounding of large numbers (1) / 21
2.5　Rounding of large numbers (2) / 23
2.6　Square kilometres (1) / 25
2.7　Square kilometres (2) / 27
2.8　Converting kilograms and grams / 29
2.9　Litres and millilitres (1) / 31
2.10　Litres and millilitres (2) / 33
Unit test 2 / 35

Chapter 3　Dividing by two-digit numbers
3.1　Speed, time and distance (1) / 39
3.2　Speed, time and distance (2) / 42
3.3　Dividing two-digit or three-digit numbers by a two-digit number (1) / 44
3.4　Dividing two-digit or three-digit numbers by a two-digit number (2) / 46
3.5　Dividing two-digit or three-digit numbers by a two-digit number (3) / 48
3.6　Dividing multi-digit numbers by a two-digit number (1) / 50
3.7　Dividing multi-digit numbers by a two-digit number (2) / 52
3.8　Practice and exercise (1) / 54
Unit test 3 / 57

Chapter 4　Comparing fractions, improper fractions and mixed numbers
4.1　Comparing fractions (1) / 61
4.2　Comparing fractions (2) / 63
4.3　Comparing fractions (3) / 65
4.4　Comparing fractions (4) / 67
4.5　Improper fractions and mixed numbers / 69
4.6　Adding and subtracting fractions with related denominators (1) / 71
4.7　Adding and subtracting fractions with related denominators (2) / 74
4.8　Multiplying fractions by whole numbers / 76

Contents

Unit test 4 / 79

Chapter 5 Consolidation and enhancement

5.1 Large numbers and rounding (1) / 83
5.2 Large numbers and rounding (2) / 86
5.3 Four operations of numbers / 89
5.4 Properties of whole number operations (1) / 91
5.5 Properties of whole number operations (2) / 93
5.6 Properties of whole number operations (3) / 95
5.7 Roman numerals to 1000 / 98
5.8 Solving problems in statistics / 100
Unit test 5 / 103

Chapter 6 Addition and subtraction of decimals

6.1 Moving the decimal point (1) / 109
6.2 Moving the decimal point (2) / 112
6.3 Addition of decimals / 115
6.4 Subtraction of decimals / 117
6.5 Addition and subtraction of decimals (1) / 119
6.6 Addition and subtraction of decimals (2) / 121
6.7 Practice and exercise (2) / 123
Unit test 6 / 125

Chapter 7 Introduction to positive and negative numbers

7.1 Positive and negative numbers (1) / 129
7.2 Positive and negative numbers (2) / 132
7.3 Number lines (1) / 135
7.4 Number lines (2) / 138
Unit test 7 / 141

Chapter 8 Geometry and measurement (1)

8.1 Knowing circles (1) / 147
8.2 Knowing circles (2) / 149
8.3 Knowing circles (3) / 151
8.4 Angle concept and notation / 153
8.5 Measurement of angles (1) / 155
8.6 Measurement of angles (2) / 158
8.7 Measurement of angles (3) / 160
8.8 Calculation of angles / 162
8.9 Angles and sides in polygons / 165
Unit test 8 / 169

Chapter 9 Geometry and measurement (2)

9.1 Volume / 173
9.2 Cubic centimetres and cubic metres (1) / 175
9.3 Cubic centimetres and cubic metres (2) / 177
9.4 Metric units and imperial units for measurement / 179
9.5 Introduction to cubes and cuboids / 181
9.6 Volumes of cubes and cuboids (1) / 183
9.7 Volumes of cubes and cuboids (2) / 185
9.8 Volume and capacity (1) / 187
9.9 Volume and capacity (2) / 189
Unit test 9 / 191

Chaper 10 Factors, multiples and prime numbers

10.1 Meaning of integers and divisibility / 195

10.2 Factors and multiples / 197

10.3 Square numbers and cube numbers / 199

10.4 Numbers divisible by 2 and 5 / 201

10.5 Prime numbers, composite numbers and prime factorisation (1) / 203

10.6 Prime numbers, composite numbers and prime factorisation (2) / 205

Unit test 10 / 207

End of year test / 209

Answers / 214

Chapter 1 Revising and improving

1.1 Multiplication and division

Learning objectives

Multiply and divide numbers with up to 4 digits

Basic questions

1. Use the column method to calculate. (Check the answers to the questions marked with *.)
   (a) $135 \times 8 =$
   (b) $25 \times 47 =$
   (c) $29 \times 508 =$

   (d) $340 \times 890 =$
   (e) *$958 \div 9 =$
   (f) *$6500 \div 50 =$

2. Work these out step by step. (Calculate smartly when possible.)
   (a) $32 \times 111 - 2058$
   (b) $76 \times 29 + 76 \times 21$
   (c) $108 \times 52 - 43 \times 71$

   (d) $(1405 - 932) \times 33$
   (e) $680 \div (122 - 102)$
   (f) $238 \times (56 + 32)$

Revising and improving

3 Fill in the brackets.

(a) The product of the greatest two-digit number and the least three-digit number is (   ).

(b) The product of 780×50 is a (   )-digit number with (   ) zero(s) at the end.

(c) In □÷9 = 12 r △, the greatest number of △ could be (   ). When △ is the greatest, □ is (   ).

(d) □74 is a three-digit number. In □74 ÷ 50, when the number in the □ is (   ), the quotient is a one-digit number. When the number in the □ is (   ), the quotient is a two-digit number.

Challenge and extension question

4 (a) Using four different digits, 2, 3, 4 and 5, to form all the possible multiplications of two two-digit numbers, which one has the greatest product and which one has the least product? Write them down and then calculate the products.

(b) Without calculation, tell which product is greater: 12 345 × 67 890 or 12 346 × 67 889.

1.2 Addition and subtraction of fractions

Learning objectives

Add and subtract fractions with the same denominator

Basic questions

1. Use fractions to represent the shaded part in each of the following figures.

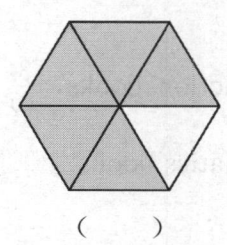

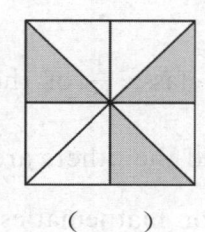

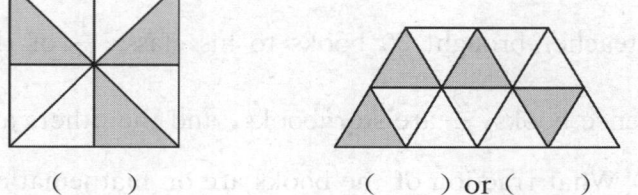

   ( )   ( )   ( ) or ( )

2. Use fractions to represent the shaded part in each of the following figures.

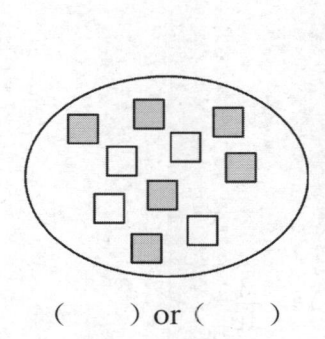

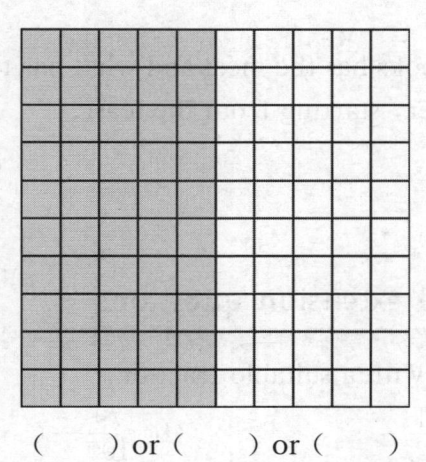

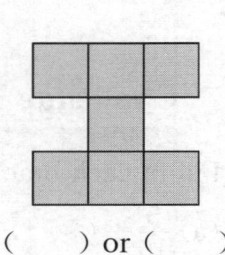

   ( ) or ( )   ( ) or ( ) or ( )   ( ) or ( )

3. Calculate.

   (a) $\dfrac{1}{5} + \dfrac{3}{5} = (\underline{})$

   (b) $\dfrac{2}{9} + \dfrac{3}{9} = (\underline{})$

   (c) $\dfrac{17}{53} + \dfrac{22}{53} = (\underline{})$

   (d) $\dfrac{56}{143} - \dfrac{36}{143} = (\underline{})$

   (e) $\dfrac{40}{87} - \dfrac{13}{87} = (\underline{})$

   (f) $\dfrac{117}{800} + \dfrac{34}{800} = (\underline{})$

   (g) $\dfrac{8}{19} - \dfrac{4}{19} + \dfrac{1}{19} = (\underline{})$

   (h) $\dfrac{52}{111} - \dfrac{51}{111} + \dfrac{50}{111} - \dfrac{49}{111} = (\underline{})$

Revising and improving

4 There are 30 pupils in a class. $\frac{3}{5}$ of the pupils are girls.

(a) What fraction of the pupils are boys?

(b) What is the difference between the number of girls and the number of the boys? First write your answer as a fraction of the total number of pupils in the class, and then write the answer using a whole number.

5 A teacher brought 50 books to his class. $\frac{1}{10}$ of them are fiction books, $\frac{3}{10}$ are science books, $\frac{2}{5}$ are storybooks, and the others are mathematics books.

(a) What fraction of the books are on mathematics?

(b) What type of books has the most and what has the least? Write the four types of books in order, starting from the least.

Challenge and extension questions

6 Fill in each bracket with a suitable fraction.

(a) $\frac{5}{16} + (\quad) = \frac{1}{2}$ (b) $\frac{79}{100} - (\quad) = \frac{3}{10}$

(c) $\frac{19}{22} - (\quad) = \frac{3}{22}$ (d) $\frac{37}{100} + (\quad) = \frac{1}{2}$

7 A storybook has 96 pages. Joshua plans to read through the whole book in three weeks. If he reads $\frac{1}{8}$ of the book in the first week, and $\frac{3}{8}$ of the book in each of the remaining two weeks, can he complete his plan? If he cannot, how many pages are remaining? (Hint: Use addition or subtraction of fractions to find your answer.)

1.3 Decimals (1)

Learning objectives

Read and write decimals and know their fraction equivalents

Basic questions

1. Think carefully and fill in the brackets.
   (a) 25.792 consists of ( ) tens, ( ) ones, ( ) tenths, ( ) hundredths and ( ) thousandths.
   (b) The number that consists of 2 hundreds, 3 tenths, and 4 thousandths is ( ).
   (c) 15.15 = 10 + ( ) + ( ) + ( )
   (d) 318.79 = 300 + ( ) + ( ) + 0.7 + ( )

2. Simplify the numbers using the property of decimals. The first one has been done for you.
   (a) 1.50 = 1.5
   (b) 0.0110 =
   (c) 6.0600 =
   (d) 120.000 =
   (e) 80.030 =
   (f) 16.200 =

3. Rewrite each of the following numbers as a decimal with three decimal places without changing its value. The first one has been done for you.
   (a) 1.2 = 1.200
   (b) 0.56 =
   (c) 3 =
   (d) 10.2 =
   (e) 50.1 =
   (f) 120.55 =

4. Write the following fractions as decimal numbers.
   (a) $\frac{1}{10} =$
   (b) $\frac{1}{5} =$
   (c) $\frac{1}{4} =$
   (d) $\frac{7}{10} =$
   (e) $\frac{29}{100} =$
   (f) $\frac{237}{1000} =$

5. Fill in each bracket with a suitable decimal number. (Note: £1 = 100p and 1 m = 100 cm.)
   (a) 1p = ( ) pounds
   (b) 15p = ( ) pounds
   (c) 220p = ( ) pounds
   (d) £5 and 5p = ( ) pounds

Revising and improving

(e) 5 cm = (　　) m　　　　　(f) 10 cm = (　　) m
(g) 550 cm = (　　) m　　　　(h) 3 m 18 cm = (　　) m

6 Round the following decimals to their nearest whole numbers.

0.09　　　　　0.9　　　　　59.3　　　　　219.5
(　　)　　　　(　　)　　　　(　　)　　　　(　　)

Challenge and extension question

7 A decimal number with two decimal places has the following features: ① The value of the whole number part is 5 greater than the greatest one-digit number. ② The sum of the digits in the tenths and hundredths places is 16. What is the number?

1.4 Decimals (2)

Learning objectives

Read, write, order and compare decimals

Basic questions

1. Work on the number line.
   (a) Mark 0.5, 10, 5.5, 19.5, 8.5, 14.5 and 16.5 on the number line.

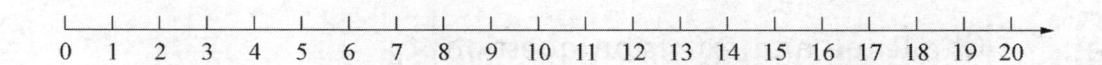

   ```
   |—|—|—|—|—|—|—|—|—|—|—|—|—|—|—|—|—|—|—|—→
   0  1  2  3  4  5  6  7  8  9 10 11 12 13 14 15 16 17 18 19 20
   ```

   (b) Which one of the numbers in question (a) is the greatest? Which one is the least?

   (c) Write the numbers in order, starting from the least.

   _____

2. Write the following decimals as fractions.
   (a) 0.1 =   (b) 0.01 =   (c) 0.23 =
   (d) 0.2 =   (e) 0.5 =   (f) 0.99 =

3. Fill in the ◯ with >, < or =.
   (a) 2.05 ◯ 1.99   (b) 0.75 ◯ $\frac{3}{4}$ (c) 32.35 ◯ 31.78
   (d) 0.909 ◯ 0.901   (e) $\frac{1}{10}$ ◯ 0.08   (f) 50.1 ◯ 49.9

4. Multiple choice questions.
   (a) There are (   ) thousandths in 0.1.
       A. 1   B. 10   C. 100   D. 1000
   (b) There are (   ) decimals with one decimal place greater than 0 but less than 1.
       A. 2   B. 5   C. 9   D. 10

Revising and improving

(c) The least decimal number with one decimal place is (   ).
   A. 0   B. 0.1   C. 0.01   D. 1

(d) The least decimal number with two decimal places is (   ).
   A. 0.99   B. 0.10   C. 0.01   D. 0.50

5 Comparing decimals.

(a) Put 0.01, 0.1, 0.001 and 0.90 in order, starting from the greatest.
   (   )>(   )>(   )>(   )

(b) Put the following measures in order, from the shortest to the longest.
   1 km 10 m, 0.91 km, 1.1 km, 1.50 km

Challenge and extension question

6 Use 0, 1, 2, 3 and the decimal point to write decimal numbers as indicated below.

(a) All the decimal numbers less than 1 and with two decimal places.

(b) All the decimal numbers greater than 2 and with three decimal places and 1 in the tenths places.

(c) All the decimal numbers between 0 and 3 and with 2 in the hundredths places.

1.5 Mathematics plaza — which area is larger?

Learning objectives

Calculate and investigate the area and perimeter of squares and rectangles

Basic questions

1. Write your answers in the brackets.
   (a) The side length of a square is 1 cm. What is the area of this square? (   )
   (b) If the side length of the square is doubled, what is the area of the square? (   )
   (c) If the side length of the square is tripled, what is the area of the square? (   )
   (d) What is the area of the square if its side length is increased so it is 4 times its original length? (   )
   And if it is increased to 5 times its original length? (   )

   What pattern do you find?
   (   )

2. (a) On the 1-cm square grid paper below, draw all the squares or rectangles that have different dimensions but with a perimeter of 20 cm.
   (b) Find their areas. Write your answers in the brackets below.

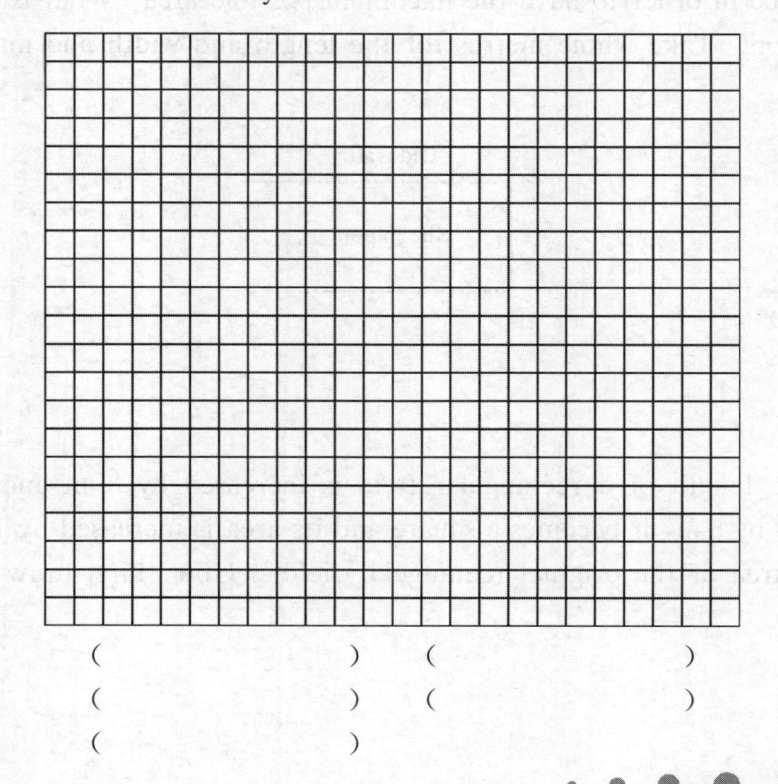

   (   )   (   )
   (   )   (   )
   (   )

Revising and improving

(c) The perimeters of the rectangles or squares drawn in question (b) are (   ), and the areas are (   ). When the length and width are (   ), the area is greatest. (Hint: Choose 'the same' or 'different' for the first two brackets.)

3 A rabbit wants to make a rectangular (excluding square) window with a perimeter of 140 cm for its home. How can the rabbit design the length and width of the window in order to have maximum possible sunlight through the window? (Note: Take whole centimetres for the length and width and make a table to analyse.)

Length (cm)				
Width (cm)				
Area (cm^2)				

Challenge and extension questions

4 Mr Wood wants to build a rectangular sheep pen and one side of the sheep pen is an old wall (as shown in the figure). Mr Wood has enough materials to build a new wall 32 m long. Help Mr Wood to design the sheep pen. How long and wide should it be in order to have the maximum possible area? What is the maximum area? (Note: Take whole metres for the length and width and make a table to analyse.)

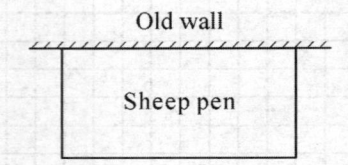

Old wall

Sheep pen

5 After the length of a rectangular field is increased by 3 m and the width is increased by 5 m, it becomes a square and its area is increased by 153 m^2. What was the area of the original rectangular field? (Hint: First draw a diagram to analyse.)

Unit test 1

1 Work these out mentally. Write the answers.
(a) $780 + 33 =$
(b) $4800 \div 60 =$
(c) $1200 - 276 =$
(d) $104 \times 4 =$
(e) $20 \times 35 =$
(f) $98 \div 7 =$
(g) $60 + 40 \div 5 =$
(h) $(48 - 33) \div 3 =$

2 Use the column method to calculate. (Check the answer to the question marked with * .)
(a) $82 \times 74 =$
(b) $860 \times 305 =$
(c) *$3400 \div 40 =$

3 Work these out step by step. (Calculate smartly when possible.)
(a) $125 \times 32 \times 25$
(b) $61 \times 89 + 61 \times 11$

(c) $385 \div (215 - 160)$
(d) $144 \times 59 \div 16$

4 Add or subtract fractions.
(a) $\frac{1}{7} + \frac{4}{7} =$
(b) $\frac{2}{15} + \frac{11}{15} =$
(c) $\frac{19}{29} - \frac{13}{29} =$
(d) $\frac{184}{365} - \frac{28}{365} =$
(e) $\frac{18}{49} + \frac{15}{49} - \frac{30}{49} =$
(f) $\frac{87}{100} - \left(\frac{33}{100} + \frac{11}{100}\right) =$

Revising and improving

5 Write the following decimals as fractions.
(a) 0.3 =	(b) 0.03 =	(c) 0.33 =
(d) 0.71 =	(e) 0.7 =	(f) 0.87 =

6 Fill in the brackets.
(a) 23.353 consists of (   ) tens, (   ) ones, (   ) tenths and (   ) hundredths and (   ) thousandths.
(b) 158.39 = 100 + (   ) + (   ) + 0.3 + (   ).
(c) Simplify the numbers using the property of decimals: 1.050 = (   ), 0.60 = (   ), and 365.00 = (   ).
(d) There are (   ) zeros at the end of the product of 150 × 60.
(e) If the quotient of 8)☐96 is a three-digit number, the least possible number in the ☐ is (   ); in this case, the quotient is (   ). If the quotient is a two-digit number, the greatest possible number in the ☐ is (   ); in this case, the quotient is (   ) and the remainder is (   ).
(f) Divide a 1 m long wire into 100 parts equally. The length of each part is (   ) m or (   ) cm. The length of 11 parts is (   ) m or (   ) cm.
(g) The length of a rectangle is 10 cm. If the length is increased by 2 cm while its width remains unchanged, then the area is increased by 16 cm². The perimeter of the original rectangle is (   ) cm.
(h) If the area of a square is 81 m², the perimeter is (   ) m.
(i) Rounding 25.49 to its nearest whole number, the result is (   ); rounding 50.50 to its nearest whole number, the result is (   ).

7 Use fractions to represent the shaded part in each of the following figures.

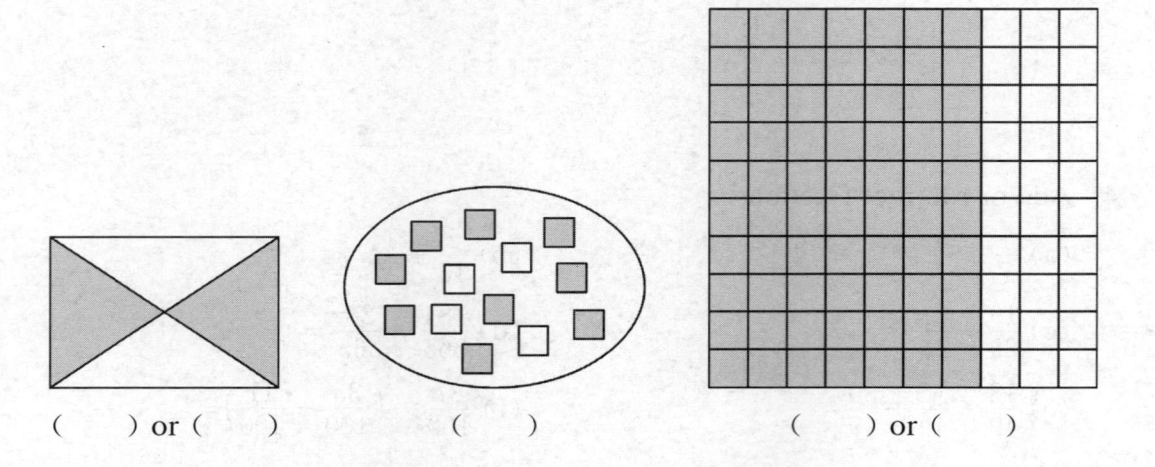

(   ) or (   )   (   )   (   ) or (   )

Revising and improving

8 Application problems.

(a) The weight of a baby bear is 69 kg. It is equal to the weight of 3 monkeys. What is the difference between the weight of a monkey and that of the baby bear?

(b) There are 60 balls in a bag. Half of them are black, one-third are white and the remaining are red. What fraction of the balls are red? How many of them are there?

(c) The perimeter of a rectangular flowerbed is 68 m. The length is 25 m. What is the area of this rectangular flowerbed?

(d) A rope is exactly long enough to enclose a rectangle with a length of 18 m and a width of 10 m. If the same rope is used to enclose a square, how big is the area of the square?

(e) Six identical squares with a side length of 3 cm are put together to form a big rectangle. What is the maximum perimeter of all the possible rectangles formed?

Chapter 2 Large numbers and measures

2.1 Knowing large numbers (1)

Learning objectives

Recognise the place value of the digits in large numbers

Basic questions

1. Understand large numbers.

   (a) Counting from the right, a large number can be separated into groups: ones group, thousands group, millions group, ..., and each group contains three places for different values: ones, tens and hundreds.
   Complete the table below.

Group	...	Millions			Thousands			Ones	
Place of value	...	Ten millions				Thousands		Tens	

   (b) The value of a digit is (   ) times the value of the same digit in the place to its right.

   (c) 378 028 867 consists of (   ) millions, (   ) thousands and (   ) ones.

   (d) When reading a large number, we start from the left with the largest group. For a number whose largest group is millions, we first read the millions group, then (   ) group and finally (   ) group. 378 028 867 is read as (   ).

   (e) When writing a large number of five or more digits in numerals, we start from the left with the largest group, and leave a space between each group (counting from right to left). Twenty-one million, one thousand and thirty-six is written as (   ).

Large numbers and measures

2 Complete the place value chart for each number and fill in the blanks. The first one has been done for you.

(a) 4019

Thousands	Hundreds	Tens	Ones
4	0	1	9

Read as: Four thousand and nineteen

4019 = 4×1000 + 0×100 + 1×10 + 9×1
     = 4000 + 0 + 10 + 9

(b) 25 198

Ten thousands	Thousands	Hundreds	Tens	Ones

Read as: _____

25 198 = ____ + ____ + ____ + ____ + ____
       = ____ + ____ + ____ + ____ + ____

(c) 412 708

Hundred thousands	Ten thousands	Thousands	Hundreds	Tens	Ones

Read as: _____

412 708 = ____ + ____ + ____ + ____ + ____ + ____
        = ____ + ____ + ____ + ____ + ____ + ____

(d) 2 395 198

Millions	Hundred thousands	Ten thousands	Thousands	Hundreds	Tens	Ones

Read as: _____

2 395 198 = ____ + ____ + ____ + ____ + ____ + ____ + ____
          = ____ + ____ + ____ + ____ + ____ + ____ + ____

15

Large numbers and measures

(e) 76 203 000

Ten millions	Millions	Hundred thousands	Ten thousands	Thousands	Hundreds	Tens	Ones

Read as: _____

76 203 000 = ____ + ____ + ____ + ____ + ____ + ____ + ____ + ____
         = ____ + ____ + ____ + ____ + ____ + ____ + ____ + ____

3. Fill in the table. The first one has been done for you.

Number in words	Number in numerals
One million, two hundred and one	1 000 201
One hundred and nineteen thousand and thirty-three	
Seventy million, seventy thousand and seven	
Nine hundred and sixty-one million, two hundred and seventy-three thousand, nine hundred and twenty-eight	
Five hundred million	

4. True or false.

(a) The number consisting of two ten thousands, two one thousand, and two ones is 2 000 020 002. (   )

(b) 50 040 600 is read as fifty thousand and forty thousand and six hundred. (   )

(c) In a five-digit number, the place with the highest value is the ten thousands place. (   )

(d) Nine hundred and nine thousand and nine is written in numerals as 909 009. (   )

Challenge and extension questions

5. Use four zeros and three sixes to form different seven-digit numbers as indicated.
   (a) Four zeros at the end: _____
   (b) Three zeros at the end: _____
   (c) Two zeros at the end: _____

6. Use six digits 3, 0, 1, 5, 7 and 9 to form the greatest and least possible six-digit numbers. What is the difference between these two numbers? (Write a number sentence to show your answer.)

2.2 Knowing large numbers (2)

Learning objectives

Compare and order large numbers

Basic questions

1. Fill in the brackets.
   (a) In a nine-digit number, the place with the highest value is in the ( ) place.
   (b) Counting from right to left, the fifth place is the ( ) place, the place to its right is the ( ) place, and the place to the left of the hundred thousands place is the ( ) place.
   (c) 2 003 500 709 contains ( ) billions, ( ) millions, ( ) thousands and ( ) ones.
   (d) In the number 10 506 000 090, '1' is in the ( ) place, standing for ( ); '5' is in the ( ) place, standing for ( ); '6' is in the ( ) place, standing for ( ); and '9' is in the ( ) place, standing for ( ).
   (e) 913 004 consists of ( ) thousands and ( ) ones. It can be also said to consist of ( ) ones.
   (f) 4000 can be seen as ( ) ones, or ( ) thousands, or ( ) hundreds.
   (g) The least seven-digit number is ( ), the least four-digit number is ( ), and the least seven-digit number is ( ) times the least four-digit number.

2. Multiple choice questions.
   (a) Two hundred and two thousand three hundred is written as ( ).
      A. 2 002 300   B. 202 000 300   C. 202 300   D. 2 020 300
   (b) In the number 6 104 510, '4' is in the ( ) place.
      A. hundreds   B. thousands
      C. ten thousands   D. hundred thousands
   (c) One billion is equal to ( ) millions.
      A. 10   B. 100   C. 1000   D. 10 000

Large numbers and measures

3 Fill in the ◯ with >, < or =.
(a) 34 796 ◯ 43 796   (b) 100 001 ◯ 99 999
(c) 900 100 ◯ 1 000 000   (d) Thirty million, three hundred thousand ◯ 30 300 000

4 Write the numbers that are greater than 69 997 and less than 70 003, and then represent them on the number line.
(a) The numbers: _____ , _____ , _____ , _____ , _____ .
(b) The number line.

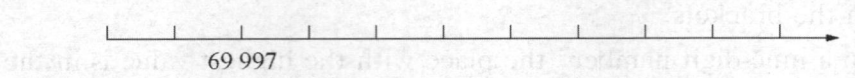

```
|___|___|___|___|___|___|___|___|___|___→
   69 997
```

5 The least five-digit number is subtracted by 23 and then added by the greatest three-digit number. What is the result?

6 Use the mental or column method to add or subtract large numbers. (Check the answers to the questions marked with *.)
(a) 608 000 + 200 000 =   (b) 236 549 − 36 000 =   (c) *720 055 − 22 000 =

(d) 32 495 − 30 001 =   (e) 225 329 + 154 019   (f) *5 800 000 − 712 012 =

Challenge and extension questions

7 Put the numbers 60 500, 50 600, 500 006, 56 000 and 65 000 in order, first from the least to the greatest, and then from the greatest to the least.

8 Find the populations of England, Scotland, Wales and Northern Ireland, and then add them up to find the total population of the United Kingdom. (State the source of your data.)

2.3 Knowing large numbers (3)

Learning objectives

Read, write, order and compare large numbers

Basic questions

1. Fill in the brackets.
   (a) 90 301 000 is a (   )-digit number. The digits '9', '3' and '1' are in the (   ) place, (   ) place and (   ) place, respectively. It is read as: (   ).
   (b) The number consisting of 60 millions, 54 thousands and 3 ones is written (   ) in numerals.
   (c) Six hundred and sixty million sixty thousand and six is written as (   ) in numerals. It is a (   )-digit number.
   (d) The digit in both the ten millions place and the thousands place is 6, the digit in the tens place is 8, and the digit in all other places is 0. The number is (   ), read as (   ).
   (e) Eight hundred thousand has (   ) ten thousands, and four hundred and thirty million has (   ) ten millions.
   (f) Adding (   ) zeros after fifty-seven, the resulting number is read as five hundred and seventy million.

2. Read the numbers underlined below and write them in the brackets in words.
   (a) According to the 2015 national statistics, the number of pupils in schools in England is 8 271 270.
   (   )
   (b) According to the Guinness World Records, the largest pizza weighed 23 250 kg.
   (   )
   (c) The Coral Sea is in the South Pacific Ocean, off the north-east coast of Australia. It contains the world largest reef system and has an area of 4 791 000 square kilometres.
   (   )
   (d) The distance between Pluto and the Sun is about 5 900 000 000 km.
   (   )

Large numbers and measures

3 True or false.
(a) The greatest seven-digit number is 9 000 000. ( )
(b) The number consisting of 70 thousands and 500 ones is 700 500. ( )
(c) A large number plus a large number is also a large number. ( )
(d) A large number minus a large number is also a large number. ( )

4 Draw a line to match each pair of the same number and then put all the numbers in order, from the greatest to the least.
(a) four hundred and five thousand and eight   A. 400 050 008
(b) forty million, fifty thousand and eight   B. 40 050 008
(c) four hundred million, fifty thousand and eight   C. 40 000 080
(d) four billion, fifty million, eight hundred   D. 405 008
(e) forty million and eighty   E. 4 050 000 800
(f) Put the numbers in order, from the greatest to the least:
_____

Challenge and extension questions

5 Given two numbers, 5976 and 1432, subtract 4 from the first number and add 4 to the second number. How many times do you have to do this before they become equal?

6 Joe and Alan are playing number games. Joe said, "I am thinking of a six-digit number, which is greater than the greatest five-digit number. The digit in its highest value place is 1, and the digit in all the other places is 0." Alan got the correct answer immediately. Do you know what the number is?

7 Remove four digits from the ten-digit number 5 704 590 212, so that, without changing the order, the six-digit number made up of the remaining six digits has the greatest value. What is the six-digit number? Repeat the activity, but this time remove four digits to leave the six-digit number with the least value. What is the number?

2.4 Rounding of large numbers (1)

Learning objectives

Round numbers to the nearest 100, 1000 and 10 000

Basic questions

1. To which whole hundred number on the number line is each of the following numbers nearest? Circle all such whole hundred numbers.

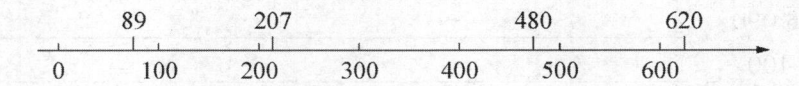

```
         89     207              480       620
    |----|-----|----|----|----|----|----|----|---->
    0   100   200  300  400  500  600
```

2. Write the whole ten thousands numbers that come before and after a, b, c, d and e. Put a √ against the ten thousands number that each number is nearest to.

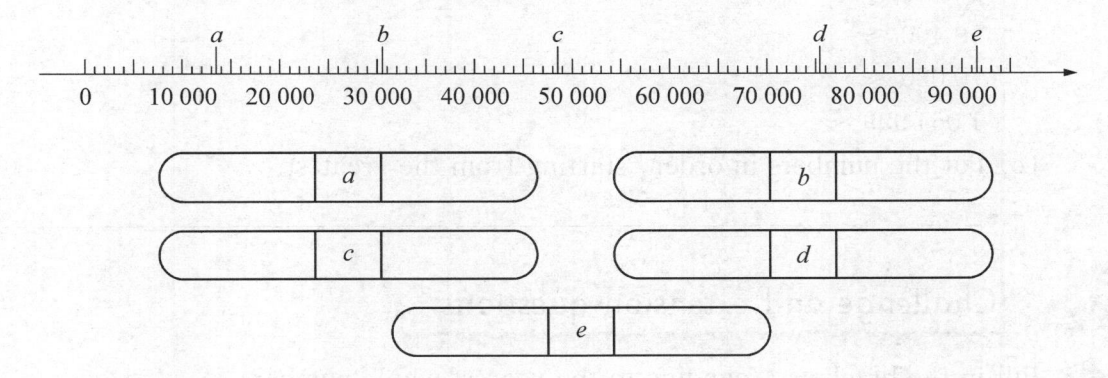

```
       a          b          c              d          e
   |---|---|---|--|---|---|---|---|---|---|-|-|---|---|-|-|---->
   0  10 000  20 000  30 000  40 000  50 000  60 000  70 000  80 000  90 000
```

( ) a ( )   ( ) b ( )

( ) c ( )   ( ) d ( )

( ) e ( )

3. Write the whole ten thousands numbers before and after each of the following numbers. Put a √ against its nearest ten thousands number.

( ) 32 108 ( )   ( ) 105 213 ( )

( ) 971 234 ( )   ( ) 120 087 ( )

( ) 6 401 239 ( )   ( ) 396 042 ( )

4. Round each of the following numbers to the nearest ten thousand.

(a) 10 999 ≈   (b) 56 089 000 ≈

Large numbers and measures

(c) 443 219 ≈   (d) 1 096 789 ≈
(e) 9167 ≈   (f) 9 950 123 ≈

5. Fill in the brackets with a suitable number.
(a) £81 023 ≈ (   ) thousand pounds
(b) 119 412 m ≈ (   ) thousand metres
(c) 2 095 802 m ≈ (   ) million metres
(d) £999 999 ≈ (   ) million pounds

6. A wholesale fruit market has 136 090 kg of apples, 59 400 kg of bananas, 70 020 kg of oranges and 1 064 999 kg of pears.
(a) Read and write these numbers in words:
136 090: _____
59 400: _____
70 020: _____
1 064 999: _____
(b) Round each number to the nearest ten thousand.
136 090 ≈
59 400 ≈
70 020 ≈
1 064 999 ≈
(c) Put the numbers in order, starting from the greatest.
_____

Challenge and extension questions

7. Fill in the brackets (rounding to the nearest whole number).
(a) Use 3 zeros and 4 sevens to make a number. The greatest number is (   ), read as (   ). Rounding it to the nearest ten thousand, the result is (   ).
(b) To make 56☐13589 ≈ 56 million true, the digit in the ☐ could be (   ). The greatest possible digit in the ☐ is (   ).
(c) To make 109☐028 ≈ 1 million and 100 ten thousands, ☐ could be (   ); the least possible digit in the ☐ is (   ).
(d) 10 056 217 101 ≈ (   ) billion.

8. Use 2 sevens and 5 zeros to make two different seven-digit numbers with the least possible difference. What are the two numbers respectively?

2.5 Rounding of large numbers (2)

Learning objectives

Round numbers to the nearest 1000, 10 000, 100 000 and 1 000 000

Basic questions

1 Write the whole hundred thousands numbers that come before and after a, b, c, d and e. Put a √ against the hundred thousands number that each number is nearest to.

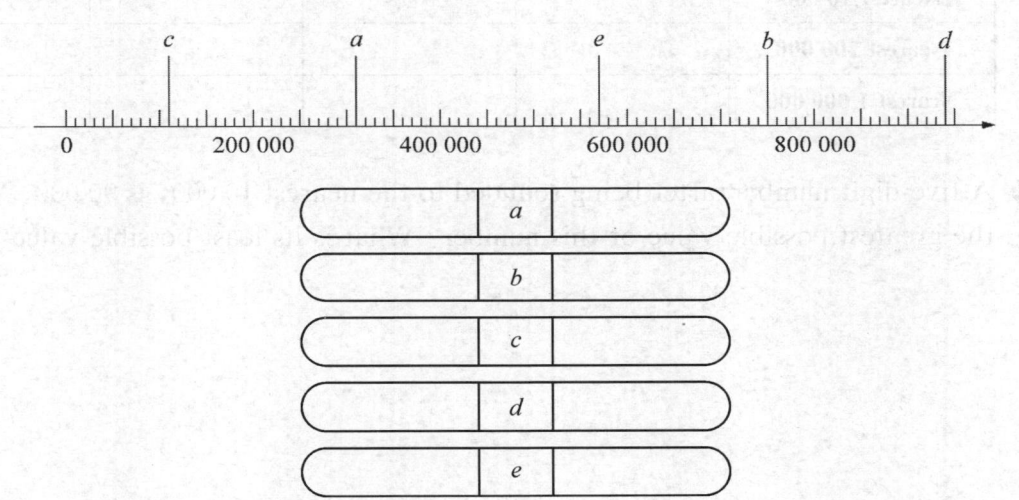

	a	
	b	
	c	
	d	
	e	

2 Write the whole ten thousands, hundred thousands and millions numbers that come before and after 56 435 900.

Whole ten thousands numbers

| | 56 435 900 | |

Whole hundred thousands numbers

| | 56 435 900 | |

Whole millions numbers

| | 56 435 900 | |

Large numbers and measures

3 Fill in the brackets.

When we round off a number, we first decide which digit is the last digit to keep. If the next digit to its right is (　) or more, it is increased by 1 and all the digits to its right become zero (known as rounding up). If the next digit is less than (　), leave it the same and all the digits to its right become zero (known as rounding down).

4 Round the following numbers to the nearest 1000, 10 000, 100 000 and 1 000 000.

	5 375 021	9 988 522	1 240 641	1 000 234
Nearest 1000				
Nearest 10 000				
Nearest 100 000				
Nearest 1 000 000				

5 A five-digit number, after being rounded to the nearest 10 000, is 90 000. What is the greatest possible value of this number? What is its least possible value?

Challenge and extension question

6 A number consists of 6 hundred thousands, 4 thousands, 5 hundreds and 3 ones. What number is it? When it is rounded to the nearest hundred thousand, what is the resulting number? What is the least number it should be added to so when the sum is rounded, the result is 610 thousand?

2.6 Square kilometres (1)

Learning objectives

Solve area problems involving square kilometres and hectares

Basic questions

1. (a) If the side length of a square is (　　), then its area is 1 square centimetre.
   (b) If the side length of a square is (　　), then its area is 1 square metre.
   (c) If the side length of a square is 1 kilometre, then its area is (　　).

2. 1 square kilometre = (　　) square metres.

3. Calculate the area of the figure as shown.

   3 km
   4 km

4. Find the area of the shaded part.

   12 km
   12 km
   6 km
   6 km

5. Multiple choice questions.
   (a) The land area of the United Kingdom is about 245 000 (　　).
      A. square kilometres   B. metres   C. square metres   D. kilometres
   (b) The total area of Greater London is about 1600 (　　).
      A. square kilometres   B. metres   C. square metres   D. kilometres
   (c) Manchester Airport occupies an area of approximately 6 (　　).
      A. square kilometres   B. metres   C. square metres   D. kilometres
   (d) The total floor area of London Olympic Stadium is approximately 108 500 (　　).
      A. square kilometres   B. metres   C. square metres   D. kilometres

Large numbers and measures

(e) The surface area of Loch Ness in Scotland is about 56 (　　).
  A. square kilometres   B. metres   C. square metres   D. kilometres

Challenge and extension question

6 Knowing new unit of measure 'hectare' (ha).

Marwell Zoo is located in the county of Hampshire, England. It is owned and run by the registered charity Marwell Wildlife and has an area of 57 hectares. Opened in 1972, it is a zoological garden where 1200 wild animals of 235 different species are kept for exhibition.

In the above context, we encountered a new unit of area, 'hectare', which is usually used to measure the area of land.

Do you know how many square kilometres 57 hectares are equal to? Let us first understand what hectare means. The area of a square with side length of 100 metres is 1 hectare, that is, 1 hectare = 10 000 square metres. So what is the relationship between hectares and square kilometres?

	Square with side length of 100 metres	The area is 100 × 100 = 10 000 square metres
1 **hectare**		
1 **square kilometre**	Square with side length of 1000 metres	The area is 1000 × 1000 = 1 000 000 square metres

Comparing the two areas in the table above, we can find that 1 000 000 square metres is 100 times 10 000 square metres, and therefore:

1 square kilometre = 100 hectares

or

1 hectare = 0.01 square kilometres

Can you use 'square kilometres' or 'hectares' to represent the areas of zoos in other cities?

	Hectares	Square kilometres
London Zoo	15	
Edinburgh Zoo	33	
Glasgow Zoo		0.4
Birmingham Zoo	49	
Welsh Mountain Zoo	15	
Belfast Zoo		0.22

2.7 Square kilometres (2)

Learning objectives

Convert between different units of metric measures for area

Basic questions

1. Write the relationships between different units of area.

1 km² = _____ m²
1 m² = _____ cm²

2. Which unit (cm², m² or km²) is most suitable to represent each of the following areas?
   (a) The area of the school field: (   )
   (b) The front cover of a mathematics book: (   )
   (c) The area of the whiteboard in classroom: (   )
   (d) The area of someone's house: (   )
   (e) The area of a postage stamp: (   )
   (f) The area of Asia: (   )

3. Fill in the brackets.
   (a) 26 km² = (   ) m²
   (b) 208 m² = (   ) cm²
   (c) 1900 cm² = (   ) m²
   (d) 13 000 m² = (   ) km²
   (e) 8 000 000 m² = (   ) km²
   (f) 5 m² + 420 cm² = (   ) cm²
   (g) 3000 m² − 2700 m² = (   ) cm²

4. Compare the measures and fill in the ◯ with >, < or =.
   (a) 11 km² ◯ 11 000 m²   (b) 8000 cm² ◯ 81 m²
   (c) 6 m² ◯ 60 000 cm²   (d) 3700 cm² ◯ 27 m²

Large numbers and measures

(e) 297 cm² + 213 cm² ◯ 5 m²   (f) 50 m² − 70 cm² ◯ 4000 cm²

5. Application problems.

(a) The United Kingdom is made up of four regions: England, Scotland, Wales and Northern Ireland. The areas of England, Scotland, Wales and Northern Ireland are 130 427 km², 78 772 km², 20 778 km² and 13,843 km², respectively. Answer the following:

(i) Which region has the largest area? Which region has the smallest area? What is the difference between the largest and smallest areas?

(ii) Which two regions have the areas that are closest to each other? What is the difference between their areas?

(b) A desk is 120 cm long and 60 cm wide. What is the surface area of the desk in cm²? What is it in m²?

Challenge and extension questions

6. A rectangular school field was 80 m long and 55 m wide. After reconstruction, both the length and the width were increased by 15 m. By how much is the area of the field increased?

7. A maximum possible square is cut out from a rectangle with length 12 cm and width 8 cm. What is the area of the remaining part of the rectangle?

2.8 Converting kilograms and grams

Learning objectives

Convert between kilograms and grams and solve measures problems

Basic questions

1. The relationship between kilograms and grams is:
   1 kilogram = _____ grams.

2. Fill in the ( ) with a suitable unit: kilograms (kg) or grams (g).
   (a) The weight of a puppy is about 2 (   ).
   (b) The weight of a bag of crisps is about 250 (   ).
   (c) The weight of a rhinoceros is about 6000 (   ).
   (d) A pear weighs 100 (   ).
   (e) Ben weighs about 30 (   ).
   (f) A rubber weighs about 6 (   ).

3. Fill in the brackets.
   (a) 307 kg = (   ) g
   (b) 17 kg = (   ) g
   (c) 6 000 000 g = (   ) kg
   (d) 1025 g + 71 kg = (   ) g
   (e) 43 000 kg + 4000 g = (   ) kg
   (f) 67 kg − 20 202 g = (   ) g

4. Fill in the ◯ with >, < or =.
   (a) 5 kg ◯ 500 g
   (b) 6000 g ◯ 6 kg
   (c) 7800 kg ◯ 8 000 000 g
   (d) 90 000 kg ◯ 9 000 000 g
   (e) 13 000 kg ◯ 1000 kg + 200 kg
   (f) 4000 kg ◯ 7000 g

5. Multiple choice questions.
   (a) A truck is loaded with 3 machine tools and 450 kg of accessories. Each machine tool weighs 800 kg. The truck is loaded with the total weight of (   ).
      A. 2050 kg   B. 2850 kg   C. 2150 kg   D. 1250 g
   (b) There is 482 000 kg of sand in a sand field. If a sand truck can be loaded with

Large numbers and measures

4000 kg of sand, how many trucks are needed to transport all the sand in one go? (   )

A. 120 trucks   B. 121 trucks   C. 122 trucks   D. 123 trucks

(c) 30 kg 900 g=(   ) g

A. 30 900   B. 903   C. 1200   D. 3900

6 Application problems.

(a) Tom's mother bought 4 bottles of sunflower oil. Each bottle weighs 2500 g. Find the total weight of the 4 bottles first in grams and then in kilograms.

(b) 8 electrical machines were loaded onto a truck which has a loading capacity of 5000 kg. The weight of each machine was 620 kg. Does the total weight of all the machines exceed the loading capacity of the truck?

(c) Mary's uncle harvested 5000 kg of pears in his orchard last year. If each box can be filled with 25 kg of pears, how many boxes can be filled with all the pears?

Challenge and extension questions

7 True or false.

(a) 1000 g of cotton is lighter than 1 kg of iron. (   )
(b) There are two 10 000 grams in 20 kilograms. (   )
(c) 1 kg is 30 g heavier than 70 g. (   )

8 The weight of a basket of apples was 46 kg inclusive of the weight of the basket. After selling half of the apples, it was 26 kg. What was the weight of the basket?

2.9 Litres and millilitres (1)

Learning objectives

Convert between litres and millilitres and solve measures problems

Basic questions

1. Fill in the brackets.
   (a) The amount of liquid is often expressed in millilitres and litres. When measuring a small amount of liquid, we usually use millilitre as the unit of measure. When measuring a (　　　) amount of liquid, we usually use (　　　) as the unit of measure.
   (b) 1 millilitre can be written as 1 ml. 1 litre can be written as 1 l or 1 L.
   1 l=(　　　) ml.

2. Which measuring cups of water can be added together to fill up a 1-litre bottle? Write the number sentence. _____

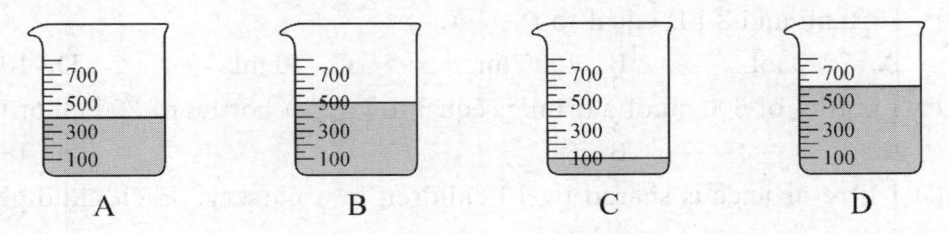

   A　　　B　　　C　　　D

3. Fill in the brackets with a suitable unit: litres or millilitres.
   (a) A tank of petrol: 30 (　　　).　(b) A bottle of refined oil: 5 (　　　).
   (c) A tub of yogurt: 250 (　　　).　(d) A bottle of eye drops: 5 (　　　).
   (e) A cup of water: 200 (　　　).　(f) A bottle of coke: 600 (　　　).
   (g) A bottle of liquid medicine: 10 (　　　).

4. Fill in the brackets.
   (a) 2 l=(　　　) ml　　　　(b) 800 l=(　　　) ml
   (c) 82 000 ml=(　　　) l　　(d) 50 l=(　　　) ml
   (e) 2 l 600 ml=(　　　) ml
   (f) 30 003 ml=(　　　) l (　　　) ml

Large numbers and measures

5 Application problems.

(a) Mary bought a bottle of 2 litres of plum juice. After pouring 400 ml into a cup, how many millilitres of plum juice were left?

(b) A 2-litre bottle of plum juice was shared equally among 8 children. How many millilitres of plum juice did each child get?

Challenge and extension questions

6 Multiple choice questions.

(a) 3 l 30 ml = (   ) ml
   A. 3300   B. 3030   C. 3003   D. 303

(b) 7000 ml and 3 l is equal to (   ).
   A. 7003 ml   B. 1000 ml   C. 10 ml   D. 10 l

(c) 4 bottles of 600 ml of a drink is equal to (   ) bottles of 200 ml of the drink.
   A. 3   B. 6   C. 12   D. 18

(d) 1 litre of juice is shared by 16 children in a nursery. Each child gets 50 ml. There are (   ) left.
   A. 800 ml   B. 20 ml   C. 2 l   D. 200 ml

7 375 ml of concentrated orange juice was added to 11 litres of water and then equally shared by 25 workers. How many millilitres of orange juice did each worker get?

2.10 Litres and millilitres (2)

Learning objectives

Convert between litres and millilitres and solve measures problems

Basic questions

1. Draw a line to match each pair.
   (a) a spoon of medicine   A. 1000 ml
   (b) a can of soft drink   B. 5 l
   (c) a bottle of cooking oil   C. 330 ml
   (d) a bottle of milk   D. 18 l
   (e) a bucket of water   E. 5 ml

2. Fill in the brackets.
   (a) When measuring the amount of liquid such as water and oil, we can use (   ) and (   ) as units of measurement.
   (b) 1000 ml of water can fill up a water bottle of (   ) litre/s.
   (c) 2 l of beverage can fill up (   ) cups of 500 ml each.
   (d) 13 l=(   ) ml
   (e) 12 000 ml=(   ) l
   (f) 10 000 ml=(   ) l
   (g) 5 l 500 ml=(   ) ml
   (h) 2 l+21 000 ml=(   ) l
   (i) 4 l 567 ml=(   ) ml
   (j) 56 010 ml=(   ) l (   ) ml
   (k) 10 700 ml=(   ) l (   ) ml

3. Put the following quantities in order.
   (a) From the greatest to the least.
       600 ml   5900 ml   7 l   5970 ml   70 l

   (b) From the least to the greatest.
       260 ml   2060 ml   2 l   200 ml   20 l

Large numbers and measures

4 Application problems.

(a) Sixteen crates of coconut milk were delivered to a supermarket. Each crate had ten 350 ml cartons of coconut milk. How many litres of coconut milk were delivered?

(b) There are 625 ml of soya milk in 5 packs of the same size. How many millilitres of soya milk are there in 8 such packs? How many litres are there?

Challenge and extension question

5 Fill in the blanks based on the diagrams shown below.

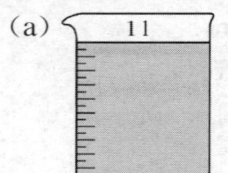

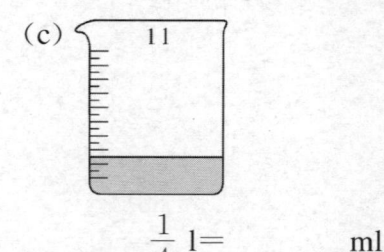

(a) 1 l = _____ ml

(b) $\frac{1}{2}$ l = _____ ml

(c) $\frac{1}{4}$ l = _____ ml

Three $\frac{1}{4}$ l = _____ ml

Two $\frac{3}{4}$ l = _____ ml

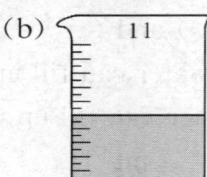

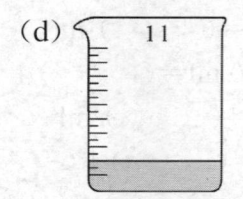

(d) $\frac{1}{5}$ l = _____ ml

Two $\frac{1}{5}$ l = _____ ml

Three $\frac{2}{5}$ l = _____ ml

Unit test 2

1 Work these out mentally. Write the answers.
(a) $90 \div 45 \times 2 =$
(b) $81 \div 3 + 9 =$
(c) $800 \div 20 - 10 =$
(d) $1000 - 90 =$
(e) $38 \div 19 \times 100 =$
(f) $240 - 15 \times 2 =$
(g) $280 \times 2 =$
(h) $4000 \div 100 =$
(i) $803 - 79 =$

2 Use the column method to calculate.
(a) $403 \times 16 =$
(b) $8098 - 909 =$

(c) $16\,018 + 994 =$
(d) $1600 \div 60 =$

3 Work these out step by step.
(a) $6129 - (715 + 1129) - 285$
(b) $3279 + 480 \div 30$

(c) $5760 \div 30 \times 72$
(d) $13\,320 - 222 \times 56$

4 Fill in the brackets.
(a) Counting from the right, the places in a number from the first place to the (   ) place are grouped as ones groups. They stand for ones, (   ) and (   ). The places from the 4th place to the (   ) place are grouped as thousands groups. They stands for thousands, (   ) and (   ). The places from the 7th place to the (   )

Large numbers and measures

place are grouped as millions group. They stand for (   ), (   ) and (   ).

(b) 9 025 000 is read as (   ).
It has (   ) millions and (   ) thousands.

(c) 70 700 000 is read as (   ).
It has (   ) thousands.

(d) 3 080 604 is read as (   ).
It has (   ) thousands and (   ) ones.

(e) It is a 6-digit number. 3 is in the highest value place. Another 3 is in the least value place. All the other digits are zeros. This number is (   ). It is read as (   ).

(f) Four million, thirty-four thousand and twenty is written as (   ) in numerals.

(g) 1 023 757 ≈ (   ) (to the nearest ten thousands)

(h) 659 313 664 ≈ (   ) (to the nearest ten millions)

(i) 90 000 m = (   ) km

(j) 70 km² = (   ) m²

(k) 20 l + 350 ml = (   ) ml

(l) (   ) kg − 3000 kg = 5300 kg

(m) 5 000 000 g = (   ) kg

(n) (   ) g = 300 kg

(o) Put the measures, 3 litres 400 millilitres, 7080 millilitres, 6 litres, and 10 litres 7 millilitres in order, starting from the least.
(   ).

5 Multiple choice questions.

(a) The two numbers that come before and after 20 000 are (   ).
A. 19 999 and 1999   B. 19 000 and 20 001   C. 19 999 and 20 001

(b) If 39☐270 ≈ 400 000 to the nearest 10 000, the numbers that can be filled in the ☐ are (   ).
A. 9, 8, 7, 6 or 5   B. 4 or 5   C. 0, 1, 2, 3 or 4

(c) Rounding £9 000 550 to the nearest 10 000 is (   ).
A. 9 million pounds   B. 9 million and 1 thousand pounds
C. 10 million pounds

(d) A rhino weighs about 2000 (   ), a bag of sugar weighs about 1000 (   ), a rabbit weighs about 8 (   ), and a bucket of water weighs about 19 (   ).
A. grams   B. kilograms   C. litres

Large numbers and measures

(e) In 805 794, the value that the digit '8' stands for is (　　) times the value that the digit '4' stands for.

 A. 20   B. 20 000   C. 200 000

(f) After adding (　　) zeros to the right of 37, it is 37 million.

 A. 4   B. 5   C. 6

6 Write the number sentences and then calculate.

(a) Subtracting a number from 330, the result is 98. Find the number.

(b) In a division, the quotient is 6 and the sum of the dividend and the divisor is 98. Find the dividend and the divisor.

(c) What is 4 times the difference between 78 and 31?

(d) The product of 23 and 105 is divided by 30. What are the quotient and remainder?

7 Application problems.

(a) How many 300 ml bottles can a bucket of water of 18 l fill up?

Large numbers and measures

(b) A canteen bought 60 bags of rice and 40 bags of flour. Each bag of both rice and flour weighs 50 kg. What is the total weight of these bags of rice and flour?

(c) 74 000 kg of cement was delivered to a construction site. The weight of yellow sand delivered to the site was 12 000 kg more than 3 times the weight of cement. What is the weight of the yellow sand delivered to the site?

(d) A rectangular footpath is 300 m long and 6 m wide. If 50 cm × 50 cm square slates are used to pave the footpath, how many slates are needed?

(e) Joan's mother bought a fish tank with a small hole in it. She turned on a tap to pour water at 300 ml per minute into the tank, but at the same time the hole was leaking water at 40 ml per minute from the tank. Five minutes later, Joan's mother noticed the leakage. At that time, how many millilitres of water were still in the fish tank? How many millilitres of water had leaked out?

Chapter 3 Dividing by two-digit numbers

3.1 Speed, time and distance (1)

Learning objectives

Calculate speed using given distance and time

Basic questions

1. Is each of the following statements correct? Put a √ for yes and a × for no in the brackets.
   (a) Speed tells how fast a moving object travels. (   )
   (b) Distance tells how much time a moving object has spent in motion. (   )
   (c) If Mr Lee walks 2 km in two hours, then his speed is 1 km per hour. (   )
   (d) If a bird flies at a speed of 2 m per second, then it can fly 120 m per minute.
   (   )
   (e) In a running race, the winner runs at the fastest speed and is the first person to cross the finish line. (   )

2. Fill in the table.

	Speed	Time	Distance
		3 hours (h)	42 km
		5 minutes (min)	4500 m
		20 seconds (s)	400 m

Dividing by two-digit numbers

3 Fill in each bracket with a suitable unit (km/h, km/min, m/min).

The pigeon flies at a speed of 65 (   ).   The lion runs at a speed of 1 (   ).

The elephant walks at a speed of 20 (   ).   The puppy runs at a speed of 330 (   ).

4 Read the following carefully, and then calculate and compare.
To celebrate a holiday, Mary, Joan, Tom and John planned to meet each other at the gate of a park at 9 o'clock to watch shows in the park. They arrived on time.
Mary left home at a quarter to nine. It is 1500 m from her home to the park. Her speed was _____.
Joan left home at 10 to nine. It is 1200 m from her home to the park. Her speed was _____.
John left home at 8 to nine. It is 1000 m from his home to the park. His speed was _____.
Tom left home at 10 to nine. It is 1300 m from his home to the park. His speed was _____.
Which of them walked the fastest? _____.

5 Application problems.
(a) Andrew walked to Jim's house for a party. The distance between their houses is 800 m. Andrew left home at 10 past 10 and arrived at 18 past 10. Find Andrew's walking speed.

(b) The distance between place A and place B is 800 km. A train leaves place A at 5 o'clock and arrives at place B at 10 o'clock. Find the speed of the train.

40

Dividing by two-digit numbers

> **Challenge and extension question**

6 The distance of the London marathon is 42 km and 195 m. Famous British marathon runner, Paula Radcliffe, is the women's world record holder in the marathon with her time of 2 hours, 15 minutes and 25 seconds. Her running speed is about (   ) m/s.

3.2 Speed, time and distance (2)

Learning objectives

Solve problems using the relationship between time, distance and speed

Basic questions

1. Fill in the blanks. The first one has been done for you.
   Distance = Speed (×) Time
   Time = _____ ( ) _____
   Speed = _____ ( ) _____

2. Compare and then fill in the brackets.
   (a) The distance between the school and the museum is 1 km. Both Bill and Jim walked to the museum from their school. Bill left at 16:00 and arrived at 16:15. Jim left at 16:05 and arrived at 16:18.
   Who walked faster? (   )
   When the distance is the same, we can compare the time. The less the time, the (   ) the speed.
   (b) Emmy and Joanne left school and walked home at 15:30. By 15:50 both of them reached their homes. The distance between Emmy's home and the school is 1500 m while the distance between Joanne's home and the school is 1650 m.
   Who walked faster? (   )
   When the time taken is the same, we can compare the distance. The longer the distance covered, the (   ) the speed is.

3. Fill in the table.

Speed	Time	Distance
	6 min	504 m
7 km/h		119 km
118 m/min	8 min	

Dividing by two-digit numbers

4 Application problems.

(a) It took Emily 5 minutes to walk 400 m while it took Samantha 4 minutes to walk 360 m. Who walked faster?

(b) Alvin and his mother left home at 7 o'clock in the morning. His mother drove to her office at a speed of 700 m/min, and Alvin cycled to school at a speed of 16 km/h. Both of them reached the office and the school at half past seven. Find out the distance between Alvin's mother's office and their home. How about the distance between Alvin's home and his school?

(c) A bicycle travels at 18 km/h and a motorcycle travels 27 km/h faster than the bicycle. How many kilometres can a motorcycle travel in 8 hours?

(d) Tim left home at 7 o'clock in the morning for school. After walking for 2 minutes he realised he had left his maths homework at home. So he went back to get his homework and arrived at the school at 28 minutes past 7. Given Tim walked at 100 m/min, and it took him 4 minutes to get home and find the homework, what is the distance between his home and the school?

Challenge and extension question

5 Four pupils were having a 100 m running race. Lily ran at 8 m/s, Anna took 13 seconds, Linda took 12 seconds and Mary ran at 7 m/s. Who ran the fastest among the four pupils?

3.3 Dividing two-digit or three-digit numbers by a two-digit number (1)

Learning objectives
Use mental and written methods to divide three-digit numbers by two-digit numbers

Basic questions

1. Work these out mentally. Write the answers.
   (a) $6 \div 2 =$
   (b) $8 \div 4 =$
   (c) $9 \div 3 =$
   (d) $21 \div 7 =$
   (e) $60 \div 2 =$
   (f) $80 \div 4 =$
   (g) $90 \div 3 =$
   (h) $210 \div 7 =$
   (i) $600 \div 20 =$
   (j) $80 \div 40 =$
   (k) $90 \div 30 =$
   (l) $210 \div 70 =$
   (m) $600 \div 200 =$
   (n) $800 \div 400 =$
   (o) $900 \div 300 =$
   (p) $2100 \div 700 =$

2. Think carefully, fill in each bracket and calculate.
   (a) In $99 \div 23 =$

   How many twenty-threes are there in 99?
   Think: How many (   ) are there in 99?
   There are (   ) (   ) in 99. The quotient is (   ).
   (   ) $\times 23 =$ (   ).
   The remainder (   ) is (   ) than the divisor.
   The quotient is (   ).

   (b) In $517 \div 63 =$

   How many sixty-threes are there in 517?
   Think: How many (   ) are there in 517?
   There are (   ) (   ) in 517. The quotient is (   ).
   (   ) $\times 63 =$ (   ).
   The remainder (   ) is (   ) than the divisor.
   The quotient is (   ).

3. Use the column method to calculate.
   $174 \div 21 =$ $195 \div 53 =$ $132 \div 22 =$

Dividing by two-digit numbers

$222 \div 43 =$ $347 \div 74 =$ $608 \div 86 =$

4 These animals are having a 1 km running race. Look at their speeds and answer the questions.

12 m/s    10 m/s    13 m/s

Position: Reason:
In 1st place is _____ _____.
In 2nd place is _____ _____.
In 3rd place is _____ _____.

Challenge and extension question

5 Which transport to hire?

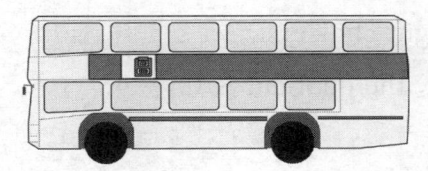

18 seats for £200 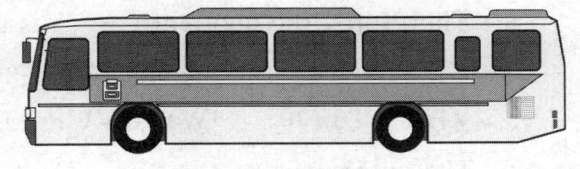   49 seats for £480

182 pupils and teachers in Year 5 are having a trip to a local science museum.

(a) If they hire 49-seated coaches, at least how many coaches do they need? What is the cost?

(b) If they hire 18-seated minibuses, how many minibuses do they need? What is the cost?

(c) Which transport should they hire?

3.4 Dividing two-digit or three-digit numbers by a two-digit number (2)

Learning objectives

Use written methods to divide three-digit numbers by two-digit numbers

Basic questions

1 Work out the following divisions.

(a) $51 \overline{)160}$ Think: When $16 \div 5$, the quotient is ( ).
We get: ( ) × 51 = ( ).

The quotient is ( ). (Choose: just right, too big or too small.)

(b) $63 \overline{)480}$ Think: When $48 \div 6$, the quotient is ( ).
We get: ( ) × 63 = ( ).

The quotient is ( ). (Choose: just right, too big or too small.)
Change the quotient to ( ).
( ) × 63 = ( ).

The remainder is ( ); it is ( ) than the divisor.
Therefore, the quotient ( ) is the right choice.

(c) $93 \overline{)360}$ Think: When $36 \div 9$, the quotient is ( ).
We get: ( ) × 93 = ( ).

The quotient is ( ). (Choose: just right, too big or too small.)
Change the quotient to ( ).
( ) × 93 = ( ).

The remainder is ( ); it is ( ) than the divisor. Therefore, the quotient ( ) is the right choice.

(d) $43 \overline{)334}$ Think: When $33 \div 4$, the quotient is ( ).
We get: ( ) × 43 = ( ).

The quotient is ( ). (Choose: just right, too big or too small.)
Change the quotient to ( ).
( ) × 43 = ( ).

The remainder is ( ); it is ( ) than the divisor. Therefore, the quotient ( ) is the right choice.

Dividing by two-digit numbers

2 Use the column method to calculate.
$505 \div 89 =$ $\qquad$ $321 \div 56 =$ $\qquad$ $317 \div 66 =$

$84 \div 22 =$ $\qquad$ $178 \div 22 =$ $\qquad$ $453 \div 57 =$

3 What is the greatest number you can fill in each set of brackets below?
$30 \times ($ $\quad$ $) < 207$ $\qquad$ $60 \times ($ $\quad$ $) < 415$ $\qquad$ $40 \times ($ $\quad$ $) < 316$
$70 \times ($ $\quad$ $) < 566$ $\qquad$ $50 \times ($ $\quad$ $) < 410$ $\qquad$ $80 \times ($ $\quad$ $) < 768$

4 Write the number sentences and then calculate.
(a) 192 is divided by 32. What is the quotient?

(b) What is 43 times 344?

(c) What is the quotient of 100 000 divided by 10?

(d) What is the quotient of 100 000 divided by 100?

5 A team of road maintenance workers is repairing an 855 metre long road. The workers have completed 162 m of the road. For the remaining part, if they repair 63 m of the road each day, how many more days do they need to complete their work?

Challenge and extension question

6 A tunnel is 760 m long. A 240 m long train is travelling at 25 m per second. How long will it take to pass through the tunnel?

3.5 Dividing two-digit or three-digit numbers by a two-digit number (3)

Learning objectives

Use written methods to divide three-digit numbers by two-digit numbers

Basic questions

1. Work out the following divisions.

   (a) 28)89̄ ( )   Think: When $80 \div 20$, the quotient is ( ).
   ( ) $\times 28 =$ ( ).

   The quotient is ( ) (Choose: just right, too big or too small); change the quotient to ( ).
   ( ) $\times 28 =$ ( ).
   The remainder is ( ); it is ( ) than the divisor. Therefore, the quotient ( ) is the right choice.

   (b) 28)80̄ ( )   Think: When $80 \div 20$, the quotient is ( ).
   ( ) $\times 28 =$ ( ).

   The quotient is ( ) (Choose: just right, too big or too small); minus 1, it is ( ).
   ( ) $\times 28 =$ ( ).
   Again minus 1, it is ( ). ( ) $\times 28 =$ ( ).
   The remainder is ( ); it is ( ) than the divisor. Therefore, the quotient ( ) is the right choice.

   (c) 38)278̄ ( )   Think: When $270 \div 30$, the quotient is ( ).
   When $270 \div 40$, the quotient is ( ).

   The quotient ( ) is the right choice.

   (d) 57)421̄ ( )   Think: When $420 \div 50$, the quotient is ( ).
   When $420 \div 60$, the quotient is ( ).

   The quotient ( ) is the right choice.

   (e) 19)134̄ ( )   Think: Both have the same first digit and $13 < 19$.
   Try the number ( ) as an initial quotient.
   $130 \div 20$, the quotient is ( ).

   The quotient ( ) is the right choice.

Dividing by two-digit numbers

(f) 78)7 3 2 ( )

Think: Both have the same first number and 73<78.
Try ( ) as an initial quotient.
730÷80, the quotient is ( ).
The quotient ( ) is the right choice.

2 Use the column method to calculate.

88 ÷ 22 =   72 ÷ 36 =   325 ÷ 38 =

188 ÷ 22 =   272 ÷ 36 =   829 ÷ 89 =

3 Write the number sentences and then calculate.
(a) How many times 48 is 384?

(b) 59 times a number is 413. What is the number?

(c) At least how much needs to be taken away from 960 so there is no remainder when it is divided by 42?

4 In a spring week, there were 1000 birds visiting an island in their migration from south to north. Among them, 130 were cuckoos. How many were other species of birds? Excluding the remainder, how many times as many as cuckoos were the other species of birds? What is the remainder?

Challenge and extension question

5 Fill in the boxes with suitable numbers to complete the column division.

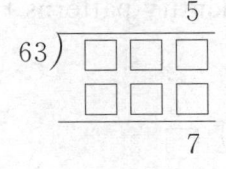

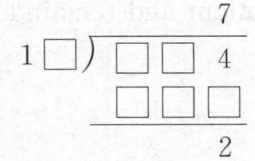

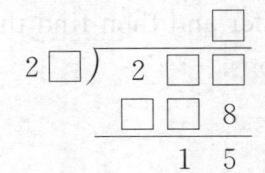

63)□□□ 5
   □□□
       7

1□)□□4 7
   □□□
       2

2□)2□□ □
   □□8
     1 5

3.6 Dividing multi-digit numbers by a two-digit number (1)

Learning objectives

Use written methods to divide multi-digit numbers by two-digit numbers

Basic questions

1 Fill in the brackets and think what you can find.

(a) $204 \div 12$
$12 \times 10 = ($ $)$
$12 \times 20 = ($ $)$
First: (   ) $\div 12 = ($ $)$
Then: $84 \div 12 = ($ $)$
Therefore: $204 \div 12 = ($ $)$

(b) $2128 \div 38$
$38 \times 50 = ($ $)$
$38 \times 60 = ($ $)$
First: (   ) $\div 38 = ($ $)$
Then: (   ) $\div 38 = ($ $)$
Therefore: $2128 \div 38 = ($ $)$

2 Try the following divisions.

$20 \overline{)500}$ $30 \overline{)500}$ $40 \overline{)500}$

3 Use the column method to calculate.

$999 \div 13 =$ $999 \div 23 =$ $999 \div 33 =$

$999 \div 43 =$ $999 \div 53 =$ $999 \div 83 =$

4 Fill in the hundreds place in each dividend below with a number starting from 1 to 9 in order and then find the quotient and remainder. Identify patterns from these divisions.

(a) $35 \overline{)\square 3\ 5}$ $35 \overline{)\square 3\ 5}$ $35 \overline{)\square 3\ 5}$

50

Dividing by two-digit numbers

$35)\overline{\square\,3\,5}$ $\qquad$ $35)\overline{\square\,3\,5}$ $\qquad$ $35)\overline{\square\,3\,5}$

$35)\overline{\square\,3\,5}$ $\qquad$ $35)\overline{\square\,3\,5}$ $\qquad$ $35)\overline{\square\,3\,5}$

(b) Pattern identified: when the hundreds place is filled in with (   ), the quotient is a one-digit number. When the hundreds place is filled in with (   ), the quotient is a two-digit number.

5 Fill in the brackets.
  (a) The quotient of $268 \div 26$ is a (   )-digit number. The highest value place of the quotient is in the (   ) place. The quotient is (   ).
  (b) The quotient of $268 \div 38$ is a (   )-digit number. The digit of the quotient in the highest value place is (   ).
  (c) When the quotient of $5\square 6 \div 53$ is a two-digit number, the least possible number in the $\square$ is (   ).
  (d) The highest value place of the quotient of $336 \div 3\square$ is in the tens place, the greatest possible number in the $\square$ is (   ).

Challenge and extension question

6 Fill in the boxes with suitable numbers to complete the column division.

3.7 Dividing multi-digit numbers by a two-digit number (2)

Learning objectives

Use mental and written methods to divide multi-digit numbers by two-digit numbers

Basic questions

① Do the following divisions.

$60\overline{)2\ 0\ 0\ 0}$ $24\overline{)2\ 0\ 0\ 0}$ $12\overline{)2\ 0\ 0\ 0}$ $16\overline{)2\ 0\ 0\ 0}$

② Use the column method to calculate.

$5000 \div 97 =$ $5000 \div 78 =$ $5000 \div 54 =$

$5000 \div 48 =$ $5000 \div 26 =$ $5000 \div 13 =$

③ Work these out step by step. (Calculate smartly when possible.)

$3265 + 806 - 265$ $35 \times 9 + 265$ $18 \times 25 + 25 \times 22$

$3333 \div 11 \times 4$ $625 \div 25 \times 40$ $158 \times 99 + 158$

Dividing by two-digit numbers

4 Write the number sentences and then calculate.

(a) When the product of 84 and 14 is divided by 49, what is the quotient?

(b) How many times 18 is the sum of the greatest three-digit number and the greatest two-digit number?

(c) When the product of two fifteens is divided by 225, what is the quotient?

5 Multiple choice questions.
(a) In the division sentences below, the quotient that is a two-digit number is (   ).
   A. $2188 \div 22$ B. $324 \div 55$ C. $843 \div 8$ D. $3838 \div 28$
(b) A four-digit number is divided by a two-digit number, the quotient is a (   ).
   A. two-digit number
   B. three-digit number
   C. one-digit number
   D. two-digit number or three-digit number

Challenge and extension question

6 Complete the column division calculations.

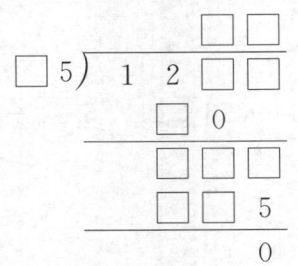

3.8 Practice and exercise (1)

Learning objectives

Solve division problems

Basic questions

1. Work them out mentally. Write the answers.
   (a) $35 \times 20 =$
   (b) $36 \times 5 \div 18 =$
   (c) $79 \times 0 \times 12 =$
   (d) $6800 \div 34 =$
   (e) $86 \times 5 - 30 =$
   (f) $100 - 100 \div 25 =$
   (g) $9300 \div 31 =$
   (h) $3000 \div 25 =$
   (i) $2000 \div 500 =$
   (j) $1000 \div 250 =$
   (k) $9000 \div 3000 =$
   (l) $10\,000 \div 100 =$

2. Use the column method to calculate. (Check the answers to the questions marked with *.)
   (a) $3025 \times 88 =$
   (b) *$3296 \div 32 =$
   (c) *$2551 \div 42 =$

3. Work these out step by step. (Calculate smartly when possible.)
   (a) $432 \times 16 \div 12$
   (b) $32 \times (275 - 75)$
   (c) $1033 \times 22 + 189 \times 9$
   (d) $2000 \div 25 \div 8$
   (e) $(2216 + 888) \div 32$
   (f) $9676 \div 41 - 6524 \div 28$

Dividing by two-digit numbers

4 Write the number sentences and then calculate.

(a) A is 4736 and it is 16 times B. What is the difference between A and B?

(b) The sum of 565 and 191 is divided by 18. What is the quotient?

5 Fill in the brackets.

(a) Find the quotients of the following division calculations.

$125 \div 25 =$ ( ) $1250 \div 25 =$ ( ) $1275 \div 25 =$ ( )

(b) When the quotient of $440 \div \square 3$ is a two-digit number, the greatest possible number in the $\square$ is ( ).

(c) When the quotient of $9\square 95 \div 95$ is a three-digit number, the least possible number in the $\square$ is ( ); in this case, the quotient is ( ) and the remainder is ( ). When the quotient is a two-digit number, the greatest possible number in the $\square$ is ( ); in this case, the quotient is ( ) and the remainder is ( ).

Challenge and extension question

6 The distance between City A and City B is 220 km. How long will it take you to get there if you have the following means of transportation?

Means of transportation	Speed	Time
On foot	5 km/h	
By scooter	20 km/h	
By motorcycle	40 km/h	
By bus	80 km/h	
By train	110 km/h	
By high speed train	275 km/h	

Unit test 3

1 Work these out mentally. Write the answers.
(a) $180 \div 15 =$
(b) $78 \times 10 =$
(c) $6300 \div 70 =$
(d) $1000 \div 25 =$
(e) $24 \times 50 =$
(f) $30 \times 99 =$
(g) $9300 \div 300 =$
(h) $10\,000 \div 200 =$
(i) $240 \div (7+3) =$
(j) $72 \div (86-74) =$
(k) $60 - 51 \div 3 =$
(l) $800 + 80 \div 40 =$
(m) $9600 \div 80 \div 30 =$
(n) $4 \times 6 \times 50 =$
(o) $75 + 25 \div 25 =$
(p) $(700 - 220) \div 60 =$

2 Use the column method to calculate. (Check the answer to the question marked with * .)
(a) $509 \times 92 =$
(b) $27 \times 6300 =$

(c) $7380 \div 36 =$
(d) * $17\,052 \div 28 =$

3 Work these out step by step.
(a) $640 \times 12 \div 80$
(b) $9090 \div 15 \times 20$

(c) $1700 \div 25 \div 4$
(d) $39 \times 75 + 9898 \div 98$

Dividing by two-digit numbers

4 Fill in the brackets.

(a) $6000 \text{ km}^2 = ($ $) \text{ m}^2$.

(b) Given $45 \times 58 = 2610$, $450 \times 5800 = ($ $)$.

(c) The quotient of 1190 divided by 17 is a (   )-digit number. The highest value place of the quotient is in the (   ) place.

(d) The quotient of $7548 \div 75$ is a (   )-digit number. The highest value of the quotient is in the (   ) place, there are (   ) zeros in the end, and the remainder is (   ).

(e) To make the quotient of $\square 784 \div 47$ a three-digit number, the digit in the $\square$ could be (   ).

(f) In $32 \overline{)\square 2 \ 3 \ 8}$, if the quotient is a three-digit number, the least possible number in the $\square$ is (   ). If the quotient is a two-digit number, the number in the $\square$ could be (   ).

5 Multiple choice questions.

(a) Bob, Hannah, Kate and Mark were having a 60-metre run. Bob took 14 seconds, Hannah took 13 seconds, Kate took 15 seconds and Mark took 16 seconds. The fastest runner was (   ).

    A. Bob   B. Hannah   C. Kate   D. Mark

(b) The number sentence that has a different answer from the calculation of 84×46 is (   ).

    A. $(80 + 4) \times 46$ B. $84 \times 40 + 84 \times 6$

    C. $80 \times 46 + 4$ D. $80 \times 46 + 4 \times 46$

(c) A four-digit number is divided by a two-digit number; the quotient is a (   )-digit number.

    A. four   B. three   C. three or two   D. Not sure

(d) In $54\,081 \div 27$, there are (   ) zeros in the middle of the quotient.

    A. 0   B. 1   C. 2   D. 3

(e) In $605\,605 \div 605$, there are (   ) zeros in the middle of the quotient.

    A. 1   B. 2   C. 3   D. 4

6 Application problems.

(a) Evan read 84 pages of a book in 3 days. The book has 504 pages. If he reads at the same speed, in how many days can he read the whole book?

Dividing by two-digit numbers

(b) A clothing factory made 60 sets of children's clothes each day on average in the first 3 days. In the next 4 days, it made 310 sets. How many sets of children's clothes has it made altogether in that week?

(c) James walks 5 km per hour. If he cycles he can be 10 km faster per hour than he walks. How many kilometers can James travel if he cycles for 3 hours?

(d) There are 4500 bottles of juice in a supermarket. 125 boxes of juice were sold. Each box has 24 bottles. How many bottles of juice were left?

7 Given that the distance from Shanghai to another Chinese city is 1328 km, find the speeds of the following means of transportation. Fill in the table with your answers (rounding to the nearest whole number).

Means of transportation	Speed	Time
By regular train	_____ km/h	9 hours and 29 minutes
By high-speed train	_____ km/h	5 hours and 18 minutes
By aeroplane	_____ km/h	1 hour and 39 minutes

Chapter 4 Comparing fractions, improper fractions and mixed numbers

4.1 Comparing fractions (1)

Learning objectives

Compare and order fractions with the same denominator

Basic questions

1. Look at the diagram and fill in the brackets.

    (a)

$\frac{1}{7}$	$\frac{1}{7}$	$\frac{1}{7}$	$\frac{1}{7}$	$\frac{1}{7}$	$\frac{1}{7}$	$\frac{1}{7}$

$\frac{1}{7}$	$\frac{1}{7}$	$\frac{1}{7}$	$\frac{1}{7}$	$\frac{1}{7}$	$\frac{1}{7}$	$\frac{1}{7}$

    $\frac{3}{7}$ means ( ) lots of $\frac{1}{7}$. $\frac{6}{7}$ means ( ) lots of $\frac{1}{7}$. Therefore, $\frac{3}{7}$ is ( ) than $\frac{6}{7}$. (Choose 'greater' or 'less'.)

    (b) For fractions that have the same denominator, the greater the numerator is, the ( ) the fraction is, and the less the ( ) is, the less the fraction is.

2. Use fractions to represent the shaded parts of the figures and fill in the ☐ with >, < or =.

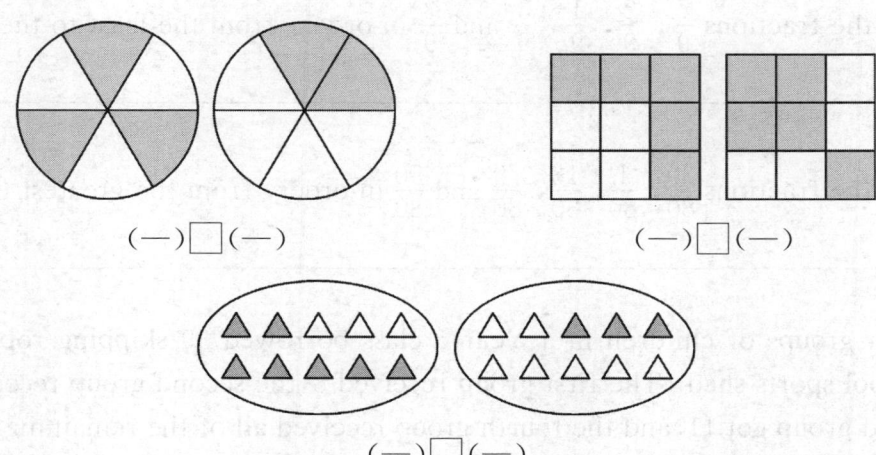

    (—)☐(—)   (—)☐(—)

    (—)☐(—)

Comparing fractions, improper fractions and mixed numbers

3 Colour $\frac{3}{8}$, $\frac{7}{8}$ and $\frac{1}{8}$ in the following diagram and put them in order, starting from the least.

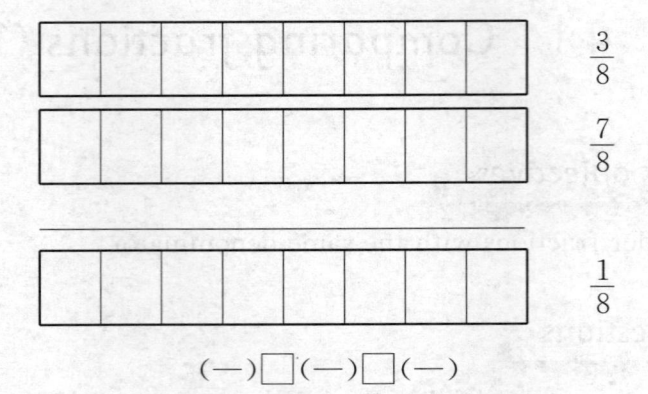

$\frac{3}{8}$

$\frac{7}{8}$

$\frac{1}{8}$

(—)☐(—)☐(—)

4 Compare the fractions and write >, < or = in the brackets.

(a) $\frac{3}{10}$ (　) $\frac{8}{10}$ (b) $\frac{6}{7}$ (　) $\frac{1}{7}$

(c) $\frac{6}{9}$ (　) $\frac{9}{9}$ (d) $\frac{5}{5}$ (　) $\frac{4}{5}$

(e) $\frac{9}{20}$ (　) $\frac{18}{20}$ (f) $\frac{53}{109}$ (　) $\frac{77}{109}$

(g) $\frac{9}{10}$ (　) $\frac{7}{10}$ (　) $\frac{1}{10}$ (h) $\frac{1}{8}$ (　) $\frac{5}{8}$ (　) $\frac{8}{8}$

(i) $\frac{13}{18}$ (　) $\frac{7}{18}$ (　) $\frac{9}{18}$

Challenge and extension questions

5 Put the fractions $\frac{7}{9}$, $\frac{2}{9}$, $\frac{1}{9}$, $\frac{5}{9}$ and $\frac{3}{9}$ in order, from the least to the greatest.

_____

6 Put the fractions $\frac{30}{80}$, $\frac{1}{80}$, $\frac{18}{80}$, $\frac{79}{80}$ and $\frac{50}{80}$ in order, from the greatest to the least.

_____

7 Four groups of children in a Year 5 class borrowed 39 skipping ropes from the school sports shed. The first group received 8, the second group received 10, the third group got 11, and the fourth group received all of the remaining ones. What fraction of the ropes did the fourth group borrow?

4.2 Comparing fractions (2)

Learning objectives
Compare and order fractions with a numerator of 1

Basic questions

1. Look at the diagram and fill in the brackets.

| $\frac{1}{6}$ | $\frac{1}{6}$ | $\frac{1}{6}$ | $\frac{1}{6}$ | $\frac{1}{6}$ | $\frac{1}{6}$ |

| $\frac{1}{3}$ | $\frac{1}{3}$ | $\frac{1}{3}$ |

| $\frac{1}{2}$ | $\frac{1}{2}$ |

(a) $\frac{1}{6}$ is (　　) than $\frac{1}{3}$. (Choose 'greater' or 'less'.)

(b) $\frac{1}{3}$ is (　　) than $\frac{1}{2}$. (Choose 'greater' or 'less'.)

(c) For fractions that have the same numerator, the greater the denominator is, the (　　) the fraction is; the less the (　　) is, the greater the fraction is.

2. Let's fill in the brackets.

(a) Use fractions to represent the shaded part in each figure below.

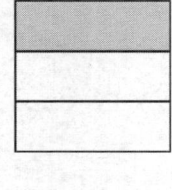

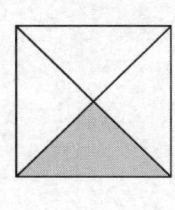

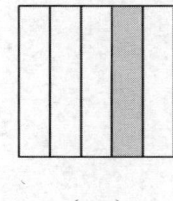

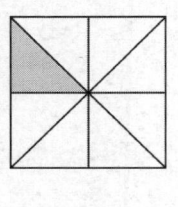

(—)　　　(—)　　　(—)　　　(—)

(b) Put the above fractions in order, starting from the greatest.

_____

(c) From the above, we found that if the whole is the same, the more parts the whole is equally divided into, the (　　) each part gets. Therefore, for a fraction with a numerator 1, the greater the denominator is, the (　　) the fraction is.

Comparing fractions, improper fractions and mixed numbers

3 Compare the fractions and write $>$, $<$ or $=$ in the brackets.

(a) $\frac{1}{10}$ ( ) $\frac{1}{8}$ (b) $\frac{1}{6}$ ( ) $\frac{1}{7}$

(c) $\frac{1}{9}$ ( ) $\frac{1}{15}$ (d) $\frac{1}{4}$ ( ) $\frac{1}{40}$

(e) $\frac{1}{21}$ ( ) $\frac{1}{20}$ (f) $\frac{1}{109}$ ( ) $\frac{1}{77}$

(g) $\frac{1}{9}$ ( ) $\frac{1}{7}$ ( ) $\frac{1}{5}$ (h) $\frac{1}{8}$ ( ) $\frac{1}{18}$ ( ) $\frac{1}{108}$

Challenge and extension questions

4 Put the fractions $\frac{1}{9}$, $\frac{1}{36}$, $\frac{1}{27}$, $\frac{1}{18}$ and $\frac{1}{81}$ in order, from the least to the greatest.

_____

5 Put the fractions $\frac{1}{10}$, $\frac{1}{20}$, $\frac{1}{70}$, $\frac{1}{100}$ and $\frac{1}{40}$ in order, from the greatest to the least.

_____

6 There are two boxes of chocolates. The first box has 30 chocolates and the second has 20 chocolates. Alex takes $\frac{1}{5}$ of the chocolates in the first box and his brother takes $\frac{1}{4}$ of the chocolates from the second box. Who takes more?

4.3 Comparing fractions (3)

Learning objectives

Compare and order fractions with the same numerator and different denominators

Basic questions

1. (a) Write a fraction in each bracket to represent the shaded part in each figure.

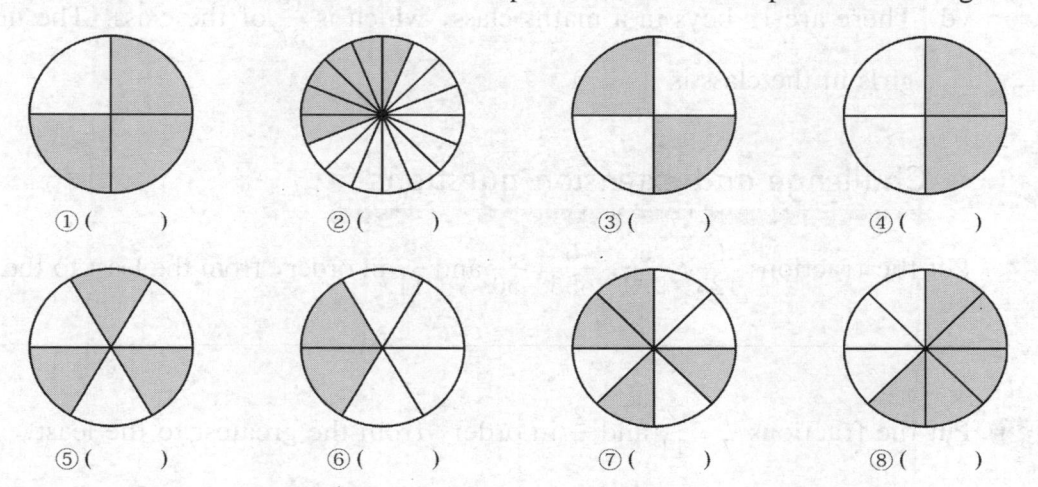

① (   )   ② (   )   ③ (   )   ④ (   )

⑤ (   )   ⑥ (   )   ⑦ (   )   ⑧ (   )

(b) Compare: The figures that have the same portion of shaded parts as figure ③ are (   ).

(c) Comparing figure ①, figure ② and figure ⑥, we can see that if the whole is the same, the fewer parts the whole is equally divided to, the (   ) each part gets, and for fractions with the same numerator, the (   ) the denominator is, the greater the fraction is.

2. Compare the fractions and write >, < or = in the brackets.

(a) $\frac{1}{63}$ (   ) $\frac{1}{36}$ (b) $\frac{3}{20}$ (   ) $\frac{3}{80}$

(c) $\frac{8}{100}$ (   ) $\frac{8}{99}$ (d) $\frac{7}{41}$ (   ) $\frac{7}{40}$

(e) $\frac{25}{200}$ (   ) $\frac{25}{300}$ (f) $\frac{11}{535}$ (   ) $\frac{11}{553}$

(g) $\frac{60}{601}$ (   ) $\frac{60}{699}$ (   ) $\frac{60}{700}$

Comparing fractions, improper fractions and mixed numbers

3 Fill in the brackets.

(a) There are ( ) lots of $\frac{1}{15}$ in $\frac{7}{15}$. After taking away 3 lots of $\frac{1}{15}$, it is ($\frac{\quad}{\quad}$).

(b) Five lots of $\frac{1}{13}$ make ( ). Four lots of $\frac{1}{13}$ make ( ). The difference between them is ($\frac{\quad}{\quad}$).

(c) A 2 m long piece of string is cut into 5 equal pieces. Each piece is ( ) of the string and it is ( ) long. Four pieces are ( ) of the string, and the length of each piece is ( ).

(d) There are 19 boys in a maths class, which is $\frac{19}{37}$ of the class. The number of girls in the class is ( ).

Challenge and extension questions

4 Put the fractions $\frac{5}{123}$, $\frac{5}{999}$, $\frac{5}{656}$, $\frac{5}{50}$ and $\frac{5}{11}$ in order, from the least to the greatest.

_____

5 Put the fractions $\frac{4}{7}$, $\frac{2}{11}$ and $\frac{2}{7}$ in order, from the greatest to the least.

_____

6 A snail and an ant had a race to climb a wall. The snail climbed $\frac{9}{15}$ m and the ant climbed $\frac{9}{20}$ m. Who climbed higher?

7 Tom and Mary had two cups of drinks with the same amount. Tom drank $\frac{3}{4}$ of his and Mary drank $\frac{2}{3}$ of hers. Who drank more?

4.4 Comparing fractions (4)

Learning objectives

Compare equivalent fractions

Basic questions

1 A story of sharing peaches.

Once upon a time, an old monkey gave young monkeys some peaches to share. The old monkey gave one of the young monkeys a basket of peaches and said: 'These are for six of you to share'. The young monkey thought it was too few and asked for more. The old monkey said: 'Okay, you can have one more basket, but to share with 12 monkeys'. The young monkey was very happy with this.

Given that each basket contains the same number of peaches, what do you think about the story?

Lee thinks: 6 monkeys share a basket of peaches. Each monkey can have $\frac{1}{6}$ of the peaches. Two baskets of peaches are shared by 12 monkeys. Each monkey has $\frac{2}{12}$ of the peaches.

Ming thinks: As learned earlier, we know different fractions can represent the same part of an object, and $\frac{1}{6}$ and $\frac{2}{12}$ are equal. Therefore, the number of peaches that each monkey has is the same either way.

Do you think Ming is right?

2 Compare the fractions and fill in the brackets.

(a) $\frac{1}{2} = \frac{2}{()} = \frac{4}{()}$

(b) $\frac{1}{5} = \frac{3}{()} = \frac{()}{30}$

(c) $\frac{6}{15} = \frac{()}{5} = \frac{4}{()}$

(d) $\frac{5}{5} = \frac{3}{()} = \frac{()}{99}$

(e) $\frac{6}{18} = \frac{12}{()} = \frac{()}{9} = \frac{24}{()} = \frac{1}{()} = \frac{2}{()}$

(f) $1 = \frac{11}{11} = \frac{33}{()} = \frac{()}{300}$

Comparing fractions, improper fractions and mixed numbers

3 Fill in the brackets.

(a) Mary was given half of half a cake, she was given $\left(\dfrac{}{}\right)$ of the cake.

(b) Write any three fractions that are equal to $\dfrac{1}{3}$: ( ), ( ) and ( ).

(c) 3 lots of $\dfrac{1}{6}$ equal ( ) lots of $\dfrac{1}{12}$.

(d) After folding a piece of square paper in half twice, each part is $\left(\dfrac{}{}\right)$ of the square.

4 An ant was crawling from Place A to Place B. The ant crawled $\dfrac{4}{12}$ m on the first day and $\dfrac{6}{12}$ m on the second day.

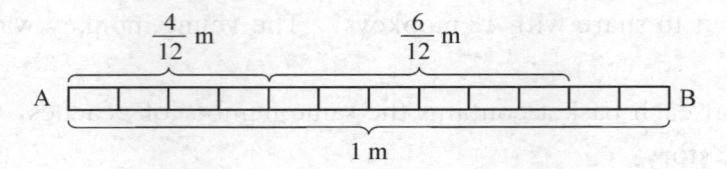

(a) How many metres did the ant crawl on these two days?

(b) How many metres away is it to Place B after the two days' crawling?

Challenge and extension questions

5 Walking from Place A to Place B took Tim $\dfrac{3}{7}$ hours and Sam $\dfrac{4}{14}$ hours. Who walked faster?

6 Three pizzas of the same size are equally shared by 4 children. How many pizzas can each child have? Show your working.

4.5 Improper fractions and mixed numbers

Learning objectives
Convert between mixed numbers and improper fractions

Basic questions

1. Fill in the brackets with the following numbers and fractions to represent the shaded part in each figure.

$$1, \frac{9}{8}, \frac{3}{8}, 1\frac{1}{8}, \frac{8}{8}$$

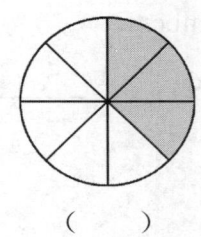

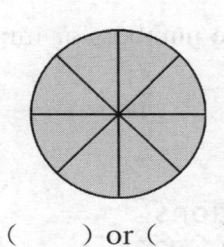

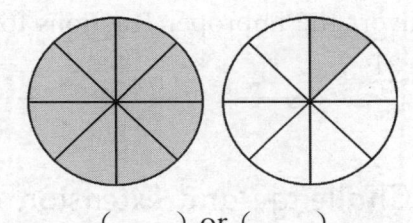

(　　)　　(　　) or (　　)　　(　　) or (　　)

2. In the following fractions, what are proper fractions, what are improper fractions and what are mixed numbers? (Fill in the blanks.)

$$\frac{7}{12}, \frac{5}{3}, 7\frac{1}{18}, \frac{3}{2}, 1\frac{4}{5}, \frac{79}{100}, 30\frac{1}{2}, \frac{181}{365}, \frac{13}{12}, \frac{19}{6}, 5\frac{1}{4}$$

Proper fractions: _____
Improper fractions: _____
Mixed numbers: _____

3. Mark the following numbers on the number line and then put them in order, from the least to the greatest.

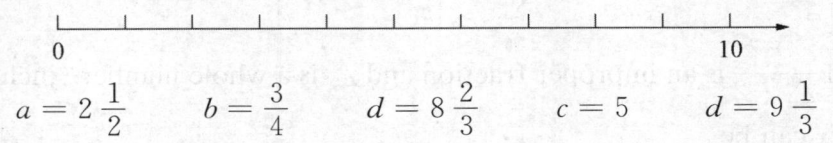

$$a = 2\frac{1}{2} \quad b = \frac{3}{4} \quad d = 8\frac{2}{3} \quad c = 5 \quad d = 9\frac{1}{3}$$

From the least to the greatest: _____

4. True or false.

   (a) $2\frac{3}{5}$ is read as two and three fifths. (　　)

Comparing fractions, improper fractions and mixed numbers

(b) All proper fractions are less than 1. ( )
(c) All improper fractions are greater than 1. ( )
(d) The numerator of a proper fraction is always less than its denominator. ( )
(e) The numerator of an improper fraction is always greater than its denominator. ( )
(f) A proper fraction can be converted to a mixed number. ( )
(g) An improper fraction can be converted to a mixed number. ( )
(h) A mixed number can be converted to an improper fraction. ( )

5 Convert the mixed numbers to improper fractions.

(a) $2\frac{1}{3} = $ _____ (b) $1\frac{5}{8} = $ _____ (c) $6\frac{7}{9} = $ _____ (d) $60\frac{37}{39} = $ _____

6 Convert the improper fractions to whole numbers or mixed numbers.

(a) $\frac{31}{7} = $ _____ (b) $\frac{53}{8} = $ _____ (c) $\frac{81}{9} = $ _____ (d) $\frac{97}{30} = $ _____

Challenge and extension questions

7 Complete the following table. The first row has been done for you.

Quantity	As decimal	As mixed number	As improper fraction
2 m 10 cm	2.1 m	$2\frac{1}{10}$ m	$\frac{21}{10}$ m
90 minutes	_____ h	_____ h	_____ h
5 kg 200 g	_____ kg	_____ kg	_____ kg
1650 ml	_____ l	_____ l	_____ l
30 km 200 m	_____ km	_____ km	_____ km
1 m² 900 cm²	_____ m²	_____ m²	_____ m²

8 (a) If $\frac{5}{\triangle + 2}$ is an improper fraction and $\triangle$ is a whole number (including 0), then $\triangle$ can be _____.

(b) If a is a whole number, $\frac{a}{9}$ is a proper fraction, and $\frac{a}{5}$ is an improper fraction, then the value of a can be _____.

4.6 Adding and subtracting fractions with related denominators (1)

Learning objectives

Add and subtract fractions with related denominators

Basic questions

1. Draw a line to link each pair of equivalent fractions.

$\dfrac{1}{2}$ $\dfrac{2}{5}$ $\dfrac{13}{18}$ $\dfrac{11}{10}$ $\dfrac{17}{20}$

$\dfrac{65}{90}$ $\dfrac{85}{100}$ $\dfrac{3}{6}$ $\dfrac{4}{10}$ $\dfrac{110}{100}$

2. Fill in the brackets.

(a) $\dfrac{1}{3} = \dfrac{(\quad)}{6}$ (b) $\dfrac{2}{5} = \dfrac{(\quad)}{10}$ (c) $\dfrac{17}{10} = \dfrac{34}{(\quad)}$

(d) $\dfrac{13}{100} = \dfrac{(\quad)}{200}$ (e) $\dfrac{31}{25} = \dfrac{93}{(\quad)}$ (f) $\dfrac{10}{17} = \dfrac{(\quad)}{(\quad)}$

3. Work these out mentally. Write the answers.

(a) $\dfrac{1}{5} + \dfrac{1}{5} =$ (b) $\dfrac{4}{7} - \dfrac{2}{7} =$ (c) $\dfrac{3}{10} + \dfrac{7}{10} =$

(d) $\dfrac{9}{13} - \dfrac{5}{13} =$ (e) $\dfrac{8}{9} - \dfrac{4}{9} =$ (f) $\dfrac{13}{23} + \dfrac{5}{23} =$

4. Add the fractions step by step and write your answers in mixed numbers if they are greater than 1. The first one has been done for you.

(a) $\dfrac{1}{3} + \dfrac{5}{6}$ (b) $\dfrac{3}{5} + \dfrac{1}{10} =$ (c) $\dfrac{9}{13} + \dfrac{7}{26} =$

$= \dfrac{2}{6} + \dfrac{5}{6}$

$= \dfrac{2+5}{6}$

$= \dfrac{7}{6} = 1\dfrac{1}{6}$

71

Comparing fractions, improper fractions and mixed numbers

(d) $\frac{1}{3}+\frac{13}{15}=$ (e) $\frac{5}{7}+\frac{18}{35}=$ (f) $\frac{20}{11}+\frac{51}{77}=$

5 Subtract the fractions step by step. The first one has been done for you.

(a) $\frac{1}{2}-\frac{3}{8}$ (b) $\frac{2}{3}-\frac{5}{9}=$ (c) $\frac{15}{22}-\frac{4}{11}=$

$=\frac{4}{8}-\frac{3}{8}$

$=\frac{4-3}{8}$

$=\frac{1}{8}$

(d) $\frac{5}{7}-\frac{5}{14}=$ (e) $\frac{61}{75}-\frac{113}{150}=$ (f) $\frac{59}{90}-\frac{4}{9}=$

6 When Andrew said how many books he had, Jason said that he had two thirds as many as Andrew, and his younger sister Amy said she had one ninth as many as Andrew. Answer the following questions. Show your working.

(a) Comparing the numbers of books Jason and Amy have, who has more books?

(b) Express the number of books Jason and Amy have in total as a fraction of what Andrew has.

Comparing fractions, improper fractions and mixed numbers

(c) Express the difference of the numbers of books Jason and Amy have as a fraction of what Andrew has.

(d) If Andrew has 18 books, how many books do Jason and Amy have altogether? (Use two different ways to find the answer.)
Method 1:   Method 2:

Challenge and extension questions

7 Calculate the following.

(a) $\dfrac{1}{2}+\dfrac{1}{4}+\dfrac{1}{8}$

(b) $1-\dfrac{1}{3}-\dfrac{1}{6}$

8 Which of the following is correct? Explain how you got the answer.

A. $\dfrac{1}{2}+\dfrac{1}{3}=\dfrac{1}{5}$ B. $\dfrac{1}{2}+\dfrac{1}{3}=\dfrac{2}{5}$ C. $\dfrac{1}{2}+\dfrac{1}{3}=\dfrac{1}{6}$ D. $\dfrac{1}{2}+\dfrac{1}{3}=\dfrac{5}{6}$

4.7 Adding and subtracting fractions with related denominators (2)

Learning objectives

Add and subtract fractions, including mixed numbers, with related denominators

Basic questions

1. Work these out mentally. Write the answers.
   (a) $\frac{1}{7} + \frac{4}{7} =$
   (b) $\frac{1}{5} - \frac{1}{5} =$
   (c) $\frac{3}{2} + \frac{1}{8} =$
   (d) $\frac{8}{9} - \frac{1}{3} =$
   (e) $\frac{5}{7} + \frac{7}{56} =$
   (f) $1 - \frac{9}{10} =$

2. Write the answers in mixed numbers.
   (a) $1 + \frac{1}{2} =$
   (b) $15 + \frac{3}{7} =$
   (c) $\frac{23}{100} + 58 =$

3. Find the differences and write the answers in mixed numbers if they are greater than 1.
   (a) $1 - \frac{1}{3} =$
   (b) $1 - \frac{2}{15} =$
   (c) $5 - \frac{17}{100} =$

4. Complete the following additions and subtractions. Write the answers as whole numbers or mixed numbers if they are greater than 1.
   (a) $\frac{10}{7} + \frac{22}{7} =$
   (b) $\frac{5}{6} + \frac{4}{3} =$
   (c) $\frac{19}{7} - \frac{15}{7} =$
   (d) $\frac{145}{99} - \frac{40}{33} =$
   (e) $1 - \frac{2}{5} + \frac{7}{25} =$
   (f) $\frac{4}{9} + \frac{23}{18} =$

5. Complete the following additions and subtractions. Write the answers as whole numbers or mixed numbers if they are greater than 1. The first one has been done for you.

74

Comparing fractions, improper fractions and mixed numbers

(a) $2\frac{3}{7} + 1\frac{5}{7}$

$= \left(2 + \frac{3}{7}\right) + \left(1 + \frac{5}{7}\right)$

$= (2 + 1) + \left(\frac{3}{7} + \frac{5}{7}\right)$

$= 3 + \frac{8}{7}$

$= 3 + 1\frac{1}{7}$

$= 4\frac{1}{7}$

(b) $10\frac{10}{13} - 5\frac{3}{13}$

(c) $3\frac{4}{9} - 2\frac{23}{18}$

(d) $12\frac{2}{3} - 10\frac{7}{12}$

6 After a number is subtracted by $\frac{5}{6}$ and then added to by $\frac{1}{3}$, it is equal to $\frac{2}{3}$. Find the number.

7 An electrician used some electrical wire to wire a new building. On the first day he planned to use $1\frac{2}{5}$ m of the wire, on the second day he planned to use $\frac{3}{5}$ m more than on the first day, and on the third day he planned to use 2 m more than on the second day. If the wire was 10 m long, would it be long enough? Why or why not?

Challenge and extension question

8 While working on addition and subtraction involving mixed numbers, Dan found another method to find the answer, that is, first convert all the mixed numbers to improper fractions and then add or subtract them.
Can you use Dan's method to find the answers to the following questions? Show your working.

(a) $9\frac{6}{19} + \frac{11}{19}$

(b) $3\frac{2}{3} - 2\frac{7}{9}$

4.8 Multiplying fractions by whole numbers

Learning objectives

Multiply fractions and mixed numbers by whole numbers

Basic questions

1. Fill in the brackets.

   (a) $2+2+2+2+2 = (\quad) \times (\quad) = (\quad)$

   (b) $\dfrac{2}{7} + \dfrac{2}{7} = \dfrac{(\quad)+(\quad)}{7} = \dfrac{(\quad)}{7}$

   (c) $\dfrac{3}{10} + \dfrac{3}{10} + \dfrac{3}{10} = \dfrac{(\quad)+(\quad)+(\quad)}{10} = \dfrac{(\quad)}{10}$

   (d) $\dfrac{1}{3} + \dfrac{1}{3} + \dfrac{1}{3} = \dfrac{(\quad)+(\quad)+(\quad)}{3} = (\quad)$

   (e) $\dfrac{5}{9} + \dfrac{5}{9} = \dfrac{(\quad)+(\quad)}{9} = \dfrac{(\quad)}{9} = (\quad)$

   (f) $\dfrac{4}{5} + \dfrac{4}{5} + \dfrac{4}{5} = \dfrac{(\quad)+(\quad)+(\quad)}{5} = (\quad)$

2. In each question below, one circle represents one whole. Use multiplication as repeated addition to find the shaded parts in total. Write your answer as a mixed number if it is greater than 1. The first has been done for you.

   (a)

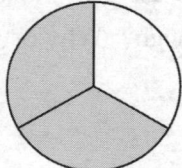

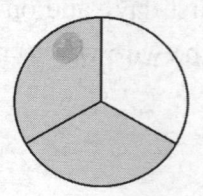

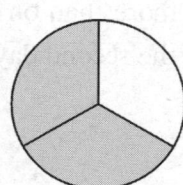

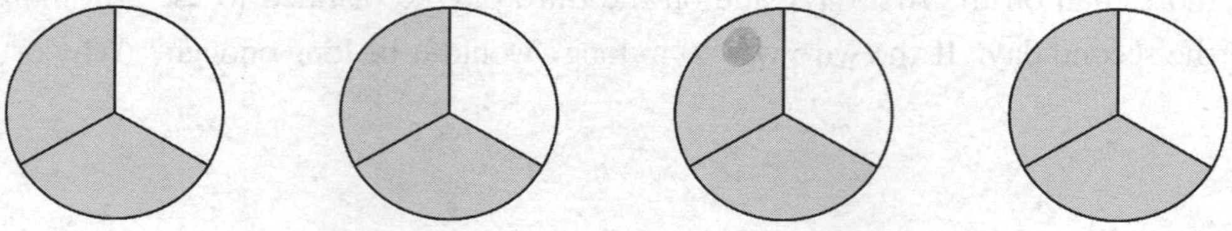

   Total shaded parts: $4 \times \dfrac{2}{3} = \dfrac{2}{3} + \dfrac{2}{3} + \dfrac{2}{3} + \dfrac{2}{3} = \dfrac{2+2+2+2}{3} = \dfrac{4 \times 2}{3} = \dfrac{8}{3} = 2\dfrac{2}{3}$

   (b)

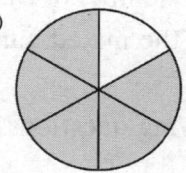

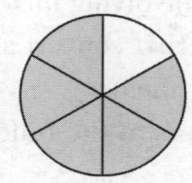

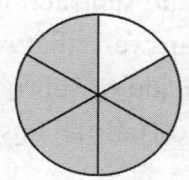

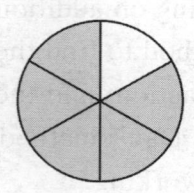

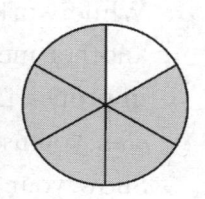

   Total shaded parts: _____

(c)

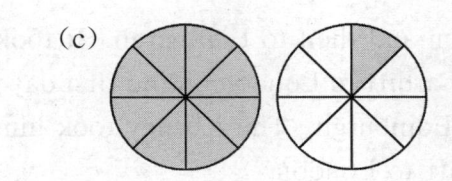

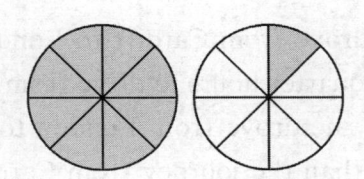

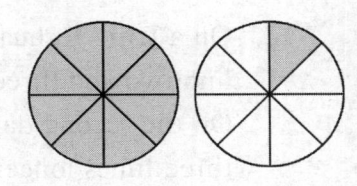

Total shaded parts: _____

3 True or false.

(a) $5 \times \frac{2}{7} = \frac{5 \times 2}{5 \times 7} = \frac{10}{35}$ ( )

(b) $3 \times 6\frac{3}{5} = (3 \times 6)\frac{3}{5} = 18\frac{3}{5}$ ( )

(c) $3 \times \frac{7}{10} = \frac{3 \times 7}{10} = \frac{21}{10} = 2\frac{1}{10}$ ( )

(d) $4 \times 2\frac{2}{9} = 4 \times \left(2 + \frac{2}{9}\right) = 4 \times 2 + 4 \times \frac{2}{9} = 8 + \frac{8}{9} = 8\frac{8}{9}$ ( )

4 Multiply fractions by whole numbers.

(a) $5 \times \frac{1}{2}$ (b) $\frac{3}{10} \times 3$ (c) $8 \times 5\frac{2}{15} + \frac{8}{15}$

(d) $12 \times 12\frac{1}{5}$ (e) $3\frac{5}{12} \times 5 - 4 \times 2\frac{1}{12}$ (f) $0 \times 6\frac{11}{100} + 1 \times 4\frac{19}{100} - 2 \times 2\frac{3}{100}$

5 A rectangular pool is 9 metres long and $5\frac{1}{2}$ metres wide. Find its perimeter and area.

Comparing fractions, improper fractions and mixed numbers

6. On a trip, Joshua drove from Cardiff to London and then to Edinburgh. It took him two and three quarter hours to drive from Cardiff to London on the first day. On the second day, he drove from London to Edinburgh. The journey took him three times longer than the journey from Cardiff to London.

(a) How long did it take Joshua to drive from London to Edinburgh?

(b) How much longer did it take Joshua to drive from London to Edinburgh than from Cardiff to London?

(c) How much time did it take Joshua to drive from Cardiff to London and then from London to Edinburgh?

Challenge and extension question

7. Calculate the following and write the answers in mixed numbers if they are greater than 1.

(a) $7 \times 5\frac{1}{2} + \frac{5}{6}$

(b) $10 \times 3\frac{11}{12} - 12 \times 2\frac{3}{60}$

Unit test 4

1 Work these out mentally. Write the answers.

(a) $12 \times 11 - 12 =$

(b) $100 \times 9 \div 30 =$

(c) $34 \div 17 + 305 =$

(d) $\frac{2}{5} + \frac{1}{5} =$

(e) $\frac{9}{15} - \frac{2}{15} =$

(f) $\frac{5}{7} + \frac{3}{14} =$

(g) $5 + \frac{3}{8} =$

(h) $4 \times \frac{4}{17} =$

(i) $10 \times 2\frac{1}{10} =$

2 Work these out step by step. Write the answers in mixed numbers when they are greater than 1.

(a) $\frac{2}{3} + \frac{7}{15}$

(b) $\frac{8}{13} - \frac{20}{39}$

(c) $2 + \frac{3}{4} + \frac{25}{48}$

(d) $3 + 2 \times \frac{5}{6}$

(e) $4 \times \frac{7}{11} - 3 \times \frac{15}{22}$

(f) $5 \times \frac{2}{3} - 2 \times \frac{5}{6} + 4 \times \frac{7}{18}$

(g) $11 + 4 \times 3\frac{4}{11}$

(h) $7 \times 5\frac{4}{9} - 11 \times 2\frac{17}{18}$

3 Fill in the brackets with numbers and the ◯ with $>$, $<$ or $=$.

(a) Colour the portion to represent the fractions given and then compare the fractions.

Comparing fractions, improper fractions and mixed numbers

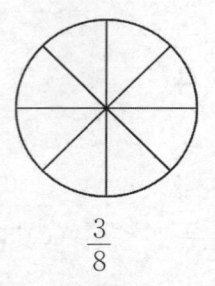

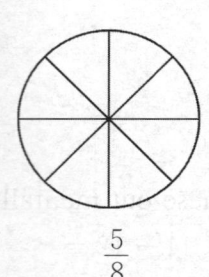

$\frac{3}{8}$ ◯ $\frac{5}{8}$

(b) Write fractions of the shaded parts shown in the squares and then compare the fractions.

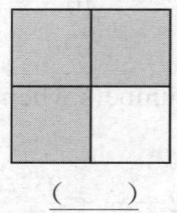

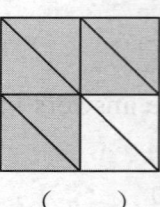

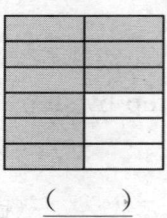

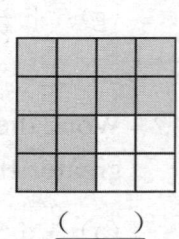

$\frac{(\quad)}{(\quad)}$ ◯ $\frac{(\quad)}{(\quad)}$ ◯ $\frac{(\quad)}{(\quad)}$ ◯ $\frac{(\quad)}{(\quad)}$

(c) The number representing three and one quarter is (   ); doubling it is (   ).

(d) The number representing three one-quarters is (   ) × (   ) or (   ); doubling it is (   ).

4 Compare the fractions and fill in the brackets with >, < or =.

(a) $\frac{1}{2}$ (   ) $\frac{1}{3}$ (b) $\frac{5}{11}$ (   ) $\frac{6}{11}$ (c) $\frac{4}{102}$ (   ) $\frac{4}{105}$

(d) $\frac{3}{12}$ (   ) $\frac{1}{4}$ (e) $\frac{10}{30}$ (   ) $\frac{12}{30}$ (f) $3\frac{1}{10}$ (   ) $2\frac{9}{10}$

5 Put the fractions in order, starting from the greatest.

(a) $\frac{8}{12}$, $\frac{4}{12}$, $\frac{4}{14}$, $\frac{1}{14}$.   (b) $\frac{1}{2}$, 1, $\frac{2}{8}$, $\frac{3}{4}$.

6 Multiple choice questions.

(a) A teacher assigned 10 mental calculation problems. Within the same amount of time, Group A finished $\frac{7}{10}$ of the questions and Group B finished $\frac{1}{2}$ of them. Which group solved the problems at a faster pace? (   )

    A. Group A   B. Group B

    C. They have the same pace   D. Cannot be decided

(b) The incorrect statement of the following is (   ).
  A. A mixed number is always greater than 1.
  B. The sum of any two mixed numbers is always greater than 1.
  C. The difference of a mixed number minus a proper fraction is always greater than 1.
  D. The product of a mixed number by a whole number except zero is always greater than 1.

7 Application problems.

(a) Ben and Jay walked from the community library to the school at the same time. It took Ben $\frac{2}{5}$ hours, while it took Jay $\frac{2}{3}$ hours. Who walked faster?

(b) Stephanie's mother bought $2\frac{1}{2}$ kg of oranges, 3 kg of apples and $1\frac{1}{2}$ kg of cherries. What is the total weight of the fruit she bought?

(c) A willow tree was $\frac{4}{5}$ m tall when it was planted. The height of the tree grew $1\frac{3}{10}$ m in the first year. In the second year, it grew twice as much as in the first year.
  (i) How much taller did the willow tree grow in the first two years?

  (ii) What was the height of the tree at the end of the second year?

(d) The width of a rectangular lawn is $5\frac{9}{10}$ m. Its length is 3 times its width.
  (i) What is the length of the rectangular lawn?

  (ii) How much longer is the length than the width?

  (iii) What is the perimeter?

Chapter 5   Consolidation and enhancement

5.1   Large numbers and rounding (1)

Learning objectives
Read, write and round large numbers

Basic questions

1. Fill in the brackets.
   (a) Counting in 100 000s.
      Forwards: 11 000, 111 000, 211 000, 311 000, (   ), (   ), 611 000
      Backwards: 1 000 000, (   ), 800 000, (   ), (   ), 500 000
   (b) In counting of large numbers, (   ) ten thousands is one hundred thousand. (   ) ten millions is one hundred million.
   (c) Ones, tens, hundreds, thousands, ten thousands, hundred thousands, millions, ten millions, hundred millions, billions, ten billions, are all units of (   ). The multiplication from one unit to the next unit is by 10.
   (d) The two nearest whole million numbers to 1 567 000 are (   ) and (   ).
   (e) 43 007 070 is read in words as (   ). It consists of (   ) thousands and (   ) ones.
   (f) In a three-digit number, the digit in the tens place is 1 greater than the digit in the ones place and 3 greater than the digit in the hundreds place. The digit in the hundreds place is half of 10. The number is (   ).

2. Read out and write the following numbers.
   (a) 4 204 322   In words: (   )
   (b) 10 025 090   In words: (   )
   (c) 20 000 200   In words: (   )
   (d) 1 010 101 010   In words: (   )

Consolidation and enhancement

3 Write the following numbers in numerals.
(a) Fifty-nine million, five hundred and eight thousand, eight hundred and eighty.
(   )
(b) Four hundred million, eight hundred and fifty-four thousand, five hundred.
(   )
(c) Two million, six hundred and sixteen thousand, three hundred and twenty-nine.
(   )
(d) One hundred and ten million, four hundred and nine thousand and eleven.
(   )

4 Multiple choice questions.
(a) The number consisting of 3 ten-millions, 6 millions and 9 thousands is (   ).
   A. 369 000   B. 3 609 000   C. 36 009 000   D. 30 609 000
(b) In a large number, from the ones place to the left, the fourth place is (   ); the place right to the hundred millions place is (   ).
   A. the thousands place   B. the ten thousands place
   C. the hundred thousands place D. the ten millions place
(c) (   ) different 4-digit numbers can be formed using the digits 0, 1, 5 and 9.
   A. 16   B. 18   C. 20   D. 24

5 Compare each pair of numbers below. Write $>$ or $<$ in the ○.
(a) 9676 ○ 9767   (b) 800 100 ○ 810 000
(c) 4 406 000 ○ 446 000   (d) 559 999 ○ 590 000
(e) 900 009 ○ 900 090   (f) 100 001 ○ 10 001

6 Round off the numbers and fill in the table.

	To the nearest ten thousand	To the nearest hundred thousand	To the nearest ten million
36 890 700			
98 970 076			
109 827 000			

Consolidation and enhancement

Challenge and extension questions

7 Use 8, 3, 5 and three zeros to form 6-digit numbers according to the conditions given.

(a) The greatest number is _____ ; rounding it to the nearest ten thousand, it is _____ .

(b) The least number is _____ ; rounding it to the nearest hundred thousand, it is _____ .

(c) The numbers with three zeros at the end are _____ _____ .

(d) The numbers without zeros next to each other are _____ _____ .

8 If a number is rounded to the nearest million, it is 5 000 000. The greatest possible value of this number is (_____) and the least possible value is (_____).

5.2 Large numbers and rounding (2)

Learning objectives

Read, write and round large numbers

Basic questions

1. Fill in the brackets.

   (a) Starting from the ones place to the left, the sixth place is the (   ) place and the ten billions place is the (   ) place.

   (b) The least seven-digit number with 3 zeros and 4 fours is (   ).

   (c) If the hundred millions place of a number is its highest value place, it is a (   )-digit number.

   (d) A number consists of 3 hundred-millions, 5 millions, 2 thousands and 1 one. The number is (   ).

   (e) Two hundred and six million and sixty is written in numerals as (   ).

   (f) One billion, eight thousand and three is written in numerals as (   ).

   (g) 25 700 890 is a (   )-digit number. The digit '5' is in the (   ) place and it represents five (   ).

   (h) Starting from the left, the first '7' in the number 7 807 321 is in the (   ) place, the second '7' is in the (   ) place, and the difference between the values they stand for is (   ).

   (i) If a number is rounded to the nearest million, the result is 258 million. The greatest possible value of this number is (   ) and the least possible value is (   ).

Consolidation and enhancement

2 Multiple choice questions.

(a) In the following numbers, the number with '2' in the millions place is (   ).
   A. 202 205 808
   B. 220 208 505
   C. 20 208 505
   D. 2 220 208 505

(b) One hundred and one thousand, three hundred is written as (   ).
   A. 1 001 300
   B. 101 000 300
   C. 101 300
   D. 1 010 300

(c) Seven billion, five hundred thousand and sixty is written as (   ).
   A. 700 050 060
   B. 700 050 060
   C. 7 000 500 060
   D. 40 070 050 060

(d) If a multi-digit number has only non-zero digits in its ten thousands place and ones place, then it is a (   ) at least.
   A. four-digit number
   B. five-digit number
   C. six-digit number
   D. seven-digit number

(e) Rounding the number 19☐ 324 to the nearest ten thousand, the result is 190 000. The least number that can be filled in the ☐ is (   ).
   A. 0
   B. 4
   C. 5
   D. 6

3 Fill in the tables according to the instructions.

(a) Rounding off the number.

	To the nearest ten thousand	To the nearest million	To the nearest hundred million
769 008 000			

(b) Rounding up the number.

	To the nearest ten thousand	To the nearest million	To the nearest hundred million
5 210 178 900			

(c) Rounding down the number.

	To the nearest ten thousand	To the nearest million	To the nearest hundred million
1 094 507 260			

Consolidation and enhancement

Challenge and extension questions

4. Think carefully and fill in blanks with suitable numbers.
   (a) For rounding off 14☐ 995 to get 150 000, the digit in the box can be _____.

   (b) For rounding off 64☐ 995 to get 640 000, the greatest possible digit in the box is _____.

   (c) For rounding off 36 74☐ 017 to get 36 750 000, the least possible digit in the box is _____.

   (d) For rounding up 99☐ 345 to get 1 000 000, the digit in the box can be _____.

   (e) For rounding down 38 74☐ 017 to get 38 740 000, the greatest possible digit in the box is _____.

5. Let's play a number game: I am thinking of a six-digit number. The first three digits starting from the left are all the same. The last three digits are consecutive whole numbers, counting down to 1. The sum of the six digits equals the two-digit number at the end of the number. What number am I thinking of?

5.3 Four operations of numbers

Learning objectives

Use the order of operations, including brackets, to solve problems

Basic questions

1. Think carefully and fill in the brackets.
   Work out the answer: 8140 − 140 ÷ 4

   Joan's working:
      8140 − 140 ÷ 4
   = 8000 ÷ 4
   = 2000   (   )

   Mary's working:
      8140 − 140 ÷ 4
   = 8140 − 35
   = 8105   (   )

   Which method is correct? Put a ✓ for yes or ✗ for no in each bracket and give your reason below.

   _____

2. First write the order of operations in each calculation below and then work it out step by step. The first one has been done for you.
   (a) 75 + 25 × 6   (b) (75 + 25) × 6
   First multiply and then add:
      75 + 25 × 6
   = 75 + 150
   = 225
   (c) 50 × 3 + 45 ÷ 3   (d) 50 × (3 + 45) ÷ 3

3. Calculate.
   (a) 960 − 78 × 12 + 18   (b) (960 − 78) × (12 + 18)

Consolidation and enhancement

(c) $(864-272) \div 16 + 24 \times 11$ (d) $[(864-272) \div 16 + 24] \times 11$

4 Multiple choice questions.

(a) $1700 - 1300 \div 25 \times 4 = ($ $)$.

  A. 4   B. 64   C. 1687   D. 1492

(b) $(1700 - 1300) \div 25 \times 4 = ($ $)$.

  A. 4   B. 32   C. 40   D. 64

(c) The sum of 60 and 20 is divided by their difference. The number sentence is ( ).

  A. $(20+60) \div (60-20)$ B. $(20+60) \div 60 - 20$
  C. $20 + 60 \div (60-20)$ D. $20 + 60 \div 60 - 20$

Challenge and extension questions

5 Fill in the brackets first. Then write number sentences with mixed operations and work out the answers.

(a) $2000 \xrightarrow{\div 4} ($ $) \xrightarrow{-323} ($ $) \xrightarrow{\times 5} ($ $)$

Number sentence: _____

(b) $($ $) \xrightarrow{\div 23} ($ $) \xrightarrow{-76} ($ $) \xrightarrow{\times 50} 600$

Number sentence: _____

6 Write the same number in the ☐ in each sentence to make the equation true.

(a) $(☐ - ☐) \times 5 + ☐ \div ☐ = 1$

(b) $(☐ + ☐ - ☐) \div (☐ \div ☐) = 2$

(c) $☐ \div ☐ + (☐ + ☐) \div ☐ = 3$

(d) $☐ \times ☐ \times 2 \div (☐ + ☐) = 4$

5.4 Properties of whole number operations (1)

Learning objectives

Solve addition and subtraction multi-step problems

Basic questions

1. Work these out mentally. Write the answers.
   (a) $79+3+6=$
   (b) $430-90-10=$
   (c) $17+20-3\times 1=$
   (d) $96-16-4=$
   (e) $80-2\times 0=$
   (f) $151-(51+11)=$

   In solving the above questions, did you use any property of subtraction operation? If so, in which questions?

   _____

2. Using the property of subtraction operation, fill in each blank with a number and each ◯ with an operation symbol. The first one has been done for you.
   (a) $101-23-77=101-(23+77)$
   (b) $132-(32+21)=$ _____ $-$ _____ ◯ _____
   (c) $277-11-$ _____ $=277-100$
   (d) $919-($ _____ ◯ $22)=$ _____ $-19-22$
   (e) _____ $-$ _____ $-$ _____ $=a-(b$ ◯ $c)$

3. Simplify first and then calculate.
   (a) $800-246-154$
   (b) $416-(16+97)$
   (c) $546-(246+55)$
   (d) $5317-(180+317)$

Consolidation and enhancement

(e) $761-122-133-45$ (f) $919-270-119$

4 A bicycle factory plans to make 1600 bikes in the first quarter. It made 520 bikes in January and 480 bikes in February. How many bikes does it need to make in March? (Use two methods to find the answer.)

Challenge and extension questions

5 Using the properties of subtraction operation, fill each blank with a number and each ◯ with an operation symbol.

(a) $190 - 165 + 65 =$ _____ $-$ (_____ ◯ 65)

(b) $142 - ($ _____ ◯ $27) = 142 - 42 +$ _____

6 Simplify first and then calculate.

(a) $288 - 73 - 27 + 12$ (b) $3156 - (927 - 844)$

(c) $483 - (216 - 183)$ (d) $775 - 167 + 215 - 233$

(e) $(351 - 178) - (51 - 22)$ (f) $6000 - 743 - 564 - 257 - 436$

(g) $1000 - 1 - 2 - 3 - 4 - 5 - \ldots - 20$

5.5 Properties of whole number operations (2)

Learning objectives
Use the order of operations, including brackets, to solve problems

Basic questions

1. Fill each blank with a number and each ◯ with an operation symbol.

   (a) $5100 \div (17 \times 25) = 5100 \div \underline{} \bigcirc \underline{}$

   (b) $1000 \div 25 \div 4 = 1000 \div (\underline{} \bigcirc \underline{})$

   (c) $128 \div 8 \div 2 = \underline{} \div (8 \bigcirc 2)$

   (d) $34 \div (\underline{} \times 2) = 34 \div 17 \bigcirc 2$

   Think carefully. The above answers are based on a property of (\underline{}) operation, that is, if a, b and c are three numbers, $b \neq 0$ and $c \neq 0$, then $a \div b \div c = a \div (b \bigcirc c)$

2. Simplify first and then calculate.

   (a) $7000 \div 8 \div 125$ (b) $3600 \div (36 \times 4)$

   (c) $850 \div (17 \times 2)$ (d) $360 \div 18 \div 2$

   (e) $2000 \div 25 \div 4 \div 2$ (f) $5400 \div 45$

Consolidation and enhancement

3 Multiple choice questions.
 (a) 1240 ÷ 62 ÷ 2 = (   ).
   A. 1240 ÷ (62 ÷ 2)   B. 1240 ÷ (62 × 2)
   C. (1240 ÷ 62) × 2   D. 1240 × (62 × 2)
 (b) 1800 ÷ (25 × 6) = (   ).
   A. 1800 × 25 ÷ 6   B. 1800 ÷ 25 × 6
   C. 1800 ÷ 25 ÷ 6   D. 1800 × (25 ÷ 6)
 (c) 9000 ÷ 125 ÷ 4 ÷ 2 = (   ).
   A. 9000 ÷ (125 × 4 × 2)   B. 9000 ÷ (125 ÷ 4 ÷ 2)
   C. 9000 × (125 × 4 × 2)   D. 9000 × (125 × 4) ÷ 2

4 240 pupils took part in the dance performance in a school's game day. They were grouped equally into 12 teams and each team was further grouped into two sub-teams. How many pupils were there in each sub-team on average? (Use two methods to find the answer.)

5 Lily's class plans to plant trees. The whole class is equally grouped into 4 teams. £240 is used to purchase saplings. Each team plants 6 saplings on average. How much does each sapling cost?

Challenge and extension question

6 Calculate smartly.
 (a) 540 000 ÷ 125 ÷ 45 ÷ 8

 (b) (91 × 27 × 84 × 76) ÷ (9 × 7 × 19 × 13)

5.6 Properties of whole number operations (3)

Learning objectives
Solve multiplication and division problems

Basic questions

1. Think carefully and then fill in the brackets.

   $24 \div 8 = ($ $)$
   $(24 \times 10) \div (8 \times 10) = ($ $)$
   $(24 \times 3) \div (8 \times 3) = ($ $)$
   $(24 \div 4) \div (8 \div 4) = ($ $)$
   $(24 \div 8) \div (8 \div 8) = ($ $)$
   $(24 \times 100) \div (8 \times 100) = ($ $)$

   Observing the calculations on the left, we can find when both the dividend and divisor are (   ) or (   ) by the same number (except zero), their (   ) remains unchanged. It is a property of (   ) operation, that is, if a, b and c are three different numbers, $b \neq 0$ and $c \neq 0$, then

   $a \div b = (a \times c) \div (b \bigcirc c)$

   $a \div b = (a \div c) \div (b \bigcirc c)$

2. Find out the number sentences with the same results as (a) and put a $\checkmark$ in the correct brackets and a $\times$ otherwise.
   (a) $375 \div 125 = 3$
   (b) $(375 \div 3) \div (125 \div 3)$ (   )
   (c) $(375 \div 5) \div (125 \div 25)$ (   )
   (d) $(375 \times 3) \div (125 \div 3)$ (   )
   (e) $(375 \times 10) \div (125 \times 10)$ (   )

3. Using the above property of division calculation, fill in the brackets.
   (a) The quotient of two numbers is 24. If the dividend is divided by 8 and the quotient remains unchanged, the divisor should be (   ).
   (b) One number is divided by another. If the dividend is divided by 10 and the divisor is also divided by 10, the quotient remains (   ).
   (c) One number is divided by another and the quotient is 71. If both the dividend and the divisor are multiplied by 11, the quotient is (   ).

Consolidation and enhancement

(d) (   ) ÷ 50 = 115 ÷ 5 = 230 ÷ (   ) = 460 ÷ (   ).

4 Use the column method to calculate. (Check the answers to the questions marked with ∗.)

(a) 3200 ÷ 160 =   (b) ∗ 2820 ÷ 170 =

(c) 6320 ÷ 90 =   (d) ∗ 63 200 ÷ 900 =

5 Calculate smartly.

(a) 1200 ÷ 25   (b) 4000 ÷ 32

(c) 6000 ÷ 125   (d) 3600 ÷ 45

(e) 13 000 ÷ 125 ÷ 8   (f) 1040 ÷ 2 ÷ 52

Challenge and extension questions

6 Multiple choice questions.

(a) The result of 4100 ÷ 700 is (   ).
   A. quotient 5 with remainder 6   B. quotient 5 with remainder 600
   C. quotient 500 with remainder 6   D. quotient 500 with remainder 600

(b) One number is divided by another number. If then dividend is multiplied by 2 and divisor is divided by 2, the quotient is (   ).
   A. unchanged   B. multiplied by 2   C. divided by 2   D. multiplied by 4

(c) In 120 ÷ 40, if the dividend increases by 120, then in order to keep the quotient unchanged, the divisor should ( ).
   A. increase by 120   B. increase by 100
   C. increase by 80   D. increase by 40

7 Think carefully and work out the answers.
   (a) Two numbers are added together. If one addend is increased by 20 and the other addend is also increased by 20, what is the change to the sum?

   (b) One number is subtracted from another number. If the subtrahend is decreased by 10 and the difference remains unchanged, what is the change to the minuend?

   (c) The quotient of two numbers is 48. If the dividend is multiplied by 10 and the divisor is divided by 10, what is the quotient now?

   (d) Two numbers are multiplied together. If one factor is multiplied by 10 and the other is divided by 10, does the product remain the same?

5.7 Roman numerals to 1000

Learning objectives

Read and recognize Roman numerals to 1000 (M)

Basic questions

1. Complete the table to show the value of each Roman numeric symbol in digits. One has been done for you.

Roman symbol		Value in digits
I		
V		
X		
L		50
C		
D		
M		

2. Write the following Roman numerals in digits.

   XIII =   LVI =   XCV =   CIV =
   CD =   DC =   MCM =   MMVII =

3. Can you recognise years written in Roman numerals? Complete the table below. The first one has been done for you.

Roman numeral	MM	MD	MDLII	MCM	MCMXCV	MMXVI
Year	2000					

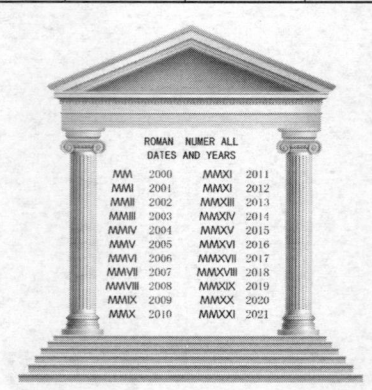

Challenge and extension question

4 Write the following years in Roman numerals. The first one has been done for you.

Year	2010	2011	2012	2013	2014	2015	2020	2100
Roman numeral	MMX							

5.8 Solving problems in statistics

Learning objectives

Complete, read and interpret data presented in different ways

Basic questions

1. The pictogram below shows the numbers of Year 5 pupils participating in different school clubs. Fill in the brackets accordingly.

△			
△	△		△
△	△	△	△
△	△	△	△
△	△	△	△
Choir	Science	Dancing	ICT

Each △ stands for 5 pupils.

Which school club has the greatest number of participating pupils? (   )
Which school clubs have the same number of participating pupils? (   )
How many more pupils are there joining choir than dancing? (   )
From the pictogram, can you tell the total number of pupils participating in different school clubs? Why or why not?

2. Read the following table carefully and then work out the answers.

Results of standing long jump test (Year 5)

	Linda	Alvin	Bob	Peter	May
Result (m)	2.42	2.56	2.61	2.28	2.19
Place					

(a) What is the difference between the longest jump and shortest jump?

Consolidation and enhancement

(b) According to the results, write each participating pupil's place in the table.

3. The bar chart shows the production of a car manufacturer quarterly in a year.

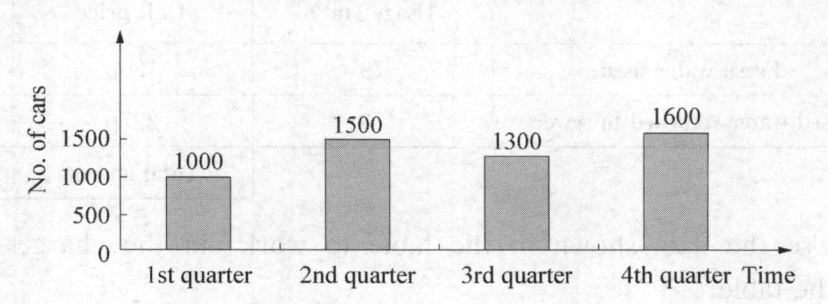

(a) The total output of the manufacturer is (　　　) cars in the year.
(b) Construct a line graph using the data represented in the bar chart.

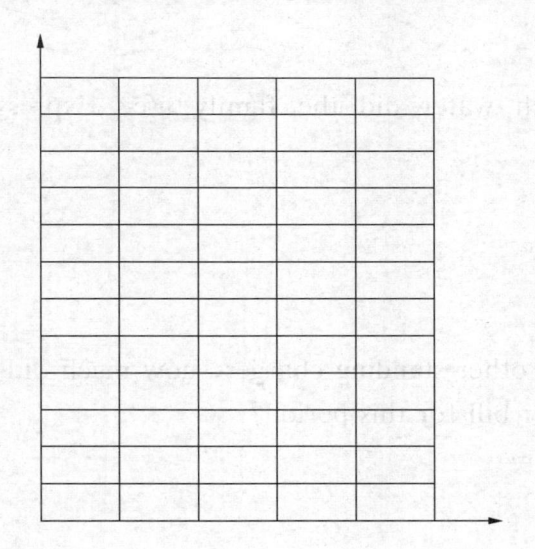

(c) According to the line graph, which of the following is true? Put a √ for true or × for false in each bracket.
  (i) The production was stable over the four quarters. (　)
  (ii) The production was steadily improving over the four quarters. (　)
  (iii) The production was steadily declining over the four quarters. (　)
  (iv) The production fluctuated over the four quarters. (　)

Consolidation and enhancement

Challenge and extension question

4. The table presents a summary of the water bill of Ivan's family for the second quarter of 2015 (the unit prices have been rounded to the nearest penny). Read it carefully and answer the questions.

	Usage (m^3)	Unit price	Charge
Fresh water used	79	120p	
Used water returned to sewer	73	227p	
		Total charge	

(a) Use the data shown in the table to work out the charges and complete the table.

(b) How much water did the family use? Express it in both cubic metres and litres.

(c) Excluding other standing charges, how much did the family need to pay for their water bill for this period?

(d) Get a recent water bill from your home and make a table like the one above. Are there other standing charges?

Unit test 5

1 Work these out mentally. Write the answers.
(a) $20 \times 50 - 80 =$
(b) $230 + 90 + 70 =$
(c) $900 - 99 + 1 =$
(d) $96 \div 12 \times 12 =$
(e) $45 \times 7 + 3 =$
(f) $75 - 75 \div 5 =$
(g) $770 \times 8 \div 70 =$
(h) $16 \times 5 \times 2 =$
(i) $32 + 8 \times 2 =$
(j) $\frac{8}{15} - \frac{11}{30} + \frac{7}{15} =$
(k) $6400 \div 200 =$
(l) $10 \text{ kg } 20 \text{ g} - 920 \text{ g} =$ g

2 Use the column method to calculate.
(a) $56\,400 \div 700 =$
(b) $180 \times 209 =$
(c) $71\,200 \div 2300 =$

3 Work these out step by step. (Calculate smartly when possible.)
(a) $412 \div (607 - 36 \times 14)$
(b) $72 \times 36 + 18 \times 36$

(c) $80 \times [(325 + 7) - 304]$
(d) $250 \times 8 - 10\,000 \div 8$

(e) $(606 - 330) \times (116 + 434 \div 14)$
(f) $36 \times [(99 - 21) \times 99 + 108]$

(g) $3\frac{6}{7} + \frac{11}{35} - \frac{33}{35}$
(h) $\frac{1}{100} + \frac{99}{100} - \frac{7}{9}$

(i) $3 \times \frac{4}{7} - 5 \times \frac{3}{14} + 7 \times \frac{5}{28}$

Consolidation and enhancement

4 Fill in the brackets.

(a) 1000 (   ) is a million. (   ) millions is a billion.

(b) 120 456 consists of (   ) thousands, (   ) hundreds, (   ) tens and (   ) ones.

(c) Put the numbers 1, $\frac{5}{6}$, $\frac{4}{7}$ and $\frac{5}{7}$ in order starting from the greatest. The second number is (   ).

(d) Pour 3 litres of vegetable oil into 450 ml bottles. (   ) bottles will be filled up and (   ) bottles are needed in total.

(e) Rounding the number 555 500 to the nearest ten thousand, it is (   ).

(f) When rounding down the number 10 700 342 to the nearest ten thousand, it is (   ). When rounding up the number to the nearest hundred thousand, it is (   ).

(g) A 1 metre long string was divided into 100 equal parts. Six parts of them are (   ) metres long.

(h) $4800 \div 160 = 480 \div ($ $) = ($ $) \div 80 = ($ $) \div ($ $)$.

(i) In $6400 \div 3200 = 2$, if the divisor is decreased to 64 and the quotient remains unchanged, the dividend should be (   ).

(j) When one number is divided by another, the quotient is 17 and the remainder is 100. If both the dividend and the divisor are multiplied by 10, then the quotient is (   ) and the remainder is (   ).

(k) After a number is rounded down to the nearest ten thousand, it is 400 thousand. The greatest value of the number could be (   ).

(l) The quotient of two numbers is 45. If the dividend remains unchanged and the divisor is multiplied by 3, then the quotient is (   ).

(m) One number is divided by another and the quotient is 6. If both the dividend and the divisor are multiplied by 74, then the quotient is (   ).

(n) Both the dividend and the divisor are divided by 100 and the quotient is 4 with the reminder 2. Given that the original divisor is 700, the original dividend is (   ).

5 True or false.

(a) $27 \div 9 = (27 \times 3) \div (9 \times 3)$ (   )

(b) $54 \div 6 = (54 \div 2) \div (6 \times 2)$ (   )

(c) In $460 \div 50$, the quotient is 9 and the remainder is 1.   (   )

(d) $560 \div 16 = (560 + 8) \div (16 + 8)$ (   )

(e) Year 2017 in Roman numerals is MXVII.   (   )

6 Multiple choice questions.

(a) The number sentence equal to $72 \div 24$ is ( ).
   A. $(72 \times 2) \div (24 \div 2)$ B. $(72 \div 24) \times (24 \times 4)$
   C. $72 \div 6 \div 2$ D. $(72 \times 3) \div (24 \times 3)$

(b) From $13 \div 4 = 3 \text{ r } 1$, we can get $1300 \div 400 = ($).
   A. 3 r 10   B. 30 r 10   C. 3 r 100   D. 300 r 100

(c) The number sentence not equal to 101×199 is ( ).
   A. $(200 + 1) \times 101$ B. $199 \times (100 + 1)$
   C. $199 \times 100 + 199$ D. $(200 - 1) \times 101$

(d) After dissolving 1 gram of sugar in 99 grams of water, the mass of the sugar water solution is ( ) the mass of the sugar.
   A. $(99 + 1) \div 1$ times   B. $99 \div 1$ times
   C. $1 \div (1 + 99)$ times   D. $1 \div 99$ times

(e) MDCXI in Roman numerals is ( ) in digits.
   A. 1609   B. 1611   C. 1409   D. 1561

7 Write the number sentences and work out the answers.

(a) Number B is 150, which is half of Number A. What is the sum of Number A and Number B?

(b) The difference between 48 and 16 is multiplied by 25 and then divided by 8. What is the quotient?

(c) The difference between a number and 12 is divided by 125, and the quotient is 8. What is the number?

Consolidation and enhancement

8 Application problems.
  (a) A school planned to donate 780 books to schools in a disaster-hit area. The actual number of books it denoted was 66 more than 3 times the number of books it planned. How many books did the school donate?

  (b) A car travelled from City A to City C via City B in 4 hours. (See the diagram below.)
    (i) What was the average speed per hour the car travelled?

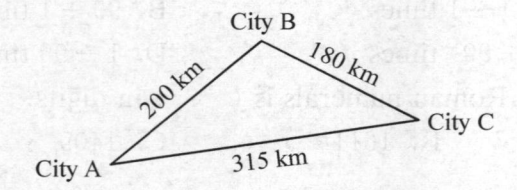

    (ii) When going back from City C straight to City A, the car travelled 10 km more per hour. How many hours did it take the car to reach City A?

  (c) A school bought 12 basketballs, which is half the number of volleyballs it bought. The number of footballs the school bought is 7 more than 3 times the total number of basketballs and volleyballs. How many footballs did the school buy?

  (d) An art studio bought 244 boxes of red-ink pens and green-ink pens. The number of green-ink pens is 12 boxes fewer than 7 times the number of red-ink pens. How many boxes of red-ink pens and green-ink pens did the studio buy?

(e) The table shows the number of pupils in a school whose birthdays fall in different quarters. Look at the table carefully and answer the questions.

	1st quarter	2nd quarter	3rd quarter	4th quarter
Number of pupils	130	180	95	155

(i) There are (   ) pupils in total in the school.

(ii) Construct a line graph using the data represented in the table.

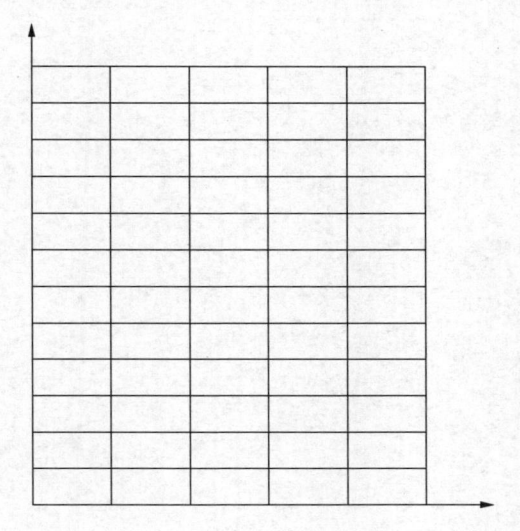

(iii) From the table or the line graph, can you tell the exact number of pupils in each year group? Can you give an estimate? Explain.

Chapter 6 Addition and subtraction of decimal numbers

6.1 Moving the decimal point (1)

Learning objectives

Multiply and divide decimals by 10, 100 and 1000

Basic questions

1. Work these out mentally. Write the answers.
   (a) $0.12 \times 10 =$
   (b) $0.12 \times 100 =$
   (c) $0.12 \times 1000 =$
   (d) $3.12 \times 10 =$
   (e) $3.12 \times 100 =$
   (f) $3.12 \times 1000 =$
   (g) $40.9 \div 10 =$
   (h) $40.9 \div 100 =$
   (i) $40.9 \div 1000 =$
   (j) $1.35 \div 10 =$
   (k) $1.35 \div 100 =$
   (l) $1.35 \div 1000 =$

2. Fill in the brackets.
   (a) When a decimal number is multiplied by 10, 100, 1000, ⋯, we just need to move the decimal point one place, two places, three places, and so on, to the (   ); when a decimal number is divided by 10, 100, 1000, and so on, we just need to move the decimal point (   ) place, (   ) places, (   ) places to the (   ). If there are not enough digits to move, add (   ) accordingly.
   (b) The result of removing the decimal point from 2.3 is the same as if it is multiplied by (   ), or moving its decimal point (   ) place(s) to the (   ).
   (c) Moving the decimal point in 45.99 (   ) place(s) to the (   ), we get 0.4599.
   (d) The unit of counting of 0.420 is (   ), and there are (   ) such units. Multiplying this number by (   ), we get 42.
   (e) 8.79 multiplied by 100 is (   ). The result further divided by 10 is (   ).
   (f) The result of inserting a decimal point in 4009 to make a decimal number with two decimal places is the same as if the number is divided by (   ).

Addition and subtraction of decimal numbers

(g) When the decimal point is removed from 1.03, the result is (   ), which is (   ) times the original number.

(h) When the decimal point in 7.77 is moved two places to the left, the result is the $\left(\dfrac{\quad}{\quad}\right)$ of the original number.

3 Fill in ○ with × or ÷, and write a suitable number in each bracket.

(a) 101.2 ○ (   ) = 10 120   (b) 36 ○ (   ) = 3.6

(c) 20.9 ○ 100 = 0.209   (d) 6.07 ÷ 10 ÷ (   ) = 0.0607

(e) (   ) × 1000 = 3256   (f) (   ) ÷ 10 ÷ 100 = 99.92

4 Multiple choice questions.

(a) Removing the decimal point in 0.022 is the same as multiplying the number by (   ).

   A. 10   B. 100   C. 1000   D. 10 000

(b) 1004.5 (   ) 10 000 is 0.10045.

   A. ×   B. ÷   C. +   D. −

(c) If we add two zeros after the decimal point in 6.7, it becomes 6.007. This number is (   ).

   A. 0.693 less than the original number
   B. 0.008 greater than the original number
   C. the same as the original number
   D. 0.792 less than the original number

(d) 0.0306 is (   ) 30.6.

   A. one tenth of   B. one hundredth of
   C. one thousandth of   D. 100 times

5 A basketball costs £23.80. How much does it cost to buy 100 such basketballs?

Addition and subtraction of decimal numbers

Challenge and extension questions

6. A school ran an oratorical contest and the results were as follows: Alvin scored 9.87 marks, James scored 9.90 marks, and Simon scored 9.96 marks.

   (a) Put the three students' scores in order, starting from the highest.

   (b) Lily's score is slightly lower than Simon's but higher than James's. Can you guess what score Lily might get?

7. Mahu is often absent-minded when doing things. Once when he was doing maths homework, he mistook 12.1 as 1.21, and he did not care about it, saying, 'It does not matter, as long as the value is close.' The decimal point in 12.1 was moved one place to the left, which became 1.21. Does it really not matter? If it matters, then what is the difference between 12.1 and 1.21?

8. A number was first multiplied by 100, then divided by 1000, and then again divided by 10. The final result is 0.017. What is the original number?

6.2 Moving the decimal point (2)

Learning objectives

Multiply and divide decimals by 10, 100 and 1000

Basic questions

1. Work these out mentally. Write the answers.
   (a) $0.25 \times 100 =$
   (b) $9.001 \times 10 =$
   (c) $0.014 \times 100 =$
   (d) $1.351 \times 1000 =$
   (e) $256.6 \div 100 =$
   (f) $100.1 \div 10 =$
   (g) $29 \div 1000 \times 10 =$
   (h) $55.5 \div 10 \div 10 =$
   (i) $0.08 \times 100 \div 10 =$
   (j) $0.06 \times 10 \times 100 =$
   (k) $630 \div 10 \times 10 =$
   (l) $2 \div 100 \times 1000 =$

2. Fill in each bracket with a suitable number.
   (a) 900 m = ( ) km
   (b) 90 cm² = ( ) m²
   (c) 1.51 t = ( ) kg
   (d) 70 cm = ( ) m
   (e) 0.48 l = ( ) ml
   (f) 789 g = ( ) kg
   (g) 20 km + 200 m = ( ) m
   (h) 9 l + 40 ml = ( ) l
   (i) £1.25 + 5p = ( ) p
   (j) 8 000 000 m² = ( ) km²

3. Write the number sentences and then calculate.
   (a) What is 1000 times 0.067?

   (b) What is one hundredth of 4.6?

   (c) How much greater is the sum of one hundred 1.5s than 10 times 7.5?

Addition and subtraction of decimal numbers

(d) The decimal point in 0.74 was moved two places to the right, and then the number was divided by 10. How many times the original number is the final result?

(e) Maria moved the decimal point of a number two places to the left, and then multiplied the number by 10. After that, she moved the decimal point one place to the right and then divided by 10 again, and got the result, which is 9.45. What was the original decimal number?

4 Fill in the brackets.
(a) 30.66 l = (　　) l (　　) ml
(b) 50 kg 500 g = (　　) kg
(c) 9 kg 9 g = (　　) kg
(d) 8004 cm = (　　) m
(e) 10.011 km² = (　　) km² (　　) m²

5 In a forest sports games, animals are having running races and their running speeds are shown in the table below.

Animal	puppy	baby elephant	pony	bunny
Speed	0.9 km per minute	400 m per minute	1.67 km per minute	1 km 200 m per minute

Based on the data above, put the animals in the correct places, starting from the 1st place.

Addition and subtraction of decimal numbers

Challenge and extension question

6 Observe the following number sentences and look for patterns.

As we know, $\frac{1}{10} = 1 \div 10 = 0.1$, $\frac{1}{100} = 1 \div 100 = 0.01$, $\frac{1}{1000} = 1 \div 1000 = 0.001$,

$34 \div 0.1 = 34 \div \frac{1}{10} = 34 \div (1 \div 10) = 34 \div 1 \times 10 = 34 \times 10$.

Conclusion: $3.4 \div 0.1 = 3.4 \times 10$.

Follow the above pattern and calculate:

569.21 ÷ 0.001 =   8.97 ÷ 0.1 =
90.1 ÷ 0.01 =   501.33 ÷ 0.001 =

Checking the answers with a calculator, we will get the same results. Hence, we can draw the following conclusion:

A number divided by 0.1, 0.01, 0.001, and so on, is equal to the number multiplied by 10, 100, 1000, and so on.

The conversion from division to multiplication makes the calculation easier. Share the finding with your friends.

6.3 Addition of decimals

Learning objectives

Add numbers with up to three decimal places

Basic questions

1 Work these out mentally. Write the answers.
(a) $0.3 + 0.9 =$
(b) $2.63 + 0.37 =$
(c) $5.3 + 3.6 =$
(d) $0.23 + 1.2 =$
(e) $1.5 + 0.8 =$
(f) $7 + 0.07 =$
(g) $0.03 + 0.06 =$
(h) $4.5 + 4 =$
(i) $4.5 + 0.4 =$
(j) $0.008 + 0.01 =$
(k) $15.6 + 0.03 =$
(l) $0.35 + 0.65 =$

2 Use the column method to calculate. The first one has been done for you. (Note: the decimal points are placed directly under each other and the numbers in columns are aligned by place value.)

(a) $46.34 + 5.7 = 52.04$

```
    4 6 . 3 4
  +     5 . 7
  -----------
    5 2 . 0 4
```

(b) $39.78 + 52.22 =$

(c) $92 + 28.97 =$

(d) $66.9 + 31 =$

(e) $8.1 + 9.089 =$

(f) $101.01 + 909.9 =$

Addition and subtraction of decimal numbers

3 Use decimals to calculate the following.

(a) 6 pounds 93 pence + 57 pence

(b) 340 cm + 1 m 15 cm

(c) 20 ml + 9 l

(d) 4 km 200 m + 900 m

(e) $\dfrac{3}{10} + \dfrac{7}{10}$

(f) $\dfrac{309}{1000} + \dfrac{276}{1000}$

4 Write the number sentences and then calculate.

(a) What number is 8.44 greater than 6?

(b) What number is 100 more than the sum of one hundred 0.759s?

(c) 0.03 is first multiplied by 1000 and then added by 69.33. What is the result?

Challenge and extension questions

5 A construction team was building a canal. In the first week, it built 1.3 km of the canal. In the second week, it built 0.15 km more than in the first week. After that, it had 1.05 km of the canal to complete. What was the total length of the canal?

6 Three identical pieces of coloured paper strips were pasted together one by one. Each piece of paper was 80 cm long and the joint area of each two pieces was 0.3 cm long. Find the total length of the paper strip formed by the 3 pieces of paper pasted together.

6.4 Subtraction of decimals

Learning objectives

Subtract numbers with up to three decimal places

Basic questions

1. Work these out mentally. Write the answers.
   (a) $0.9 - 0.8 =$
   (b) $0.09 - 0.05 =$
   (c) $0.007 - 0.003 =$
   (d) $7.8 - 2.8 =$
   (e) $1 - 0.6 =$
   (f) $3.6 - 1.8 =$
   (g) $5.4 - 0.6 =$
   (h) $1 - 0.06 =$
   (i) $5.2 - 2.6 =$
   (j) $8 - 2.5 =$
   (k) $1 - 0.01 =$
   (l) $1.1 - 0.04 =$

2. Use the column method to calculate. The first one has been done for you. (Check the answers to the questions marked with *.)
   (a) $30.74 - 11.32 = 19.42$

   $$\begin{array}{r} 3\,0.7\,4 \\ -\ 1\,1.3\,2 \\ \hline 1\,9.4\,2 \end{array}$$

   (b) *$21.1 - 8.57 =$

   (c) $60 - 6.07 =$
   (d) $27.4 - 18.09 =$

   (e) $60.3 - 13.55 =$
   (f) *$87.5 - 1.01 =$

3. Use decimals to calculate the following.
   (a) 10 pounds 38 pence − 2 pounds 46 pence
   (b) 9 km − 4 km 140 m

Addition and subtraction of decimal numbers

(c) 36 m² 600 cm² − 9900 cm² (d) $\dfrac{303}{1000} - \dfrac{28}{1000}$

(e) 2 l 20 ml − 1 l 600 ml (f) $\dfrac{84}{100} - \dfrac{19}{100} - \dfrac{13}{100}$

4. Write the number sentences and then calculate.
   (a) 0.8 is subtracted by one tenth of 0.8. What is the difference?

   (b) The quotient of 21.9 divided by 10 is added to the difference between 0.58 and 0.25. What is the sum?

Challenge and extension questions

5. When working on a subtraction sentence, Andy misread 9 as 6 in the ones place in the minuend and 8 as 2 in the tenths place. Therefore, he got a result of 3.6. What is the correct answer?

6. Bob planned to drive from Place A to Place B, which were 210.8 km apart. After he had travelled 66.8 km, he realised that he had left something important at home. He drove back to Place A to get the item and then continued his journey to Place B. How many kilometres more did he drive than planned?

6.5 Addition and subtraction of decimals (1)

Learning objectives

Add and subtract numbers with up to three decimal places

Basic questions

1 Work these out mentally. Write the answers.
(a) $0.9 + 10.1 =$
(b) $5.5 - 0.78 =$
(c) $0.56 + 0.405 =$
(d) $4.05 - 3.9 =$
(e) $0.45 + 0.056 =$
(f) $0.34 + 0.66 =$
(g) $1.1 - 1.056 =$
(h) $9.04 + 2.1 =$
(i) $1 - 0.099 =$
(j) $4.78 + 0.98 =$
(k) $12.99 - 3.99 =$
(l) $10.1 + 2.09 =$

2 Work these out step by step. (Calculate smartly when possible.)
(a) $9.06 - 2.87 - 4.13$
(b) $4.9 + 8.7 + 11.1$

(c) $8.67 - (4.67 - 2.7)$
(d) $7.35 - (2.87 + 2.35)$

(e) $14.4 - 3.908 - 0.092$
(f) $23.43 - 6.56 - 3.44 - 5.43$

3 Write the number sentences and then calculate.
(a) The sum of Number A and Number B is 63.5. Number A is 24.5. What is Number B?

Addition and subtraction of decimal numbers

(b) Number A is 30.52, which is 8.8 greater than Number B. What is the sum of Number A and Number B?

(c) Number A is 42.62. Number B is half of Number A. Number C is 2.8 greater than Number B. What is Number C?

4. Sue bought two books from a used bookstore, one for £41.80 and the other for £38.20. She paid the cashier £100. How much change should she get?

Challenge and extension questions

5. Find the perimeter of the figure below.

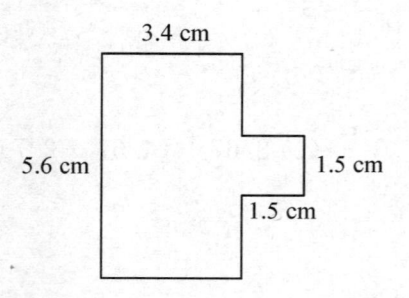

3.4 cm
5.6 cm
1.5 cm
1.5 cm

6. Mum bought some food from a market. She bought some green vegetables for £4.75, prawns for £23.80, pies for £10.25 and meats for £6.20. How much did she spend in total?

7. When a pupil was working on an addition problem, in one of the addends, he misread 0 in the tenths place as 9, and got a sum of 16.98. What is the correct sum? When he was working on a subtraction problem, in the subtrahend he again mistakenly wrote 5 in the hundredths place as 3. Therefore, the difference was 23.56. What is the correct difference?

6.6 Addition and subtraction of decimals (2)

Learning objectives

Add and subtract numbers with up to three decimal places

Basic questions

1. Work these out mentally. Write the answers.
   (a) $2.4 + 11.8 =$
   (b) $2.5 + 0.57 =$
   (c) $3.9 - 3 =$
   (d) $2.8 - 0.28 =$
   (e) $5.6 + 6.5 =$
   (f) $13.3 - 0.8 =$
   (g) $9 - 0.05 =$
   (h) $1 - 0.999 =$
   (i) $5.3 + 0.78 =$
   (j) $10 - 0.42 =$
   (k) $29 + 0.17 =$
   (l) $0.06 - 0.023 =$

2. Work these out step by step. (Calculate smartly when possible.)
   (a) $108.43 + 15.84 + 24.16$
   (b) $125.47 - 26.46 - 73.54$

   (c) $86.5 - (18.5 + 3.7) - 26.3$
   (d) $2.54 - 0.27 + (1.46 + 1.73)$

   (e) $200 - [36.8 - (6.8 - 2.9)]$
   (f) $985 \div 125 \div 8$

   (g) $6.4 \times 7 + 6.4 \times 3$
   (h) $2200 \div [436 \div (192 - 83)]$

3. Write the number sentences and then calculate.
   (a) How much greater is 90.5 than the sum of 7.1 and 12.9?

Addition and subtraction of decimal numbers

(b) How much greater is the sum of 56.04 and 0.99 than the difference between 14.6 and 0.26?

(c) The difference between 6.1 and 0.61 is multiplied by 100. What is the product?

4 A science laboratory produced 8.92 kg of a new product each day in the first ten days. It produced a total of 21.45 kg of the same product in the following two days. What was the total weight of the product the laboratory produced in the twelve days?

Challenge and extension questions

5 Calculate.
(a) $680 \times 3.4 + 34 \times 32 =$

(b) $23.02 + 48.303 + \dfrac{362}{1000} - 20.72 - \dfrac{121}{100} =$

6 Three bags have the same amount of sweets. Tina took one of the bags. Henry divided the sweets in the second bag into 10 equal parts and he took 3 parts for himself. Alice divided the sweets in the third bag into 100 parts and she took 7 parts for herself. How many bags of sweets did the three of them take in total? (Express your answer in decimals.)

6.7 Practice and exercise (2)

Learning objectives

Add and subtract numbers with up to three decimal places

Basic questions

1. Work these out mentally. Write the answers.
   (a) $85.3 + 2.7 =$
   (b) $50 \div 100 =$
   (c) $9.1 \times 100 =$
   (d) $4.65 + 2.45 =$
   (e) $765 \div 1000 =$
   (f) $12 - 9.3 =$
   (g) $0.231 \times 1000 =$
   (h) $120 \div 24 =$
   (i) $20 - 18.06 =$
   (j) $5.5 + 5 =$
   (k) $3.5 \times 100 =$
   (l) $7.66 \div 10 \times 1000 =$

2. Use the column method to calculate. (Check the answers to the questions marked with *.)
   (a) $202.78 + 10.89 =$
   (b) *$34.416 - 4.78 =$

   (c) $90.4 - 9.08 =$
   (d) *$4.69 + 5.039 =$

3. Work these out step by step. (Calculate smartly when possible.)
   (a) $24.25 - 11.08 - 0.266$
   (b) $335.39 + 0.78 - 335.39$

   (c) $49.9 + 199.9 + 1999.9 + 0.3$
   (d) $(200 + 100 \div 50) \times 16$

   (e) $199.69 - (57 + 39.69)$
   (f) $(2.5 \times 39 + 2.5 \times 61) \times 4$

Addition and subtraction of decimal numbers

4 Compare the quantities below and put them in order, starting from the greatest.
0.24 km, 2040 m, 2 km 400 m

_____

5 Fill in the brackets.
(a) When 2.015 is multiplied by 100, it is (   ). When the result is further divided by 10, it is (   ).
(b) The result of 0.03 × 100 ÷ 1000 is to move the decimal point in 0.03 (   ) place(s) to the (   ).
(c) Adding (   ) 0.001s is the same as the sum of five 0.1s and one 0.001.
(d) After moving the decimal point in Number A two places to the right, it is equal to Number B. Number B is (   ) times Number A.
(e) 71 m² + 6 cm² = (   ) m²
(f) 0.112 kg + 20 g = (   ) g

Challenge and extension questions

6 Jane spent £70.50 on a schoolbag and a pencil box in total. If the cost of one schoolbag is twice the cost of two pencil boxes plus £19.50, what are the unit prices of the schoolbag and the pencil box?

7 There are three numbers: A, B and C. If the decimal point in A is moved two places to the right, and the decimal point in B is moved three places to the left, then the two new numbers are both equal to C. If A is 3.01, then what are B and C?

Unit test 6

1 Work these out mentally. Write the answers.
(a) $6 \div 1000 =$
(b) $8.4 - 6.5 =$
(c) $4.8 \times 100 =$
(d) $31.05 - 0.5 =$
(e) $0.8 + 6.28 =$
(f) $25 \times 4 \div 5 =$
(g) $500 \div 1000 =$
(h) $30.08 \times 10 =$
(i) $66 \div 11 \times 6 =$

2 Use the column method to calculate. (Check the answers to the questions marked with *.)
(a) $20.208 + 89.9 =$
(b) *$300 - 41.78 =$

(c) $26.6 - 4.543 =$
(d) *$18.9 + 0.11 =$

3 Work these out step by step. (Calculate smartly when possible.)
(a) $25.29 - (16.29 + 6.2)$
(b) $10.9 - 5.2 - 4.8 + 9.1$

(c) $6400 \div (64 \times 50)$
(d) $33.08 + (2.713 + 7.92) + 0.287$

(e) $3900 \div (39 \times 4) \div 25$
(f) $116.77 + 38.49 - (6.77 - 61.51)$

Addition and subtraction of decimal numbers

4. Use decimals to calculate the following.

(a) $\frac{9}{10} + 4.7 - \frac{56}{100}$

(b) $5 - \frac{8}{10} - \frac{344}{1000}$

(c) 0.5 kg $+ 5$ g

(d) 96 m$^2 + 96$ cm^2

5. Multiple choice questions.
   (a) The correct statement of the following is (   ).
   A. Moving the decimal point one place to the right is the same as the number being divided by 10.
   B. Decimal numbers are always less than whole numbers.
   C. The second place to the right of the decimal point is the hundredths place and the third place to the left of the decimal point is the thousands place.
   D. To read the decimal part of a number is to start with the decimal point and then read each digit from the left to the right.

   (b) 24 m$^2 = ($ $)$ cm^2
   A. 24   B. 2400   C. 2400.00   D. 240 000

   (c) Compare 4.00 and 4. The two numbers are (   ).
   A. the same both in value and in unit of counting
   B. the same in value but different in unit of counting
   C. different in value but the same in unit of counting
   D. different both in value and in unit of counting

   (d) In a decimal number, the unit of counting for the digit in the tenths place is (   ) less than the unit of counting for the digit in the ones place.
   A. 0.09   B. 0.9   C. 1.0   D. 10

   (e) Move the decimal point in a number four places to the right and then move it two places to the left. It means the original decimal number is (   ).
   A. divided by 1000   B. divided by 100
   C. multiplied by 100   D. multiplied by 3

6. Write the number sentences and then calculate.
   (a) In a decimal number, how much greater is the value represented by 9 in the

Addition and subtraction of decimal numbers

hundreds place than that represented by 9 in the tenths place?

(b) How much less is the least decimal number with three decimal places than the greatest pure decimal with one decimal place?

(c) How much greater is the sum of one thousand 2.2s than 10 times 99.5?

7 Application problems.
(a) Scott spent £28.60 on drinks. The money his mum spent on food is £74.50 more than the amount Scott spent on drinks. How much did they spend in total?

(b) A full bottle of purified water weighed 19 kg. After 9.1 kg of water was used to make lemonade, half the water was left in the bottle. What is the weight of the empty bottle?

(c) The length of a rectangle is 0.85 m, which is 12 cm longer than the width. What is the perimeter of the rectangle?

(d) The prices of four book collections are as follows: *A Collection of Cartoons* — £54.70, *A Collection of Short Stories* — £20.88, *A Collection of Children's Songs* — £19.40 and *Best Selections of Comics* — £25.10. Which three collections will cost less than £100 in total? Show your working.

Chapter 7 Introduction to positive and negative numbers

7.1 Positive and negative numbers (1)

Learning objectives

Interpret and use negative numbers in context

Basic questions

1. The thermometers show the lowest temperatures recorded in January in three cities. Write them in the table below.

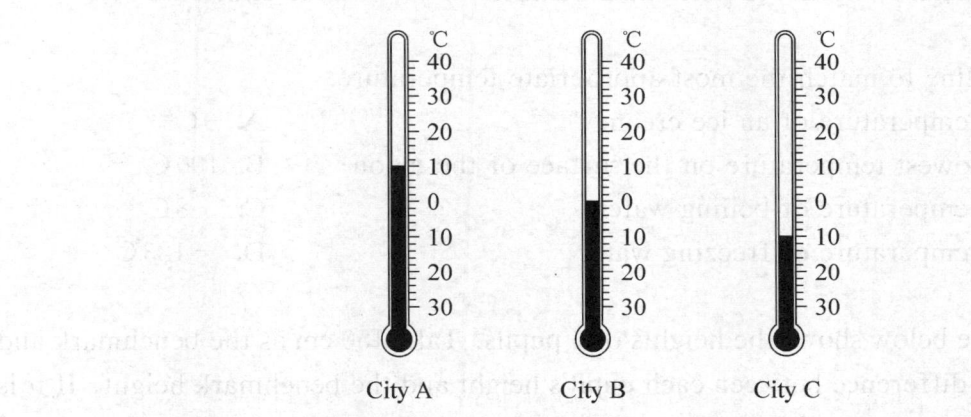

	City A	City B	City C
Lowest temperature recorded in January			

2. Put the numbers in the correct circles.

$$3.2,\ -18,\ +20.1,\ 0,\ -6.9,\ 37,\ -\frac{9}{10}$$

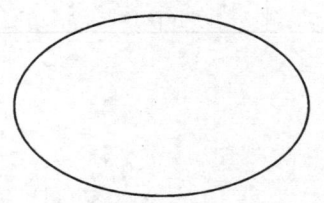

Positive numbers

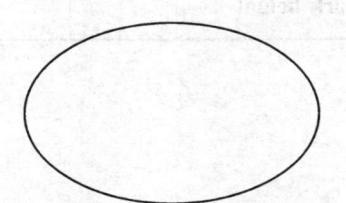

Negative numbers

Introduction to positive and negative numbers

3 Link each pair of words that have the opposite meaning. One has been done for you.

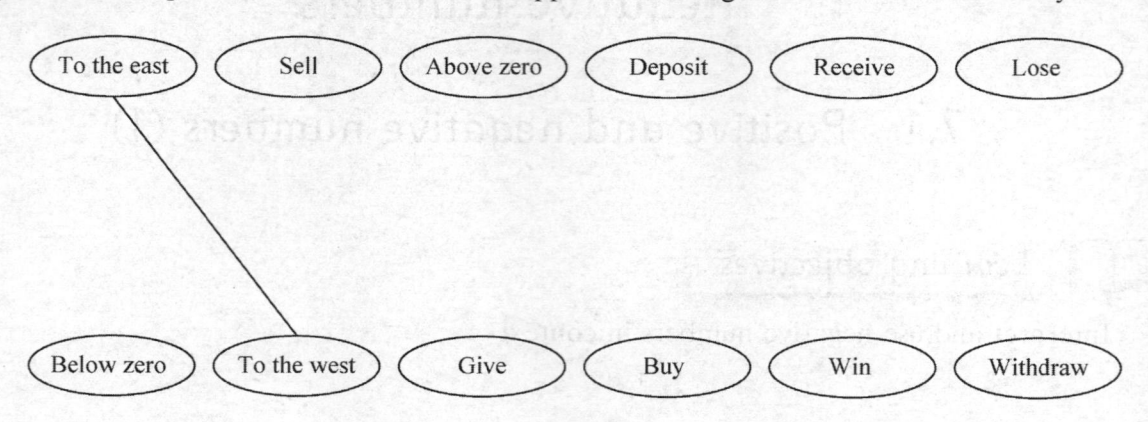

(To the east)   (Sell)   (Above zero)   (Deposit)   (Receive)   (Lose)

(Below zero)   (To the west)   (Give)   (Buy)   (Win)   (Withdraw)

4 Fill in the brackets with 'can' or 'cannot'.
(a) The sign '+' before a positive number (　　) be omitted.
(b) The sign '−' before a negative number (　　) be omitted.

5 Draw a line to match the most appropriate temperature.
① The temperature of an ice cream　　　　　　　　　　A. 0℃
② The lowest temperature on the surface of the moon　　B. 100℃
③ The temperature of boiling water　　　　　　　　　　C. −8℃
④ The temperature of freezing water　　　　　　　　　　D. −183℃

6 The table below shows the heights of 6 pupils. Take 150 cm as the benchmark and find the difference between each pupil's height and the benchmark height. If it is above the benchmark, write the difference as positive, and if it is below the benchmark, write the difference as negative, and fill in the table.

Pupil	1	2	3	4	5	6	Benchmark
Height (cm)	140	148	160	135	155	162	150
Difference from the benchmark height							

Introduction to positive and negative numbers

Challenge and extension questions

7 The income of Julie's family in May was £5800. The bills for water, electricity and gas totalled £270. The phone bill came to £180. The following table is to record the family's income and expenditure in May.

Item	Expense (pounds)
Family income	+5800
Bills for water, electricity and gas	
Telephone bill	
Other expenses	

(a) Help Julie record her family's expenses for water, electricity, gas and telephone bills in May in the table.

(b) Julie's mum deposited the surplus of £2500 in May to the bank. Can you work out the family's other expenses in May? Add them to the table.

8 A, B and C are three places on some land. If the elevation of Place A is +10 m, Place B is +36 m, and Place C is −3 m, then the highest place is (   ) and the lowest place is (   ).

7.2 Positive and negative numbers (2)

Learning objectives
Solve problems involving positive and negative numbers

Basic questions

1 Fill in the brackets.
   (a) In recording the change of the number of passengers on a bus, if $+8$ represents 8 passengers getting on the bus, then -5 people represents (   ).
   (b) Jane's mum received her salary of £2500, and it is recorded as $+£2500$. She spent £120 buying some books for Jane, and it should be recorded as (   ).
   (c) In a maths competition, every right answer gets 5 marks and every wrong answer loses 5 marks. If the former is recorded as $+5$, then the latter is recorded as (   ). A team got 25 right answers, recorded as (   ) marks, and 4 wrong answers, recorded as (   ) marks. Their final score was (   ) marks.
   (d) The label on a pack of sugar shows the net weight is (500 ± 5) g. It means that the maximum weight of the sugar is (   ) g and the minimum weight is (   ) g.
   (e) Due to global warming and snow melting, the sea level is rising over time. The average height of the Maldives in the Indian Ocean is only 1.5 m higher than sea level, noted as (   ) m. If the sea level rises 2 cm every year, in about (   ) years, all the areas of the Maldives below the average height will be completely flooded by the sea.

2 True or false.
   (a) In recording temperature, 10℃ and $+10$℃ have the same meaning.   (   )
   (b) In representing elevation of sea level, -230 m means 230 m below the sea level.   (   )
   (c) If today's lowest temperature is 2℃ lower than yesterday's, then today's lowest temperature is -2℃.   (   )
   (d) If the average maths score, 87 marks, is used as a benchmark, and Tim got 95 marks, then his score can be denoted by $+95$ marks.   (   )

Introduction to positive and negative numbers

3. Multiple choice questions.
   (a) If walking 200 m from the school to the south is recorded as $+200$ m, then -360 m means walking 360 m from the gate to the (   ).
   A. east   B. south   C. west   D. north
   (b) With every increment of 1 km in height, the temperature decreases by 6℃. If the ground temperature is 12℃, then the temperature at the high altitude of 4 km is (   ).
   A. -6℃   B. -12℃   C. -18℃   D. -24℃
   (c) Six pupils took part in an environmental protection knowledge competition. The teacher used 80 marks as the benchmark and recorded their scores simply as $+5$, -3, $+8$, 0, -2 and -5. The lowest score among the 6 pupils was (   ) marks.
   A. 88   B. 70   C. 80   D. 75
   (d) A building has 15 floors, including 2 floors below the ground floor. If the 12th floor above the ground floor is denoted as $+12$ floor, then the first floor below the ground level is denoted as (   ) floor.
   A. $+1$ B. 0   C. -1 D. -2

4. The table shows some information about the heights of pupils in a school choir.

	Anne	Ruth	Beth	Chloe	Gemma	Grace
Height (cm)	147			140		
Difference from average height	$+2$	-1	$+5$		0	$+13$

(a) Who is the tallest person? Who is the shortest?

(b) What is the difference in height between the tallest and the shortest?

Introduction to positive and negative numbers

Challenge and extension question

5. Because of the Earth's rotation, there are different time zones around the world. Let's take Greenwich Mean Time (GMT) as the benchmark, so the time earlier than GMT is positive and the time later than GMT is negative.

   For example: Beijing time is 8 hours earlier than GMT, which can be denoted as +8 hours. New Zealand time is 12 hours earlier than GMT, which can be denoted as +12 hours.

   (a) New York time is 5 hours later than GMT, which can be denoted as (   ) hours. Tokyo time is 9 hours earlier than GMT, which is denoted as (   ) hours.

   (b) If GMT is 12:00, then Beijing time is (   ), New Zealand time is (   ), New York time is (   ), and Tokyo time is (   ).

   (c) If using Beijing time as the benchmark, then the time earlier than Beijing time is positive and later is negative, so London time, when it is on GMT, can be denoted as (   ) hours, New York time as (   ) hours and New Zealand time as (   ) hours. (Note: during Daylight Saving Time each year, London time is one hour ahead of GMT.)

7.3 Number lines (1)

Learning objectives
Solve problems involving positive and negative numbers on number lines

Basic questions

1. Count and then fill in the brackets.
   (a) Forwards in tens: 0, 10, 20, ( ), ( ), ( ), ( ), ( ), 80.
   (b) Backwards in ones: 5, 4, 3, ( ), ( ), ( ), ( ), ( ),
       ( ), ( ), −5.
   (c) Backwards in fives: 10, 5, 0, ( ), ( ), ( ), −20.
   (d) Forwards in hundreds: −500, −400, −300, ( ), ( ), ( ),
       ( ), 200.

2. Write what number the points A, B, C and D represent on the number line.

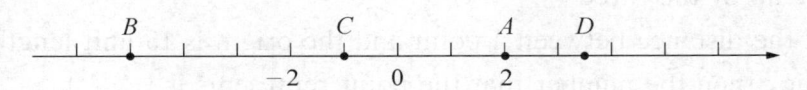

   Point A represents the number ( ).   Point B represents the number ( ).
   Point C represents the number ( ).   Point D represents the number ( ).

3. Locate the points on the number line representing −4, +3, 0, −5.5 and +0.5, and use A, B, C, D and E to denote them in the same order.

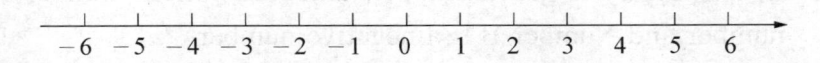

4. Look at the number line below and fill in the brackets.

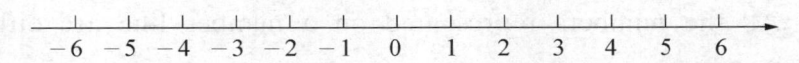

   (a) The point represented by +2 is on the ( ) of the origin and is ( ) units away from it.
   (b) The point represented by −4 is on the ( ) of the origin and is ( ) units away from it.

Introduction to positive and negative numbers

(c) The point represented by (　) is on the left of the origin and is 5 units away from it.

(d) The point represented by (　) is on the right of the origin and is 2.5 units away from it.

(e) The points 3 units away from the origin are (　) and (　).

(f) +6 and −6 are both (　) units away from the origin.

5 On a number line, points representing positive numbers are on the (　) of the origin, and points representing negative numbers are on the (　) of the origin.

6 All (　) numbers are greater than 0, and all negative numbers are (　) than 0. Positive numbers are (　) than negative numbers.

7 Multiple choice questions.

(a) A number line has the following elements defined: (　).

　A. an origin

　B. a positive direction

　C. a unit length

　D. all of the three

(b) If the distance between a point and the origin is 15 unit lengths on a number line, then the number that the point represents is (　).

　A. +15

　B. −15

　C. +15 or −15

　D. uncertain

(c) In the following statements, the correct one is (　).

　A. If Number A is greater than Number B, then Number A is a positive number and Number B is a negative number.

　B. A number line does not need to have an origin and a positive direction.

　C. If two points are 5 unit lengths apart on a number line, then the difference between the numbers represented by the two points is 5.

　D. All the numbers represented on a number line are either positive or negative.

Introduction to positive and negative numbers

8 Mark points represented by each of the following numbers on the number line, and answer the questions.

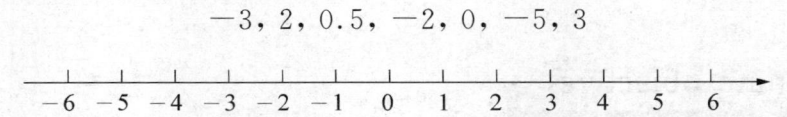

$$-3, 2, 0.5, -2, 0, -5, 3$$

```
 ┼──┼──┼──┼──┼──┼──┼──┼──┼──┼──┼──┼──►
-6 -5 -4 -3 -2 -1  0  1  2  3  4  5  6
```

(a) Which numbers are represented by the two points that are of the same distance from the origin?

(b) How many unit lengths are the difference between the point represented by −2 and that represented by 3?

Challenge and extension questions

9 On the number line below, first move the point representing −1 to the right for 3 unit lengths and then move it to the left for 5 unit lengths. What number does the new point represent? If considering these two moves as one step, then after taking 10 such steps what number does the final point represent?

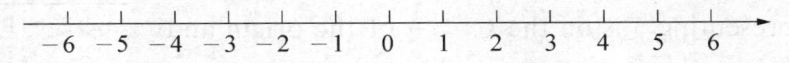

```
 ┼──┼──┼──┼──┼──┼──┼──┼──┼──┼──┼──┼──►
-6 -5 -4 -3 -2 -1  0  1  2  3  4  5  6
```

10 Mark five points on the number line to represent +1, −7.5, −2, +6 and −10.

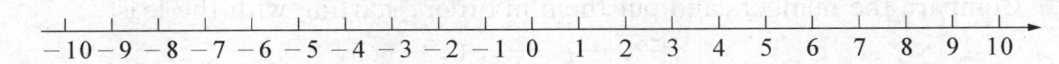

```
 ┼──┼──┼──┼──┼──┼──┼──┼──┼──┼──┼──┼──┼──┼──┼──┼──┼──┼──┼──┼──►
-10 -9 -8 -7 -6 -5 -4 -3 -2 -1  0  1  2  3  4  5  6  7  8  9  10
```

Among these points, (   ) points are on the right of the origin and (   ) points are on the left of the origin. Points representing (   ) and (   ) are the closest to each other, and they are (   ) units apart. Points representing (   ) and (   ) are the farthest from each other and they are (   ) units apart.

7.4 Number lines (2)

Learning objectives
Solve problems involving positive and negative numbers on number lines

Basic questions

1. Use the number line to compare the numbers. Fill in the ◯ with < or >.

   ```
   -6 -5 -4 -3 -2 -1  0  1  2  3  4  5  6
   ```

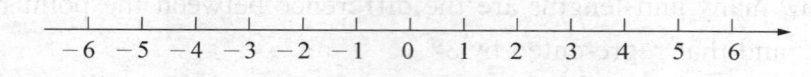

   (a) -4 ◯ $+6$ (b) -5 ◯ -2 (c) 0 ◯ -3

   (d) 6 ◯ -6 (e) $+1.5$ ◯ -1.5 (f) $+4$ ◯ -4.5

   (g) -1 ◯ -7 (h) -3.2 ◯ -2.3 (i) -5 ◯ -0.5

2. Fill in the brackets.
   (a) Write 4 whole numbers less than $+7$ (　　).
   (b) Write 4 whole numbers greater than -7 (　　).
   (c) There are (　　) whole numbers between $+7.5$ and -7.5.
   (d) The diagram shows a number line. The point representing 5 is on the (　　) of the origin and its distance from the origin is (　　) units of length. The point representing -8 is on the (　　) of the origin and its distance from the origin is (　　) units. The distance between the point representing 5 and the point representing -8 is (　　) units.

   ```
   -2 -1  0  1  2
   ```

3. Compare the numbers and put them in order, starting with the least.
   $$+2,\ +7,\ -4,\ 0,\ -6.5,\ -3$$

4. True or false.
   (a) On a number line, the farther a point is apart from the origin, the greater the number it represents. (　　)
   (b) Every number can be represented by a point on a number line. (　　)

(c) As zero means none, none of the points on a number line represents zero.
( )

(d) On a number line, there is only one number whose distance from the origin is 0.5.
( )

5 Multiple choice questions.
(a) In the following statements, the incorrect one is ( ).
A. The least whole number is 0.
B. There is no greatest negative number.
C. There is no least negative number.
D. The greatest whole number exists.

(b) Comparing -3.2, $+6$ and -1, the result is ( ).
A. $-3.2 > -1 > +6$ 　　　　　　B. $+6 > -1 > -3.2$
C. $-3.2 > +6 > -1$ 　　　　　　D. $+6 > -3.2 > -1$

(c) A beetle started crawling from point A on a number line at a speed of 3 units per second. The number represented by point A is -4. The beetle moved to the right for 2 seconds and reached point B. The number represented by point B is ( ).
A. 2　　　　　B. -2　　　　　C. 4　　　　　D. -4

(d) The point representing -7.5 is ( ) on the number line.
A. between -6 and -7 　　　　B. between -7 and -8
C. between 7 and 8 　　　　　　D. between 6 and 7

6 Boat A and Boat B exchanged goods at Place A, and then travelled in opposite directions, with Boat A heading south and Boat B heading north. After 1 hour, Boat A travelled 12 nautical miles and Boat B travelled 7 nautical miles. What was the distance between the two boats? (Note: 1 nautical mile=1852 metres.)

Challenge and extension questions

7 Is each of the following statements correct? (Note: whole numbers are 0, 1, 2, 3, and so on, natural numbers are 1, 2, 3, and so on, and integers are, for example. -3, -2, -1, 0, 1, 2, 3, and so on.)
(a) All natural numbers are whole numbers.
( )

Introduction to positive and negative numbers

    (b) All whole numbers are natural numbers. ( )
    (c) All integers are positive numbers. ( )
    (d) The greatest negative integer is -1. ( )
    (e) Non-positive numbers are negative numbers. ( )
    (f) There is only one integer on a number line with distance from the origin less than 2. ( )

8 An insect creeps backwards and forwards along a straight line. Starting from point A, when it creeps to the right, it is regarded as positive, and when it creeps to the left it is regarded as negative. The route the insect crept, in sequence, was $-3, +4, +3, -5, -7$ and $+6$ (unit: cm).

(a) Was the insect on the left or the right of point A in the end?

(b) What was the farthest place the insect reached from point A?

(c) What was the total distance the insect travelled?

Unit test 7

1 Fill in the brackets.

(a) When a warehouse receives 150 tons of goods, it is denoted as $+150$ tons. When 200 tons of goods are dispatched from the warehouse, it is denoted as (   ) tons.

(b) The point representing -7 on a number line is on the (   ) of the origin, (   ) units apart from it.

(c) In $+4$, 1.7, -3, -5.6, 0, $-\frac{1}{2}$, 3, -1, $+2$ and -8, the positive numbers are (   ) and the negative numbers are (   ). The numbers less than -5 are (   ) and the numbers greater than -3 but less than $+3$ are (   ). The two numbers with the same distance from the origin are (   ).

(d) Putting -1, $+3$, 0, 2 and -4 in order from the greatest to the least, the fourth number is (   ). The difference between the greatest number and the least number is (   ).

(e) Among 4, -3, -2 and 3, the number nearest to 0 is (   ).

(f) On one day, the temperature at noon was 7℃ and at 17:00 it was 4℃ lower; the temperature at 04:00 in the early morning was 8℃ lower than that at noon. The temperature at 17:00 was (   )℃ and at 04:00 it was (   )℃.

(g) Some people were on a bus before it reached a bus stop. Taking the number of people getting on the bus as positive and the number of people getting off as negative, the numbers of people getting on or off the bus in the next four stops were noted as: -5, 3, 8 and -10. After the four stops, how many more or fewer people were on the bus than the original number? (   ).

(h) The number represented by any point on a number line is always less than the number represented by a point on its (   ).

(i) In a military defence exercise, the elevation of the location of one submarine from the red group is -200 m. Another submarine from the blue group is 160 m above the submarine in the red group. The elevation of the location of the submarine from the blue group is (   ) m.

(j) Taking the gate of a residential park as the origin and walking to east as positive, if Jason walked -100 m to east, it means that Jason actually walked 100 m (   ). If Jason first walked 50 m east from the gate, and then walked

Introduction to positive and negative numbers

west 80 m, Jason's position is (　　) m from the gate.

(k) In a maths test, 10 pupils recorded their test scores with 90 marks as the benchmark. The marks above 90 were denoted as positive and the marks below 90 were denoted as negative. The results are as follows: $+3$, -5, $+8$, $+1$, $+9$, -4, -3, $+6$, $+5$ and -2. The highest score is (　　) and the lowest score is (　　).

2 True or false.

(a) Non-negative numbers are positive numbers. (　　)

(b) The numbers represented by two different points at the same distance from the origin are equal. (　　)

(c) The farther a point is from the origin, the greater the number it represents. (　　)

(d) Of all the numbers less than 0, the greatest is -1. (　　)

(e) The numbers greater than -3 and less than $+3$ are -2, -1, 0, $+1$ and $+2$. (　　)

3 Multiple choice questions.

(a) A (　　) with an origin, a positive direction and a unit length is known as a number line.

　　A. point　　　　B. circle　　　　C. curve　　　　D. straight line

(b) Barbara walked backwards and forwards on a straight line. Starting from the origin (point A), she first walked 3 steps to the right, and then 7 steps to the left. She walked another 8 steps to the right, and 5 steps to the left. She stopped at point B. If the length of each step was the same, then the distance between point A to point B was (　　) steps.

　　A. 1　　　　　B. -2　　　　　C. 3　　　　　D. -1

(c) Look at the following table. The biggest temperature change in the five days took place from (　　).

	Monday	Tuesday	Wednesday	Thursday	Friday
Average temperature	0℃	6℃	-2℃	-5℃	-8℃

　　A. Monday to Tuesday　　　　　B. Tuesday to Wednesday
　　C. Wednesday to Thursday　　　D. Thursday to Friday

(d) In the following statements, the incorrect one is (　　).

　　A. Positive numbers are greater than negative numbers.

B. Zero is less than all positive numbers.

   C. Negative numbers closer to the origin must be greater than negative numbers further from it.

   D. Positive numbers closer to the origin must be greater than positive numbers further from it.

(e) There are three groups of numbers A, B and C. Group A consists of numbers greater than -10 and less than or equal to $+5$. Group B consists of numbers greater than or equal to -6 and less than $+9$. Group C consists of the numbers that belong to both Group A and Group B. The numbers in Group C are (   ).

   A. greater than -6 and less than $+5$

   B. greater than or equal to -6 and less than $+5$

   C. greater than -6 and less than or equal to $+5$

   D. greater than or equal to -6 and less than or equal to $+5$

4 Application problems.

(a) The table below shows the temperatures of seven tourist areas on a particular day.

	Area 1	Area 2	Area 3	Area 4	Area 5	Area 6	Area 7
Temperature (℃)	11~1	8~4	3~ -2	27~19	8~ -8	15~1	0~ -5

(i) Which tourist area had the least temperature difference between the high and the low on the day?

(ii) Which tourist area had the greatest temperature difference on the day?

(iii) Which two tourist areas had the same temperature difference on the day?

(b) Allan's house is 3 km east of the school and Nara's house is 3 km north of Allan's house. May's house is 3 km west of Nara's house. How far is May's house away from the school, and in what direction?

Introduction to positive and negative numbers

(c) A toy car moves backwards and forwards along a straight line. Starting from point O, when it moves to the right, it is recorded as positive, and when it moves to the left, it is recorded as negative. The first 6 moves the toy car made were, in sequence, -1, $+2$, -3, $+4$, -5 and $+6$ (unit: cm). Taking the 6 moves the toy car made as one round, the toy car repeated the same pattern of movement many times.

(i) After the toy car moved 9 rounds, was it on the left or right of point O? How far was it away from point O?

(ii) In the first 2 rounds the toy car moved, what was its farthest distance from point O?

(iii) After the toy car had moved for 50 rounds, what was the total distance it had covered?

(d) Ben's house is 1 km west of Lily's house. Between Ben's house and Lily's house there is a school, a market, and a post office, which are all located on a straight street. The market is 300 m east of Ben's house, and the post office is 200 m west of Lily's house. The school is 150 m east of the market.

(i) How far are Ben's house and Lily's house away from the school, respectively?

(ii) One day, after Lily visited the post office, she walked to the school at an average speed of 70 m per minute. At the same time, Ben walked from his home to the school. If he wanted to reach the school at the same time as Lily, what should be his average speed?

Introduction to positive and negative numbers

(iii) One morning, Ben and Lily went jogging. They started from their own houses at the same time and ran towards each other. Ben ran 260 m per minute and Lily ran 240 m per minute. When they met each other, in what direction in relation to the school were they? How far were they away from the school? In what direction in relation to the market were they, and how far were they away from it? In what direction in relation to the post office were they and how far were they away from it?

Chapter 8 Geometry and measurement (1)

8.1 Knowing circles (1)

Learning objectives

Identify, name and draw parts of a circle

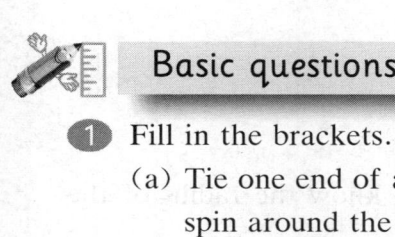

Basic questions

1. Fill in the brackets.
   (a) Tie one end of a string tightly onto a fixed point and allow the other end to spin around the point; a (   ) is formed. The distances from any point on the circle to the point are equal, known as the (   ) and the point is known as the (   ) of the circle.
   (b) The figure on the right shows a circle, in which point O is the (   ) and r is a (   ) of the circle. 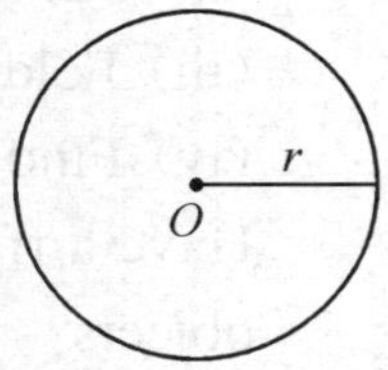
   (c) The length of the diameter of a circle is (   ) its radius.
   (d) A PE teacher was drawing a circle on the sports field with a little trolley. The length of the string between the fixed point and the trolley was 4 m. The radius of the circle was (   ).

2. Multiple choice questions.
   (a) Based on the circle shown, the correct statement is (   ). 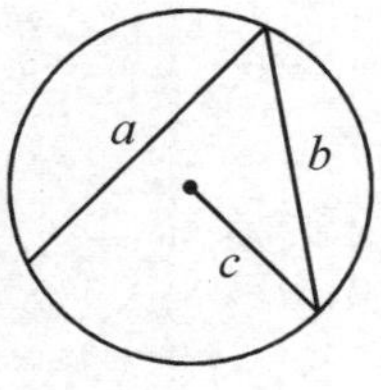
       A. a is a diameter
       B. b is a radius
       C. c is a radius
       D. b is a diameter
   (b) In the same circle, if the diameter, or d, is 40 cm, then the radius is (   ).
       A. 2 cm
       B. 40 cm
       C. 20 cm
       D. 80 cm
   (c) In the figure on the right, if the diameter of each small circle is 2 cm, then the radius of the big circle is (   ) cm. 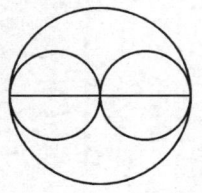
       A. 2
       B. 4
       C. 6
       D. 8

Geometry and measurement (1)

3 Draw a radius of the circle below on the left and a diameter of the circle on the right and then measure. Write your answers in the brackets (keep one decimal place).

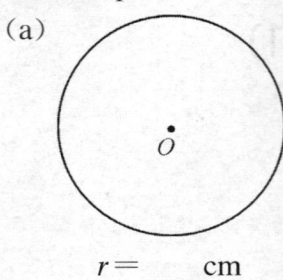

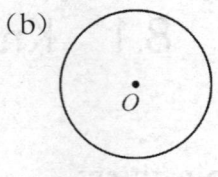

(a) r = ____ cm

(b) d = ____ cm

Challenge and extension question

4 Do you have a mug with a circular base? If so, do you know the radius of the base? Follow the steps below:
(i) Draw a circle around the base of your mug on a piece of blank paper.
(ii) Cut out the circle.
(iii) Fold the circle in half and then in half again.
(iv) Find the centre and measure the radius.
Have a try. Can you measure the radius of other circular objects?

8.2 Knowing circles (2)

Learning objectives

Identify, name and draw parts of a circle

Basic questions

1. Fill in the brackets.
   (a) In the same circle, all radiuses are (　　) and all diameters are (　　).
   (b) In the same circle, if the diameter is d and radius is r, then $d=$ (　　) or $r=$ (　　). If the diameter of a circle is 20 cm, then its radius is (　　) cm.
   (c) In the figure on the right, the length of the rectangle is 6 cm and the two circles have the same size. Therefore, $d=$ (　　) cm and $r=$ (　　) cm.

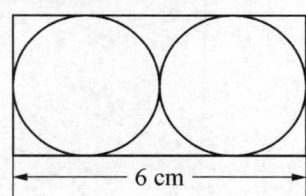

2. Use a pair of compasses to draw circles.
   (a) Draw a circle with a radius of 2 cm.　(b) Draw a circle with a diameter of 30 mm

   (c) Draw a circle with $d=4$ cm.　(d) Draw a circle with $r=1$ cm.

Geometry and measurement (1)

(e) Draw a circle with *O* as the centre and *OA* as the radius.

O ———— *A*

(f) Draw a circle with *O* as the centre and *OB* as the diameter.

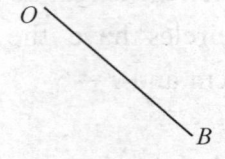

O ———— *B*

Challenge and extension question

3 Hands-on activity.
   (a) Draw a circle with point *A* as the centre and a radius of 2 cm.
   (b) Draw a circle with point *B* as the centre and a diameter of 6 cm.

8.3 Knowing circles (3)

Learning objectives

Identify properties of a circle

Basic questions

1. Fill in the brackets.
   (a) A circle has (   ) centre, (   ) radiuses and (   ) diameters. (Hint: fill in the brackets with 'one' or 'infinitely many'.)
   (b) Fold a circle in half. The folding line is a (   ) of the circle. Its length is (   ) the radius. The intersection of two different folding lines is the (   ).
   (c) The diameter of a bigger circle is 3 times the diameter of a smaller circle. If the diameter of the bigger circle is 15 cm, then the diameter of the smaller circle is (   ) cm.
   (d) In the figure on the right, the radiuses of both circles are 3 cm and the area of the rectangle is (   ).

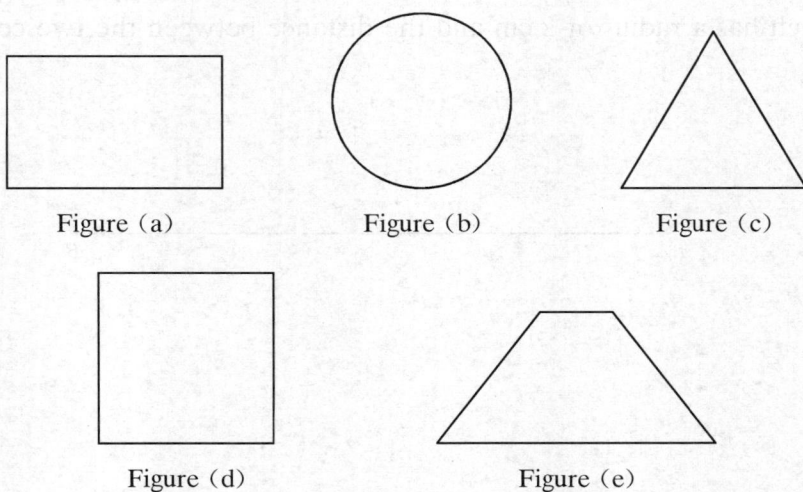

2. In the following figures, Figure (   ) has only 1 symmetrical line, Figure (   ) has 2 symmetrical lines and Figure (   ) has infinitely many symmetrical lines.

Figure (a)   Figure (b)   Figure (c)

Figure (d)   Figure (e)

Geometry and measurement (1)

3 True or false.

(a) The distance between the centre of a circle and any point on the circle is the same. (　)

(b) In the same circle, the number of radiuses is less than the number of diameters. (　)

(c) If the radius of a circle is decreased by 1 cm, then its diameter is decreased by 2 cm. (　)

(d) Using a pair of compasses to draw a circle with a diameter of 36 cm, the two toes of the compasses should be set 18 cm apart. (　)

(e) Fold a circle in half. The folding line is a symmetry line of the circle. (　)

Challenge and extension question

4 Hands-on activity.

(a) Draw a maximum circle in the rectangle below.

(b) A and B are the endpoints of the part of the line shown below and AB = 8 cm. Take two points between A and B as the centres to draw two circles so that each has a radius of 2 cm and the distance between the two centres is 4 cm.

A　　　　　　　　　　　　　　　　　　　　B

8.4 Angle concept and notation

Learning objectives

Identify line segments, rays and straight lines.

Basic questions

1. Fill in the brackets.

   (a) Two straight lines starting from a common endpoint form an (   ). The endpoint is called the (   ) of the angle. The two lines are called the (   ) of the angle. The symbol for angle is (   ).

   (b) Which of the following are angles? Fill in the brackets.

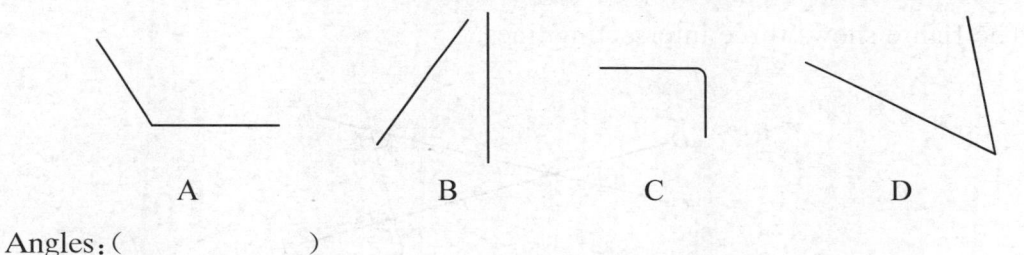

   A   B   C   D

   Angles: (   )

2. Do you know how to describe the following angles? Fill in the brackets with your answers.

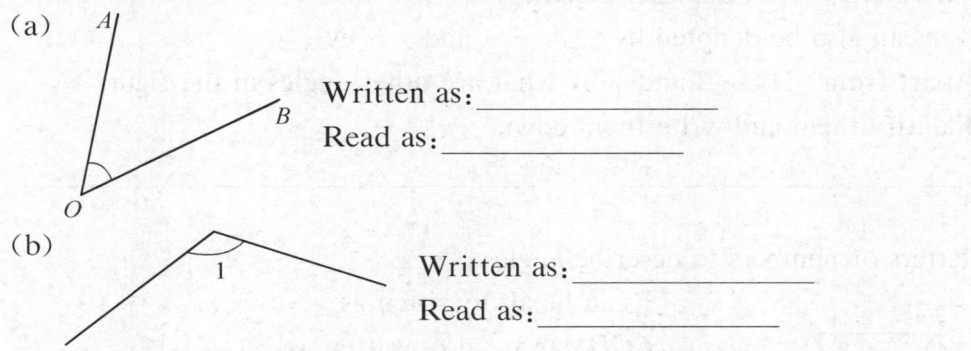

   (a) Written as: _____
       Read as: _____

   (b) Written as: _____
       Read as: _____

   (c) Mark seven angles in the following figures in order with ∠1, ∠2, ∠3, and so on.

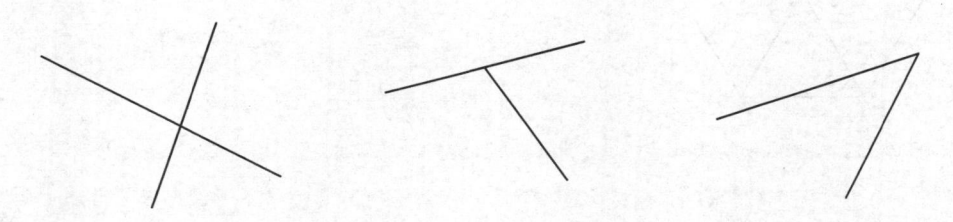

Geometry and measurement (1)

3 Look at the figure and fill in the brackets.
   (a) ∠1 and ( ) are vertically opposite angles.
   (b) ∠2 and ( ) are vertically opposite angles.

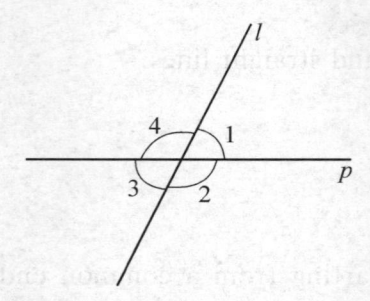

Challenge and extension questions

4 The figure shows three intersecting lines.

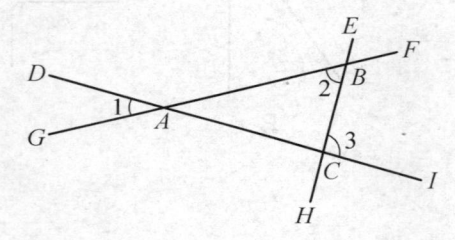

   (a) There are ( ) angles altogether.
   (b) ∠1 can also be denoted by ∠( ) and ∠3 by ∠( ).
   (c) Apart from ∠1, ∠2 and ∠3, what are other angles in the figure? Identify them and write them down.

   _____

5 Use letters or numbers to describe angles.

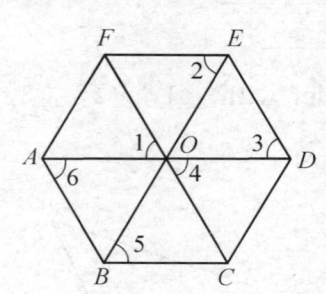

   ∠1 can be also written as ∠( );
   ∠COD can be also written as ∠( );
   ∠6 can be also written as ∠( ).

8.5 Measurement of angles (1)

Learning objectives

Identify angles at a point and on straight lines

Basic questions

1. Fill in the brackets.
   (a) A full angle=(   ) degrees. A straight angle=(   ) degrees. A right angle=(   ) degrees.
   (b) An angle less than a right angle is called an (   ) angle.
   An angle greater than a right angle but less than a straight angle is called an (   ) angle.
   An angle greater than a straight angle but less than a full angle is called a (   ) angle.
   (c) A full angle=(   ) straight angles=(   ) right angles.
   A straight angle=(   ) right angles.
   (d) If a straight angle is divided into six angles equally, each of the six angles is (   ) degrees. They are all (   ) angles.
   (e) At 9 o'clock in the morning, the angle formed by the hour hand and minute hand on a clock face is a (   ) angle.
   (f) At 6 o'clock, the angle formed by the hour hand and minute hand is a (   ) angle.
   (g) A 68 degree angle is (   ) degrees less than a right angle and (   ) degrees less than a straight angle. When it is increased by (   ) degrees, it is a full angle.
   (h) On a clock face, from ten past twelve to twenty past twelve, the minute hand turned (   ) degrees.

2. Multiple choice questions.
   (a) A 40° angle under a 3× magnifier will be (   ).
      A. 40°   B. 80°
      C. 120°   D. 160°
   (b) The sum of two acute angles is (   ).
      A. an obtuse angle   B. an acute angle
      C. a right angle   D. uncertain

Geometry and measurement (1)

(c) If $\angle AOB = 135°$, then $\angle AOB$ is ( ).
  A. a straight angle B. a right angle
  C. an obtuse angle D. an acute angle

(d) Putting the angles in order, starting from the greatest, the correct answer is ( ).
  A. a full angle > a reflex angle > a straight angle > an obtuse angle > an acute angle
  B. an obtuse angle > an acute angle > a full angle > a straight angle > a reflex angle
  C. a full turn > a reflex angle > an acute angle > a right angle > a straight angle
  D. a full turn > a reflex angle > a straight angle > an acute angle > a obtuse angle

(e) When two lines intersect at a point, four angles are formed. These angles are all ( ).
  A. acute angles B. obtuse angles C. right angles D. uncertain

3 True or false.
 (a) At half past 3, the angle formed by the hour hand and minute hand on a clock face is a right angle. ( )
 (b) An angle greater than 90° is an obtuse angle. ( )
 (c) Half of an obtuse angle is an acute angle. ( )
 (d) A reflex angle is greater than 180°. ( )

4 Write the angles into the circles as indicated.
125°, 76°, 91°, 179°, 2°, 45°, 103°, 89°

Acute angles   Obtuse angles

5 What types of angles are these? Fill in the brackets.

( )   ( )   ( )

156

Challenge and extension question

6 Count and write the angles.

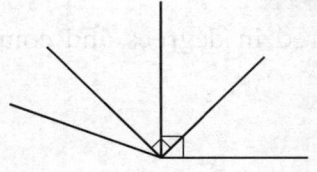

In the figure, there are (   ) acute angles, (   ) obtuse angles and (   ) right angles. There are (   ) angles altogether.

8.6　Measurement of angles (2)

Learning objectives

Know that angles are measured in degrees and compare different acute, obtuse and reflex angles

Basic questions

1. Fill in the brackets.
   (a) A straight angle is twice a (　　　) angle and half of a (　　　) angle.
   (b) At 3 o'clock in the afternoon, the angle formed by the hour hand and minute hand on a clock is (　　　) degrees. It is a (　　　) angle.
   (c) Two lines intersect and form four angles. If one of the angles is 90 degrees, then the other three angles are all (　　　) angles.
   (d) When a straight angle is divided into two angles, these two angles can both be (　　　) angles, or one could be an (　　　) angle and the other an (　　　) angle.

2. Multiple choice questions.
   (a) When measuring an angle with a protractor, the centre of the protractor should line up with (　　).
       A. a side of the angle
       B. the vertex of the angle
       C. any point on one of the sides of the angle
       D. anywhere near the vertex
   (b) When drawing an angle of 75° with a set square, use the set for angles (　　) and (　　).
       A. 90°　　　　B. 60°　　　　C. 30°　　　　D. 45°
   (c) When drawing an angle of 135° with a set square, use the set for angles (　　) and (　　).
       A. 90°　　　　B. 60°　　　　C. 30°　　　　D. 45°
   (d) The hour hand on a clock face should turn (　　) degrees in 24 hours.
       A. 180　　　　B. 360　　　　C. 540　　　　D. 720

Geometry and measurement (1)

3 Use a protractor to measure the angles and write your answers in the brackets below.

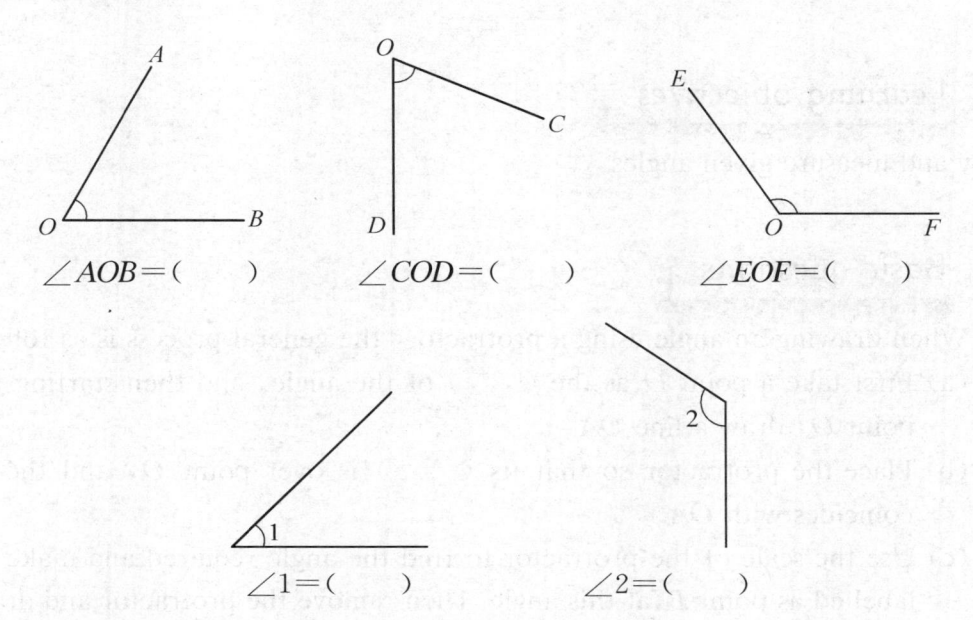

∠AOB=(   )   ∠COD=(   )   ∠EOF=(   )

∠1=(   )   ∠2=(   )

Challenge and extension questions

4 Do you still remember the sizes of the angles in the set square?
Fill in the brackets.

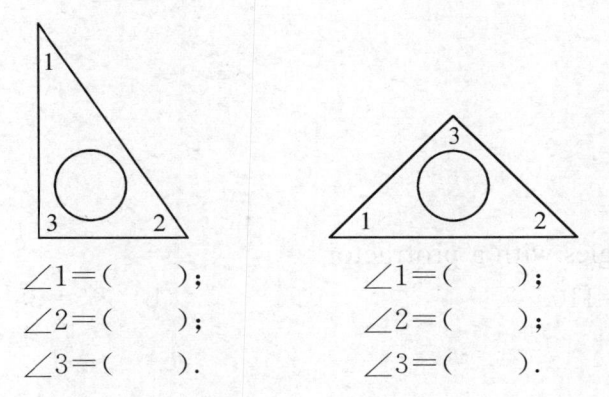

∠1=(   );   ∠1=(   );
∠2=(   );   ∠2=(   );
∠3=(   ).   ∠3=(   ).

5 Can you make the following angles with a set square? Put a ✓ for yes and ✗ for no in each bracket.

105°   120°   180°   75°   135°   150°
( )   ( )   ( )   ( )   ( )   ( )

8.7 Measurement of angles (3)

Learning objectives
Draw and measure given angles

Basic questions

1. When drawing an angle using a protractor, the general process is as follows:
   (a) First take a point O as the (   ) of the angle, and then starting from the point O, draw a line OA.
   (b) Place the protractor so that its (   ) is over point O, and the baseline coincides with OA.
   (c) Use the scale of the protractor to find the angle required and make a mark, labelled as point B, at this angle. Then remove the protractor and draw a line starting from the point (   ) and passing through the point (   ).
   (d) (   ) is the angle required.

2. Use a protractor to draw $\angle AOB$, with O as the vertex.
   (a) $\angle AOB = 80°$
   (b) $\angle AOB = 120°$

3. Draw the angles with a protractor.
   (a) $\angle COD = 110°$
   (b) $\angle 5 = 38°$

   (c) $\angle A = 175°$
   (d) $\angle AOB = 90°$

Geometry and measurement (1)

4 In each of the following figures, draw an angle as indicated.

(a) ∠ABC = 35°

(b) ∠B = 100°

(c) ∠CDE = 150°

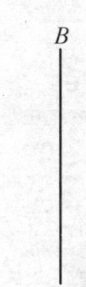

(d) ∠AOC = 240°

Challenge and extension question

5 Hands-on activity.

(a) Draw ∠AOB so that it is 80°.

(b) Mark a point D on side OB so that OD = 3 cm. Mark another point E on the other side OA, so that OE = 3 cm.

(c) Connect points D and E.

(d) Measure to find: ∠ODE = (   ) and ∠OED = (   ).

8.8 Calculation of angles

Learning objectives
Calculate angles

Basic questions

1. Think carefully and then fill in the brackets.
   (a) One third of a straight angle is (   ). An angle that is 40° greater than a right angle is (   ). 115° is (   ) less than a straight angle. A full angle is (   ) greater than 15°.
   (b) Given $\angle 1 + \angle 2 = 150°$ and $\angle 1 = 67°$, then $\angle 2 = ($ $)$.
   (c) Given $\angle 1 + \angle 2 = 180°$ and $\angle 2 = 100°$, then $\angle 1 = ($ $)$. If 5 times $\angle 3$ is a straight angle, then $\angle 3 = ($ $)$.
   (d) If $\angle 1 = \angle 2 = \angle 3$, and $\angle 1 + \angle 2 + \angle 3 = 120°$, then $\angle 2 = ($ $)$.

2. Calculation questions.
   (a) In the figure, given $\angle 2 = 135°$, find $\angle 1$.

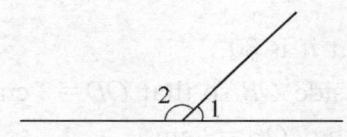

   (b) In the figure, given that $\angle ABC$ is a right angle and $\angle ABD = 70°$, find $\angle 1$.

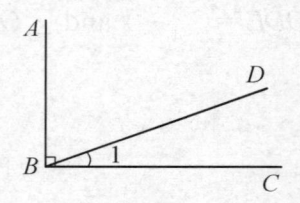

   (c) In the figure, given that $\angle BOC$ is a right angle and $\angle COD = 15°$, find $\angle AOB$.

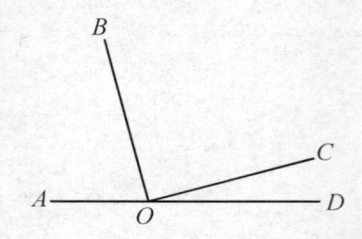

Geometry and measurement (1)

(d) In the figure, find ∠1 and ∠2.

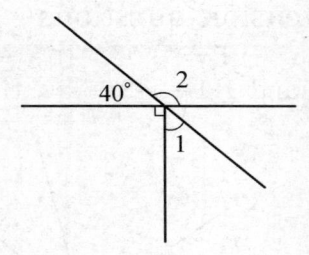

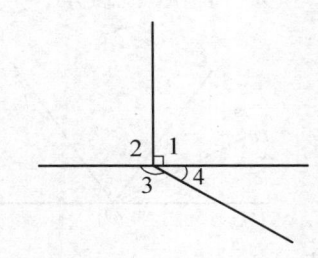

(e) In the figure, given ∠4=30°, find ∠3.

(f) In the figure, two pairs of angles, ∠1 and ∠3, and ∠2 and ∠4 are vertically opposite angles, respectively. Given ∠1=55°, find the other three angles.

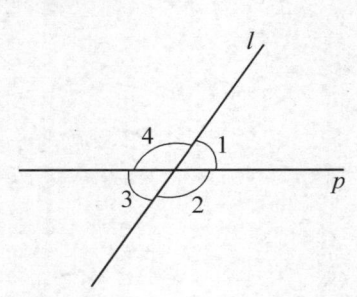

Geometry and measurement (1)

Challenge and extension questions

3 Given that $\angle EOF = 140°$ and $\angle 1 = \angle 3 = 35°$, find $\angle 2$.

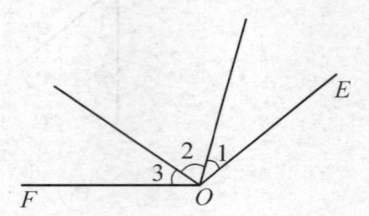

4 In the figure below, A, O and B are on the same line. OE is the bisector of $\angle AOC$, i.e., $\angle AOE = \angle EOC$, OF is the bisector of $\angle BOC$, i.e., $\angle BOF = \angle FOC$, and $2\angle AOE = \angle BOF$. Find $\angle BOF$, $\angle AOE$ and $\angle EOF$.

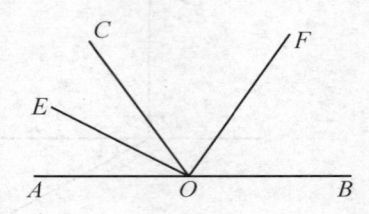

8.9 Angles and sides in polygons

Learning objectives
Identify angles at points on straight lines

Basic questions

1. Complete the table about polygons. The first one has been done for you.

Name of polygon	No. of angles	No. of sides	Figure
Triangle	3	3	
Quadrilateral			
Pentagon			
Hexagon			
Octagon			

2. Write the following into the circles as indicated.
   Straight lines, squares, cubes, circles, cuboids, equilateral triangles, prisms

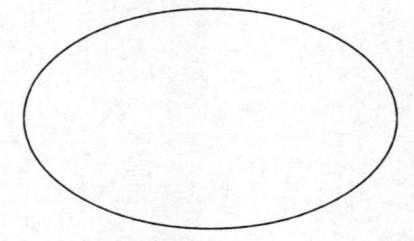

Polygons   Non-polygons

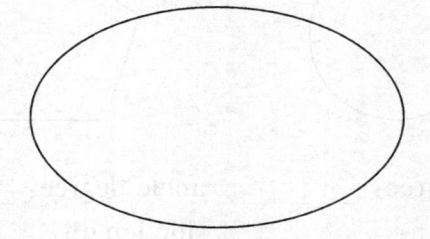

Geometry and measurement (1)

3 True or false.
(a) The numbers of angles and sides are the same in a polygon. ( )
(b) A polygon has all angles equal and all sides equal. ( )
(c) A square is a special regular polygon. ( )
(d) A right-angled triangle is not a regular polygon. ( )
(e) A square has four equal angles and four equal sides. ( )
(f) A rectangle has four equal angles and four equal sides. ( )
(g) A regular polygon has all angles equal and all sides equal. ( )

4 Look at the 2-D figures below. Measure and then put a ✓ for a regular polygon and × for an irregular polygon in each bracket. If it is a regular polygon, write its angle degree and side length. Otherwise, write N/A (not applicable) accordingly.

( )　　　　　　　　( )　　　　　　　　( )
angle degree: _____　angle degree: _____　angle degree: _____
side length: _____　　side length: _____　　side length: _____

( )　　　　　　　　( )　　　　　　　　( )
angle degree: _____　angle degree: _____　angle degree: _____
side length: _____　　side length: _____　　side length: _____

( )　　　　　　　　( )
angle degree: _____　angle degree: _____
side length: _____　　side length: _____

Geometry and measurement (1)

5. The angles inside a polygon are also called interior angles of the polygon. Look at the pentagon shown on the right. ∠1, ∠2, ∠3, ∠4 and ∠5 are its interior angles. Accordingly, ∠6, ∠7, ∠8, ∠9 and ∠10 are called its exterior angles.
What is the relationship between an interior angle and an exterior angle that have the same vertex and one common side in a polygon (for example, ∠1 and ∠6)? If ∠1=110°, find ∠6.

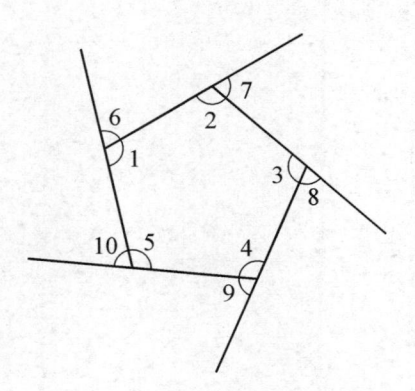

Challenge and extension question

6. Look at the pentagon shown in question 5. What can you say about the relationships between the exterior angles? Are they always equal? If not, in what kind of polygons are they equal?

Unit test 8

1 Work these out mentally. Write the answers.

(a) $52 \div 26 \times 13 =$ (b) $50 \times 25 \div 10 =$ (c) $1000 \div 100 + 101 =$

(d) $54 \div 6 \times 9 =$ (e) $70 \div 35 \times 0 =$ (f) $3232 \div 32 - 100 =$

(g) $140 \div 1 + 140 =$ (h) $24 \times 3 \div 24 =$ (i) $100 \div 5 \div 5 =$

(j) $90 - 15 + 15 =$ (k) $16 \times 101 =$ (l) $12 - 12 \div 3 =$

2 Use your preferred methods to calculate. Show your working.

(a) $(125 + 19) \times 8$ (b) $666 - (309 + 266)$

(c) $75 \times 2 \times 7 \times 4$ (d) $125 \times (800 - 8)$

(e) $24 \times 24 + 76 \times 24$ (f) $5000 - 666 \div 37 \times 34$

(g) $29 \times 75 + 72 \times 75 - 75$ (h) $7800 \div [300 + 5 \times (66 + 134)]$

3 Fill in the brackets.

(a) Twice a straight angle equals (   ) degrees. It is a (   ) angle. It is (   ) times a right angle.

(b) A full angle=(   ) angle×2=(   ) angle×4=(   )×6.

(c) The distance between any point on a circle and its centre is called the (   ) of the circle.

(d) Fold a circle in half. The folding line is a (   ) line of the circle, which is also the (   ) of the circle. If the circle is folded in half twice, the angle that is formed by the two folding lines is (   ) degrees. The vertex of the angle is the (   ) of the circle.

Geometry and measurement (1)

(e) At 6 o'clock, the angle formed by the hour hand and minute hand on a clock face is (   ). At 9 o'clock, the angle formed by the hour hand and minute hand is (   ).

(f) In a right-angled triangle, if one acute angle is 11°, then the other acute angle is (   ).

(g) The largest obtuse angle that can be formed by a set square is (   ). (The two set squares are not overlapping each other, and one side from each is coinciding.)

(h) The smallest acute angle that can be formed by a set square is (   ).

(i) Among right-angled triangles, isosceles triangles, equilateral triangles, rectangles, squares and circles, the symmetrical figures are (
).

4 Multiple choice questions.

(a) A full angle has (   ) coinciding sides.
    A. 1   B. 2   C. 3   D. infinite

(b) In the following statements, the correct one is (   ).
    A. A polygon can have 2 sides.
    B. A regular polygon has all angles equal and all sides equal.
    C. A rectangle is a special regular polygon.
    D. A cube is a special regular polygon.

(c) At 3 o'clock, the angle formed by the hour hand and minute hand on a clock face is (   ).
    A. 90°   B. 180°   C. 270°   D. 360°

(d) When the minute hand on a clock face makes a full turn, the hour hand makes a turn of (   ).
    A. 360°   B. 180°   C. 90°   D. 30°

(e) At half past 1, the angle formed by the hour hand and minute hand on a clock face is (   ).
    A. 80°   B. 100°   C. 110°   D. 135°

(f) When the diameter of a circle is increased by 6 mm, its radius is increased by (   ).
    A. 2 mm   B. 3 mm   C. 6 mm   D. 12 mm

5 Hands-on activities.

(a) Draw a circle that has a radius of 25 mm, and mark d, r and the centre.

(b) Measure the degree of the angle shown in the figure below.

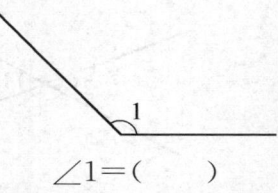

$\angle 1 = ($ $)$

(c) Use a protractor to draw angles as indicated.
$\angle AOB = 80°$. $\angle C = 140°$.

(d) In each figure, draw the angle with one side given.
$\angle A = 115°$. $\angle MOP = 25°$.

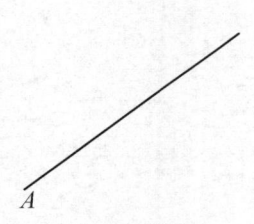

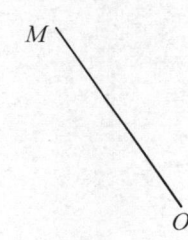

6 Calculate.

(a) Given $\angle AOB = 115°$ and $\angle 2 = 87°$, find $\angle 1$.

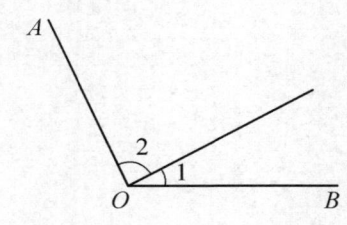

(b) Given $\angle 1 = 40°$, find $\angle 2$.

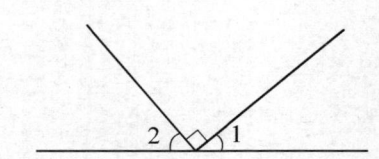

Geometry and measurement (1)

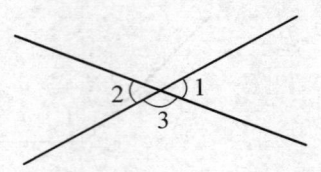

(c) Given ∠1=50°, find ∠3 and ∠2.

(d) Give that in a regular hexagon, the sum of its angles is 720°, what is the degree of each of its angles?

Chapter 9　Geometry and measurement (2)

9.1　Volume

Learning objectives

Estimate the volume of different objects

Basic questions

1. Fill in the brackets.
   (a) The amount of the space that an object takes up is called (　　　　　).
   (b) Both 'volume' and 'area' represent the size of an object, but the area represents the size of a (　　)-dimensional figure, while the volume represents the space taken up by a (　　)-dimensional figure.

2. True or false.
   (a) After Joe poured a carton of fruit juice into a glass, the volume of the juice changed (assuming no loss of the juice in the process). (　　)
   (b) The volume of an object changes as the shape changes (assuming no loss of the object in the process). (　　)
   (c) If two books have the same cover and page size, the thicker book has a greater volume. (　　)
   (d) There are two pieces of round timber with different thicknesses and lengths. Their volumes must also be different. (　　)

3. Short answer questions. (Hint: use 'changed' or 'unchanged' for the answers.) Bob was playing with a piece of play dough. Help him answer the following questions.
   (a) He first rolled the play dough into a long strip. What happened to the volume of the play dough? (　　　　)
   (b) He then made the play dough into a little monkey. What happened to the volume of the play dough? (　　　　)
   (c) He finally made the play dough into a rabbit. What happened to the volume of the play dough? (　　　　)

Geometry and measurement (2)

④ Let's put cubes into different shapes. Six cubes are stacked together. Answer the following questions. (Hint: use 'changed' or 'unchanged' for the answers.)
(a) Tom took the 6 cubes apart into separate pieces. What happened to the volume of the 6 cubes? (   )
(b) Tom put the cubes into a row. What happened to the volume of the 6 cubes? (   )
(c) Tom put the cubes into two rows. What happened to the volume of the 6 cubes? (   )

Challenge and extension question

⑤ Put some water into a cubic glass and then immerse a stone in the water. How would you find the volume of the stone?

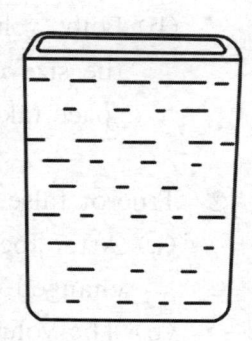

9.2 Cubic centimetres and cubic metres (1)

Learning objectives

Calculate, estimate and compare volume of objects made from cubes

Basic questions

1. Fill in the brackets.
   (a) If the edge length of a cube is 1 cm, its volume is (   ) cubic centimetres or (   ) cm³.
   (b) Using 5 cubes of edge length 1 cm to form a 3-D figure, its volume is (   ) cm³.
   (c) To use cubes of edge length 1 cm to form a bigger cube, at least (   ) cubes are needed. In this case, its volume is (   ) cm³.

2. Each of the following cuboids is made up of cubic blocks of 1 cm³. What is the total volume of the five cuboids below?

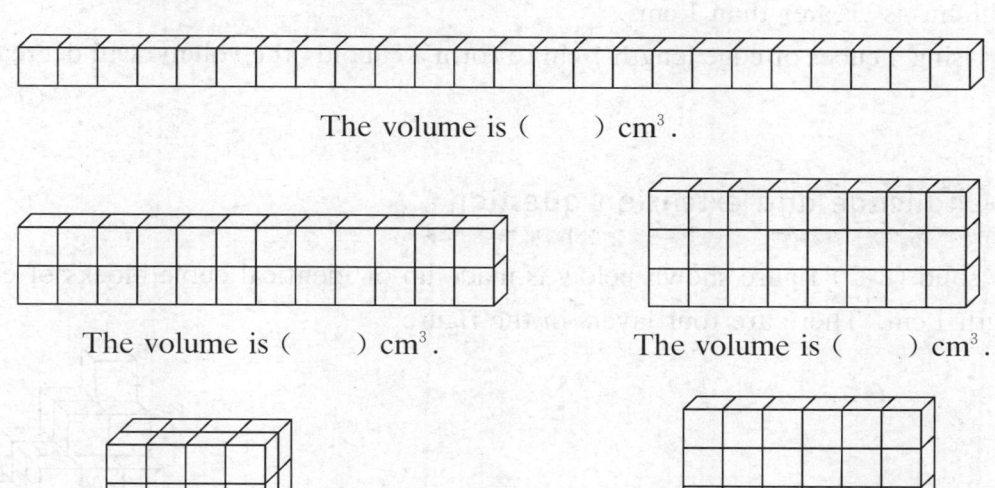

   The volume is (   ) cm³.

   The volume is (   ) cm³.

   The volume is (   ) cm³.

   The volume is (   ) cm³.

   The volume is (   ) cm³.

   What did you find from the above? Fill in the brackets below.
   The shapes of the above cuboids are (   ). Their volumes are (   ).

Geometry and measurement (2)

3 Look at the 3-D figures below, and write a suitable number in each bracket. (The edge length of each small cube is 1 cm.)

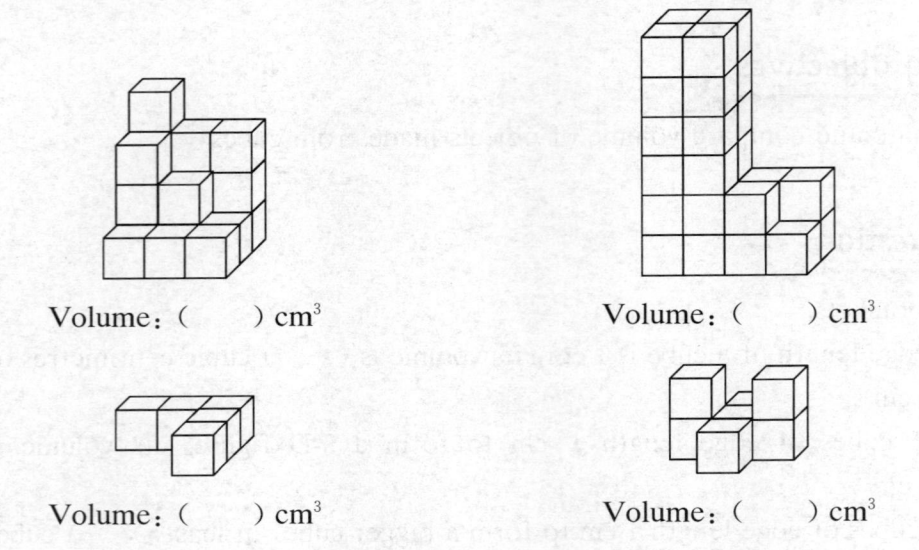

Volume: (   ) cm³

Volume: (   ) cm³

Volume: (   ) cm³

Volume: (   ) cm³

4 True or false.

(a) The edge length of a small cube is 1 cm. A figure is made of 12 such cubes. Its volume is 12 cm³. (   )

(b) 1 cm³ is greater than 1 cm². (   )

(c) Using 4 cubes of edge length 1 cm to form a cuboid, the volume will decrease. (   )

Challenge and extension question

5 The solid (3-D) figure shown below is made up of identical cubic blocks of edge length 1 cm. There are four layers in the figure.

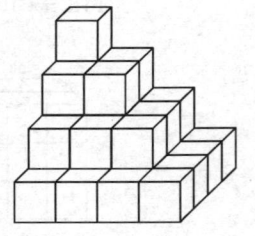

(a) What is the volume of this solid figure?

(b) Following the pattern from top to bottom, add more layers to the 3-D figure until the 10th layer is completed. What is the volume of the new figure?

9.3 Cubic centimetres and cubic metres (2)

Learning objectives

Calculate, estimate and compare volume of objects using standard units

Basic questions

1. Fill in the brackets.
   (a) The volume of a cube of edge length 1 m is (   ) cubic metre or (   ) m³. It can also be considered as the volume of a cube of edge length 100 cm, which has a volume of (   ) cubic centimetres. Therefore, 1 cubic metre = (   ) cubic centimetres or 1 m³ = (   ) cm³.
   (b) Centimetres and metres are both units of (   ).
   Square centimetres and square metres are both units of (   ).
   Cubic centimetres and cubic metres are both units of (   ).

2. Write a suitable unit in each bracket.
   (a) The length of a rubber is about 6 (   ).
   (b) The volume of a refrigerator is about 2.1 (   ).
   (c) The volume of a washing machine is about 1.2 (   ).
   (d) The volume of a mobile phone is about 85 (   ).

3. Fill in each bracket with a suitable number.
   (a) 2.8 m³ = (   ) cm³
   (b) 8 500 000 cm³ = (   ) m³
   (c) 61 500 cm³ = (   ) m³
   (d) 0.04 m³ = (   ) cm³
   (e) 700 000 cm³ = (   ) m³
   (f) 6 m³ and 990 000 cm³ = (   ) m³

Geometry and measurement (2)

4 Multiple choice questions.

(a) 1000 cm³ is ( ).

A. 1 m³   B. 0.1 m³   C. 0.01 m³   D. 0.001 m³

(b) The edge length of a cube is 100 cm and its volume is ( ).

A. 100 000 cm³   B. 1000 m³   C. 100 m³   D. 1 m³

(c) The volume of an English dictionary is about 5000 ( ).

A. m³   B. km³   C. cm³   D. mm³

(d) The volume of a finger tip is about ( ).

A. 1 m³   B. 1 cm³   C. 1 km³   D. 1 mm³

(e) The edge length of each small cube is 10 cm. There are 19 such cubes and their ( ) is 19 000 cm³.

A. perimeter   B. volume   C. area   D. weight

Challenge and extension question

5 The solid figure shown below is made up of identical cubic blocks of edge length 10 cm. There are four layers in the figure.

(a) What is the volume of this 3-D figure?

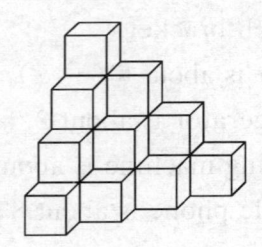

(b) Take the longest side of the figure as the edge to expand it into a new cube with more cubic blocks of edge length 10 cm. What is the volume of the new cube? How many more block cubes are needed to form the new cube?

9.4 Metric units and imperial units for measurement

Learning objectives

Understand and use equivalences between metric units and common imperial units

Basic questions

1. Look at the following imperial units of measurement, and write them into the circles below.

   inch, foot, gallon, mile, ounce, pound, pint, yard

   Length   Weight/Mass   Volume/Capacity

2. Fill in the brackets.
   (a) 1 mile is (   ) yards. 1 yard is (   ) feet. 1 foot is (   ) inches.
   (b) 1 pound is (   ) ounces, or 1 lb = (   ) oz. 80 oz are (   ) lbs.
   (c) 1 gallon is (   ) pints. 4 pints are (   ) gallons.

3. Write a suitable imperial unit in each bracket.
   (a) Jason is about 6 (   ) tall.
   (b) The distance between London and Shanghai is about 5700 (   ).
   (c) The tank capacity of a car is 15.4 (   ).
   (d) The area of a typical football pitch is about 1.5 (   ).

4. Given 1 metre ≈ 3.28 feet, fill in the brackets below. Show your working.
   (a) 1 km ≈ (   ) ft
   (b) 1 km² ≈ (   ) ft²

   From (b), can you find how many square feet are in 1 square metre? Fill in the brackets below.
   (c) 1 m² ≈ (   ) km² ≈ (   ) ft²

Geometry and measurement (2)

5 Given 1 mile is approximately 1.6 km, convert the following speed limits for cars and motorcycles in the United Kimgdom from imperial units to metric units. Fill in the table.

	miles per hour (mph)	kilometres per hour (km/h)
Motorway	70	
Dual carriageway	70	
Single carriageway	60	
Built-up area	30	

6 In a supermarket, a certain type of potato is priced at 99p for one pound or £0.99/lb and a brand of butter is at £12 for every 8 ounces. Mr Becker wants to buy 100 kg of the potato and 10 kg of the butter for his restaurant. How much does he need to pay? (Note: take 1 kg = 2.2 lbs; 1 lb = 16 oz.)

7 The area of a football pitch is about 1.75 acres. Given that 1 acre is about 4000 m^2, what is the area of the football pitch in m^2 and km^2, respectively?

Challenge and extension question

8 The tank capacity of a van is 50 litres. Given 1 litre is about 0.22 gallons, approximately how many gallons is the capacity of the tank? If on average the van can travel 68 miles per gallon (mpg) of fuel, approximately how many kilometres can the van travel with a full tank of petrol?

9.5 Introduction to cubes and cuboids

Learning objectives

Identify properties of cubes and cuboids

Basic questions

1. Complete the table.

	Features in common			Different features		
	Length of edges	No. of faces	No. of edges	No. of vertices	Shapes of faces	Areas of faces
Cuboid		6			All faces are rectangles.	
Cube						All faces have the same area.

2. Fill in the brackets.
   (a) The two cuboids shown below are made of identical small cubes of edge length 1 cm. Find their lengths, widths, and heights and put them into the brackets.

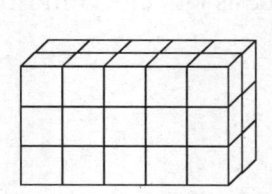

   Length (   ), width (   ), height (   )

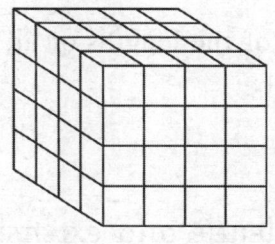

   Length (   ), width (   ), height (   )

   (b) In a cuboid, the measures of three edges meeting at the same vertex are called (   ), (   ) and (   ) of the cuboid, respectively.
   (c) A cuboid with its length, width and height being all equal is called a (   ).
   (d) A cube has 12 edges of (   ) length. If the length of an edge is 3 cm, then the total length of all of its edges is (   ) cm.
   (e) A cuboid has 12 edges. Among them, the measures of (   ) edges are called lengths, the measures of (   ) edges are called widths, and the measures of

Geometry and measurement (2)

( ) edges are called heights.

(f) In a cuboid, the sum of the lengths of three edges from one vertex is 0.75 m. The sum of the lengths of all the edges of this cuboid is (　　) m.

(g) A cuboid has (　　) faces. It is possible that the shapes of all the faces are (　　　　). It is also possible that the shapes of 2 faces are (　　　　) and 4 faces are (　　　　).

(h) A (　　　　) is a special cuboid.

3 True or false.

(a) The measures of three edges of a cuboid are called length, width and height, respectively. (　)

(b) Among the 12 edges of a cuboid, any 4 parallel edges have the same length. (　)

(c) A cuboid whose bottom face is a square must be a cube. (　)

(d) One edge of a cuboid is 6 cm long. The sum of the lengths of all the edges is 72 cm. (　)

(e) 16 identical small cubes can form a bigger cube. (　)

(f) Six squares can form a cube. (　)

4 A cuboid is 3.2 cm long, 3 cm wide and 2.5 cm high. Find the sum of the lengths of all the edges.

5 The sum of the lengths of all the edges of a cube is 540 cm. Find the edge length of the cube.

Challenge and extension questions

6 The sum of the lengths of all the edges of a cuboid is 90 cm. The length is twice the height and the width is 1.5 times the height. What are the length, width and height of the cuboid?

7 A piece of iron wire is used to form a cuboid frame with length 45 cm, width 38 cm and height 25 cm. If the same length of iron wire is used to form a cube, what is the edge length of the cube?

9.6 Volumes of cubes and cuboids (1)

Learning objectives
Calculate, estimate and compare volume of cubes and cuboids using standard units

Basic questions

1. Given that a cuboid has three dimensions: length (l), width (w) and height (h), and a cube has all edges of length a, fill in the brackets.
   Volume of a cuboid = length × ( ) × ( ) = l × ( ) × ( )
   Volume of a cube = length × ( ) × ( ) = ( )³

2. Calculate the volume of each cuboid. (The edge length of each small cube is 1 cm.)

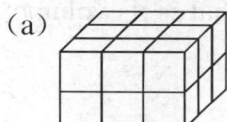

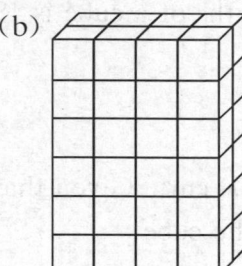

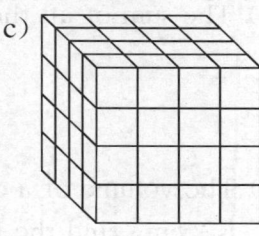

   (a)   (b)   (c)

   The volume is ( ).   The volume is ( ).   The volume is ( ).

3. Find the volumes of the cuboid and the cube (unit: cm).

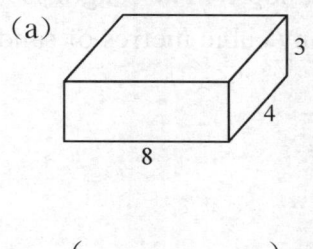

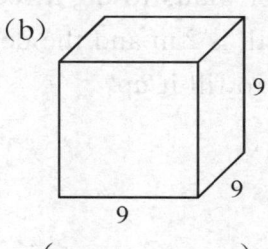

   (a) 8, 4, 3   (b) 9, 9, 9

   (   )   (   )

4. Fill in the brackets.
   (a) 450 000 cm³ = ( ) m³
   (b) 3.9 m³ = ( ) cm³
   (c) The length of the edge of a cube is 6 cm. Its volume is ( ) cm³.
   (d) The length of a cuboid is 28 cm, the width is 12 cm and the height is 25 cm. The volume of the cuboid is ( ) cm³.

Geometry and measurement (2)

(e) The volume of a cube is 125 cm³. The length of the edge is (   ) cm.

(f) Two identical cubes are put together to form a cuboid. Given the length of the cuboid is 10 cm, the volume is (   ) cm³.

(g) The length of a cuboid is a m, the width is b m and the height is h m. If the length is increased by 5 m and the width and the height remain unchanged, then the volume is increased by (   ) m³. If the length and the width remain unchanged and the height is decreased by 2 m, then the volume of the cuboid is (   ) m³.

5 Application problems.

(a) The length of a brick is 24 cm. The width is half the length and the thickness is 5 cm. What is the volume of the brick?

(b) The sum of all the edge lengths of a cube is 480 cm. What is its volume?

(c) The volume of a cuboid is 100 cm³. Given that the length is 10 cm and width is 2 cm, find the height of the cube.

(d) A school wants to dig a rectangular box-shaped sandpit. The length is 4 m, the width is 2 m and the depth is 0.4 m. How many cubic metres of sand are needed to fill it up?

Challenge and extension question

6 Two identical cubic boards are put together to form a cuboid. The sum of the lengths of all the edges of the cuboid formed is 48 cm. Find its volume.

9.7 Volumes of cubes and cuboids (2)

Learning objectives

Calculate, estimate and compare volume of cubes and cuboids using standard units

Basic questions

1. Fill in the brackets.
   (a) Putting together 3 identitical cubes of edge length 20 cm into a cuboid, the volume of the cuboid is (   ) cm³.
   (b) An iron wire of 180 cm is used to form a maximum frame of a cube. The volume of the cube is (   ) cm³.
   (c) A cubic piece of wood of edge length 12 cm is cut into small cubes with edge length of 3 cm. It can be cut into (   ) such small cubes.
   (d) A cube has an edge length of 50 cm. If the edge length is increased by 10 cm, then its volume is increased by (   ) cm³.
   (e) The length of a piece of cuboid steel is 0.2 m, the width is 6 cm and the height is 2 cm. The volume is (   ) cm³.
   (f) If the length, width and height of a cuboid are all increased to 3 times the orginal values, then the volume will be increased to (   ) times the original value.

2. True or false.
   (a) If the volumes of two cuboids are equal, then their lengths, widths and heights must also be equal. (   )
   (b) Putting together the two identical cubes of edge length 6 cm into a cuboid, the volume of the cuboid is 512 cm³. (   )
   (c) Since $2^2 = 2 \times 2$, we can get $2^3 = 6$. (   )
   (d) Two cubes have difference sizes. If the edge length of the bigger cube is twice that of the smaller one, the volume of the bigger one is 8 times that of the smaller one. (   )

3. Application problems.
   (a) The area of one face of a cube is 3600 cm². Find its volume.

Geometry and measurement (2)

(b) A piece of cubic steel of edge length 60 cm is melted and formed into a piece of cuboid steel of length 0.9 m and width 40 cm. What is the height of the cuboid steel?

(c) If the height of a cuboid is increased by 3 cm, it becomes a cube and the volume is increased by 243 cm^3. What is the volume of the cuboid?

(d) The length of a piece of iron wire is exactly enough to form a cubic frame of edge length 8 cm. If it is used to form a cuboid frame of length 10 cm and width 7 cm, what is the volume of the cuboid?

(e) A concrete mixture of sand, cement and gravel is used to pave a rectangular box-shaped site of 60 m long, 50 m wide and 10 cm thick. If for every 10 m^3 of the site, the mixture needs to be blended twice, then for the whole site, how many times does the mixture need to be blended?

(f) A cuboid-shaped steel plate is 80 cm long, 20 cm wide and 5 cm thick. What is the volume of the steel plate? Given every 1 cm^3 of the steel plate weighs 7.8 g, what is the weight of the steel plate in kg?

Challenge and extension question

4. Four identical cubes are put together to form a cuboid. The sum of the lengths of all the edges of the cuboid is 120 cm. Find the volume of the cuboid. (Note: there are two possible combinations.)

9.8 Volume and capacity (1)

Learning objectives

Calculate, estimate and compare volume of composite shapes

Basic questions

1. Fill in the brackets.
   (a) The (   ) of the objects that a container, for example, glass bottle, bucket and cargo container, can contain is usually called the (   ) of the container.
   (b) To measure the size of a container, we can usually use the units of (   ). However, when measuring the volume of liquid, we usually use the units of (   ). They are (   ) and (   ).
   (c) 1 litre＝(   ) cubic centimetres; 1 millilitre＝(   ) cubic centimetre; 1 litre＝(   ) millilitres

2. Use capacity units to indicate the volumes of the following containers.

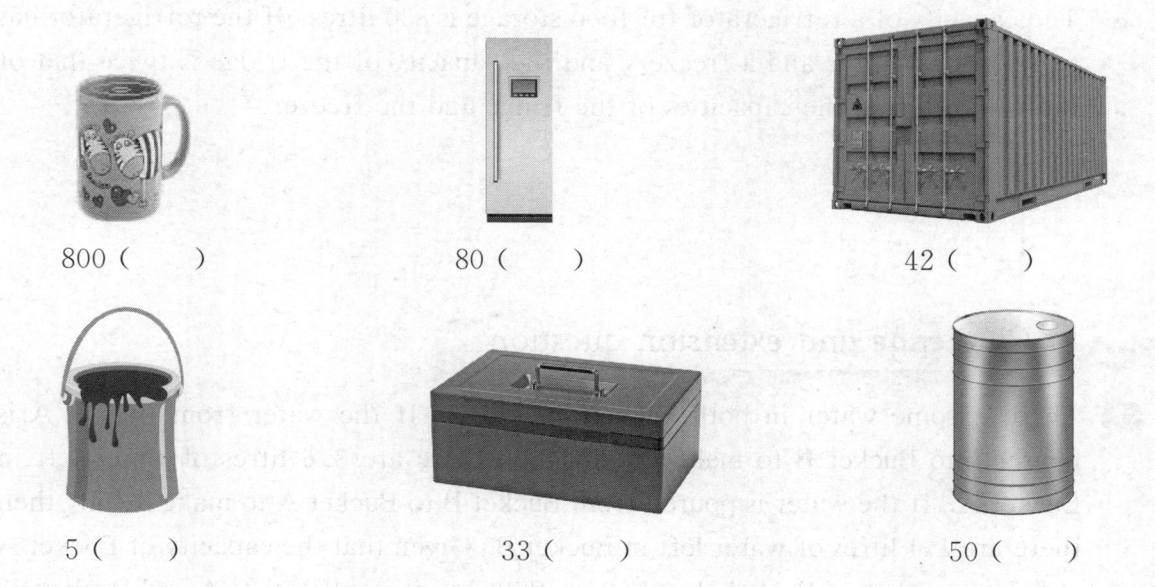

   800 (   )   80 (   )   42 (   )

   5 (   )   33 (   )   50 (   )

3. Converting between units.
   (a) 11 litres＝(   ) cubic centimetres
   (b) 7 millilitres＝(   ) cubic centimetres

Geometry and measurement (2)

(c) 3.5 litres = ( ) cubic centimetres
(d) 78 litres 8 millilitres = ( ) litres
(e) 4.4 cm³ = ( ) ml   (f) 20.2 cm³ = ( ) l
(g) 0.23 l = ( ) ml   (h) 4.38 l = ( ) ml
(i) 8 l 12 ml = ( ) l = ( ) ml   (j) 6080 ml = ( ) l ( ) ml

4 Fill in each bracket with a suitable unit.
(a) A water bottle has 280 ( ) of water.
(b) A peanut oil bottle has 2.48 ( ) of peanut oil.
(c) The capacity of a water heater is 60 ( ).
(d) The capacity of a warehouse is 480 ( ).
(e) A petrol tank has 115 ( ) of petrol.
(f) An ink bottle has 100 ( ) of ink.

5 A bucket has 5 l of water. If Matthew drinks 800 ml of water from the bucket every day, then how many days will it take Matthew to drink all the water?

6 The capacity of a refrigerator for food storage is 330 litres. If the refrigerator has two parts, a fridge and a freezer, and the capacity of the fridge is twice that of the freezer, find the capacities of the fridge and the freezer.

Challenge and extension question

7 There is some water in both buckets A and B. If the water from Bucket A is poured into Bucket B to make it full, then there are 3.6 litres of water left in Bucket A. If the water is poured from Bucket B to Bucket A to make it full, then there are 1.4 litres of water left in Bucket B. Given that the capacity of Bucket A is 1.5 times that of Bucket B, what are the capacities of Bucket A and Bucket B, respectively?

9.9 Volume and capacity (2)

Learning objectives

Solve problems involving volume and capacity

Basic questions

1. Fill in the brackets.
   (a) A cuboid petrol tank is 90 cm long, 50 cm wide and 40 cm high. There are ( ) litres of petrol in the tank when it is full.
   (b) A cuboid water tank is 50 cm long, 40 cm wide and 20 cm high. Its capacity is ( ) l.
   (c) A cuboid ice storage unit is 12 m long, 6 m wide and 3 m high. Its capacity is ( ) m^3.
   (d) The sum of all the edge lengths of a cubic box is 240 cm. Its capacity is ( ) cm^3.

2. True or false.
   (a) The volume formulae can also be used to calculate the capacity of an object. ( )
   (b) 5.6 litres = 560 cubic centimetres. ( )
   (c) The volume of a storage box made of wood is the same as its capacity. ( )

3. The inside of a cuboid wooden crate measures 95 cm long, 64 cm wide and 40 cm deep. What is the capacity of the crate?

4. The edge length of a cubic water tank is 100 cm. If the height of water in the tank is 85 cm, how many litres of water are there in the tank?

Geometry and measurement (2)

5 The inside of a cuboid fish tank measures 60 cm long, 30 cm wide and 40 cm high. The water level is 6 cm from the top of the tank. How many litres of water are there in the fish tank?

6 A cuboid water tank measures 36 cm by 25 cm by 18 cm. What is the capacity of the tank in cubic centimetres? What is the capacity in terms of litres?

7 The carriage of a refrigerated truck is a cuboid and its capacity is 22 500 litres. The inside of the carriage measures 4.5 m long and 2.5 m wide. What is the height of the carriage?

8 A cuboid glass tank without a top is made of 1-cm thick glass. The dimensions of the tank are 32 cm × 27 cm × 25 cm.
  (a) What is the capacity of the tank in litres?

  (b) If 15 litres of water is poured into the tank, how far is the water level from the top of the tank?

Challenge and extension question

9 The inside of a cuboid swimming pool measures 50 m long and 25 m wide. If water is pumped into the pool through two water pipes A and B at a speed of 1200 m³/h and 1300 m³/h respectively, what is the depth of water after the water ran into the pool for 15 minutes?

Unit test 9

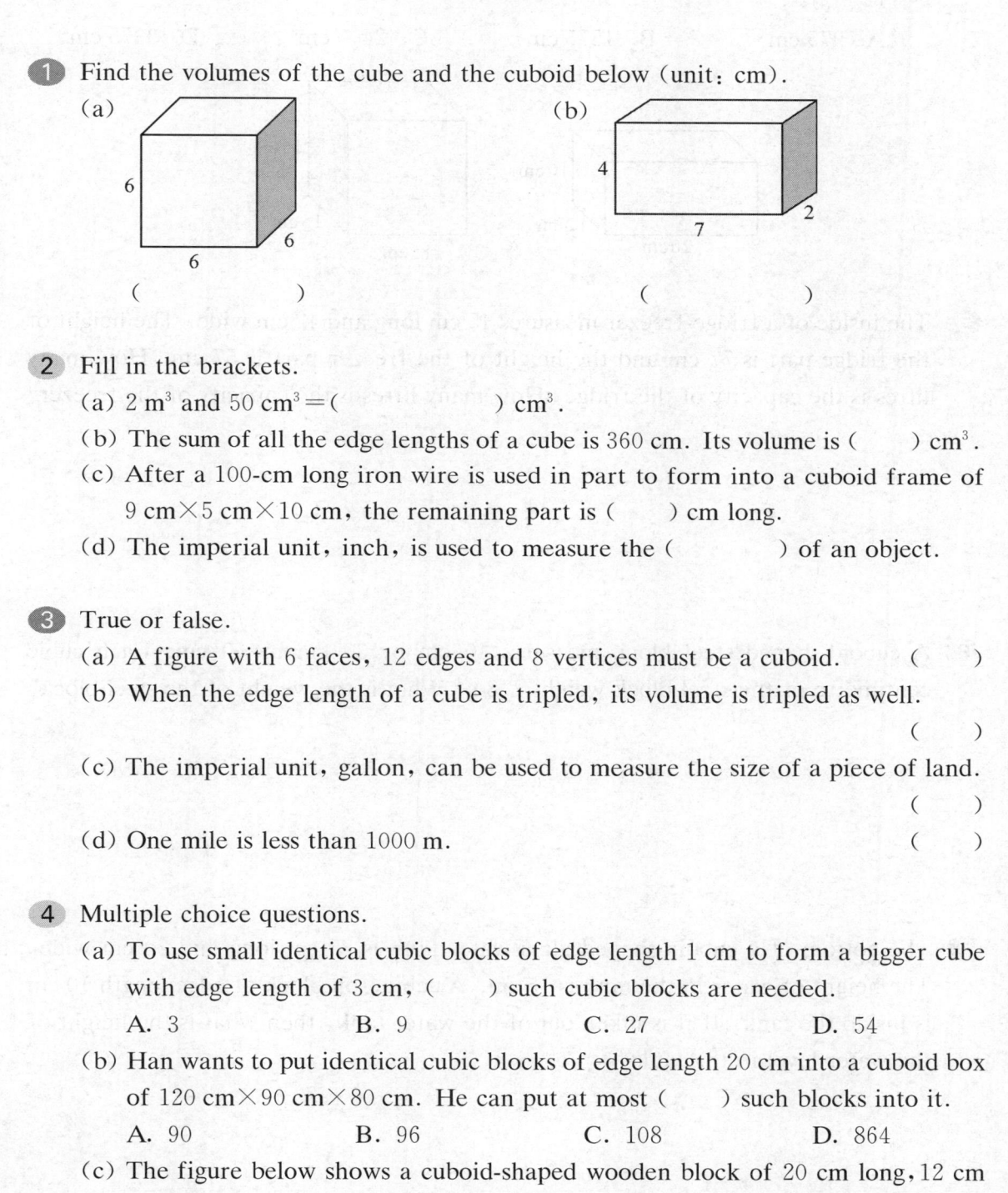

1. Find the volumes of the cube and the cuboid below (unit: cm).

   (a)
   6, 6, 6
   (   )

   (b)
   4, 7, 2
   (   )

2. Fill in the brackets.
   (a) 2 m³ and 50 cm³ = (   ) cm³.
   (b) The sum of all the edge lengths of a cube is 360 cm. Its volume is (   ) cm³.
   (c) After a 100-cm long iron wire is used in part to form into a cuboid frame of 9 cm×5 cm×10 cm, the remaining part is (   ) cm long.
   (d) The imperial unit, inch, is used to measure the (   ) of an object.

3. True or false.
   (a) A figure with 6 faces, 12 edges and 8 vertices must be a cuboid.   (   )
   (b) When the edge length of a cube is tripled, its volume is tripled as well.
                                                                            (   )
   (c) The imperial unit, gallon, can be used to measure the size of a piece of land.
                                                                            (   )
   (d) One mile is less than 1000 m.   (   )

4. Multiple choice questions.
   (a) To use small identical cubic blocks of edge length 1 cm to form a bigger cube with edge length of 3 cm, (   ) such cubic blocks are needed.
      A. 3   B. 9   C. 27   D. 54
   (b) Han wants to put identical cubic blocks of edge length 20 cm into a cuboid box of 120 cm×90 cm×80 cm. He can put at most (   ) such blocks into it.
      A. 90   B. 96   C. 108   D. 864
   (c) The figure below shows a cuboid-shaped wooden block of 20 cm long, 12 cm wide and 10 cm high, and a cubic container of edge length 15 cm. Place the wooden block vertically so its bottom base is the surface of 10 cm×12 cm,

Geometry and measurement (2)

and then put it into the cubic container (leaving part of the wooden block outside the container). The volume of the unoccupied part of the container is ( ).

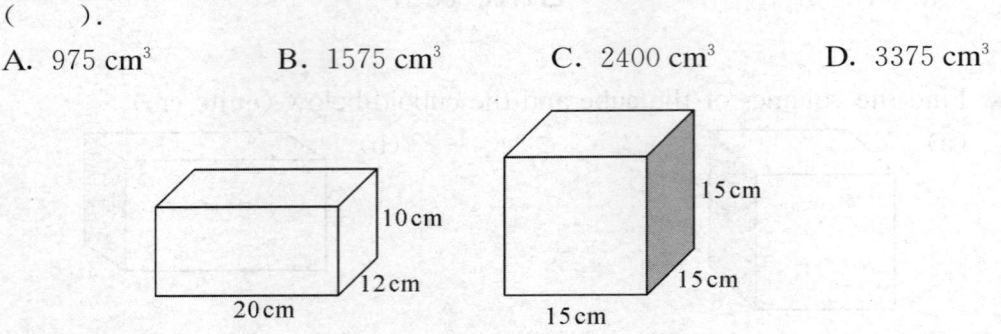

A. 975 cm³   B. 1575 cm³   C. 2400 cm³   D. 3375 cm³

5. The inside of a fridge-freezer measures 45 cm long and 42 cm wide. The height of the fridge part is 77 cm and the height of the freezer part is 57 cm. How many litres is the capacity of the fridge? How many litres is the capacity of the freezer?

6. A cuboid-shaped steel block measures 40 cm by 30 cm by 50 cm. Each cubic centimetre of the steel block weighs 7.8 g. What is the weight of the steel block?

7. The bottom of a cuboid-shaped glass water tank is 25 cm long and 20 cm wide. The height of water in the tank is 15 cm. A cubic iron block of edge length 10 cm is inside the tank. If it is taken out of the water tank, then what is the height of the water level in the tank?

Geometry and measurement (2)

8 A sealed cuboid container is 40 cm long, 30 cm wide and 20 cm high. The height of the water inside the container is 15 cm. If the front face of the container is laid down forward so it is the base of the container, what is the height of the water inside the container?

9 A cuboid fish tank is 40 cm long, 25 cm wide and 20 cm high. The height of the water in the tank is 12 cm.

(a) If 10 small steel balls are put into the tank, the water level will be raised by 0.4 cm. What is the volume of each small steel ball?

(b) If more small steel balls are put into the tank at a speed of 10 balls per minute, will the water overflow after 20 minutes? If so, how many millilitres of water will overflow? Otherwise, how many centimetres is the water level from the top of the tank?

Chapter 10 Factors, multiples and prime numbers

10.1 Meaning of integers and divisibility

Learning objectives

Know the meaning of integers and divisibilty

Basic questions

1. Write the name for each set of numbers in the brackets below. (Choose from natural numbers, whole numbers and integers.)

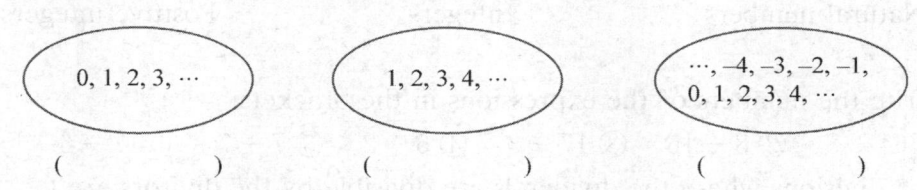

   (0, 1, 2, 3, ⋯)   (1, 2, 3, 4, ⋯)   (⋯, −4, −3, −2, −1, 0, 1, 2, 3, 4, ⋯)

   (   )   (   )   (   )

2. Multiple choice questions.
   (a) In the following statements, the incorrect one is (   ).
       A. There is no smallest integer.
       B. The smallest natural number is 1.
       C. The greatest negative integer is −1.
       D. All integers can be classified into two categories: positive integers or negative integers.
   (b) In the following pairs of numbers, the pair in which the first number is divisible by the second number is (   ).
       A. 4 and 10   B. 13 and 39   C. 16 and 4   D. 5 and 2
   (c) If 10 is divisible by a, then a has (   ) possible values.
       A. 2   B. 3
       C. 4   D. infinitely many

3. Fill in the brackets.
   (a) (   ) integers are called natural numbers. (   ) and the natural numbers are whole numbers.
   (b) When we talk about divisibility, it meets the conditions: (   ) and

Factors, multiples and prime numbers

(　　　) are all integers; and when (　　　) is divided by (　　　), the quotient is an (　　　) and the remainder is (　　　). (Choose from dividend, divisor, integer and zero.)

(c) 5 is divisible by the numbers (　　　).

(d) If a is divisible by 2, then the smallest number a can be is (　　　).

(e) If a is divisible by 3 and 12 is divisible by a, then $a=$ (　　　).

4 Choose suitable numbers from 15, -1, 0.25, 0, $\frac{1}{4}$ and 100, and write them into the circles below.

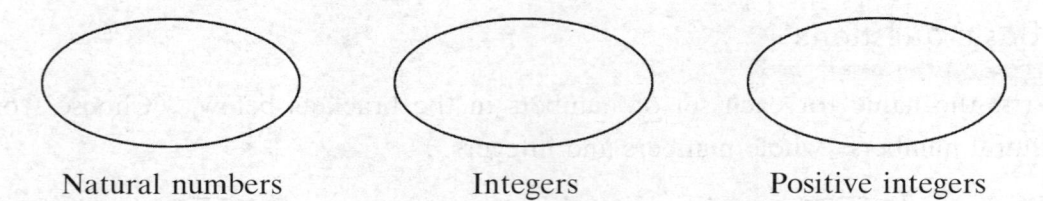

　　Natural numbers　　　　Integers　　　　Positive integers

5 Write the numbers of the expressions in the brackets.
① $64 \div 8$　② $8 \div 16$　③ $17 \div 3$　④ $5 \div 2$　⑤ $7 \div 7$　⑥ $17 \div 6$

The divisions where the dividends are divisible by the divisors are (　　　).

The divisions with non-zero remainders are (　　　).

6 Using 10 numbers 2, 3, 5, 6, 8, 9, 10, 12, 15 and 20, write all the expressions of division showing divisibility of two numbers. (Hint: for example, $6 \div 2 = 3$.)

Challenge and extension question

7 If two integers a and b $(a > b)$ are both divisible by integer c, are their sum, difference and product also divisible by c? Give your reason.

10.2 Factors and multiples

Learning objectives
Identify multiples and factors

Basic questions

1 Multiple choice questions.

(a) In the following pairs of numbers, the pair in which the first number is a multiple of the second number is (   ).

    A. 4 and 40   B. 5 and 1

    C. 2 and 8   D. 26 and 4

(b) There are (   ) factors of 16.

    A. 3   B. 4

    C. 5   D. infinitely many

(c) The correct statement of the following is (   ).

    A. A positive integer has at least two factors.

    B. 0.5 is the factor of 1.5.

    C. A factor of a number must be less than the number itself.

    D. There are infinitely many multiples of an integer.

2 Fill in the brackets.

(a) If a is divisible by b, then a is called a (   ) of b and b is called a (   ).

(b) There are (   ) factors of 6. There are (   ) multiples of 6 within 20.

(c) In all the factors of 18 and 24, the same factors of them are (   ).

(d) A number is a multiple of 5 as well as a factor of 15. The number is (   ).

(e) If the greatest factor of a number is 25, then there are (   ) factors of the number.

(f) The sum of the greatest factor of a number and the least multiple of the number is 10. This number is (   ).

Factors, multiples and prime numbers

3. The difference between the greatest factor of a number and the least factor of the number is 8. Write all the factors of the number.

4. Choose suitable numbers from 1, 2, 9, 31, 39, 57, 61 and 91, and write them into the circles below.

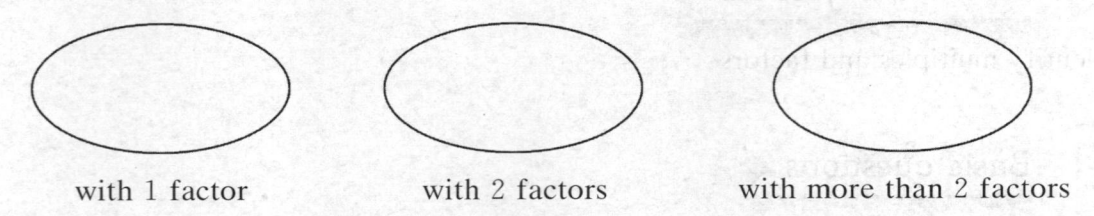

with 1 factor   with 2 factors   with more than 2 factors

5. Put 24 identical squares into a rectangle. How many combinations are there? Show your working.

Challenge and extension question

6. Find all the numbers less than 20 that have 3 factors, 4 factors, 5 factors and 6 factors, respectively.

10.3 Square numbers and cube numbers

Learning objectives
Recognise and use square numbers and cube numbers

Basic questions

1. Multiple choice questions.
   (a) There are (   ) square numbers from 1 to 20, both inclusive.
      A. 1   B. 2   C. 3   D. 4
   (b) There are (   ) cube numbers from 1 to 20, both inclusive.
      A. 1   B. 2   C. 3   D. 4
   (c) In all the factors of 100, (   ) of them are square numbers.
      A. 1   B. 2   C. 3   D. 4
   (d) In all the factors of 128, (   ) of them are cube numbers.
      A. None   B. 1   C. 2   D. 3
   (e) If the side length of a square is an integer, then (   ) of the square is a square number.
      A. the side length   B. the diagonal   C. the perimeter   D. the area

2. Fill in the brackets.
   (a) If a is a positive integer, then $a \times a$, denoted as a^2, is called a (   ).
   (b) If a is a positive integer, then $a \times a \times a$, denoted as a^3, is called a (   ).
   (c) From 2 to 101, the smallest square number is (   ) and the largest square number is (   ).
   (d) From 2 to 101, the smallest cube number is (   ) and the largest cube number is (   ).
   (e) Within 100, the numbers that are both a square number and a cube number are (   ).
   (f) The product of all the cube numbers from 1 to 100 is (   ).

3. Find the sum and product of all the square numbers from 20 to 50.

Factors, multiples and prime numbers

4 Choose suitable numbers from 1, 5, 8, 99, 144, 121, 64, 100 and 1000 and write them into the circles below.

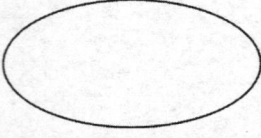

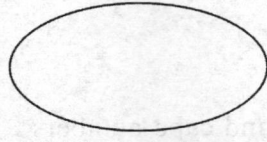

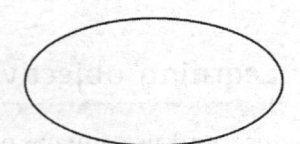

　　　Square numbers　　　　　Cube numbers　　　　　Numbers that are neither square numbers nor cube numbers

5 Calculate.
(a) $2^2 + 3^2$　　　　(b) $12^3 - 9^3$　　　　(c) $11^2 + 100^2 - 32^2$

Challenge and extension question

6 Find all the numbers from 1 to 10 000, both inclusive, that are both square numbers and cube numbers.

10.4 Numbers divisible by 2 and 5

Learning objectives

Identify numbers that are divisible by 2 and by 5

Basic questions

1. Multiple choice questions.
   (a) Write a number in ☐ so that the three-digit number 23☐ is divisible by 2, but not by 5. There are (   ) numbers that can be filled in the ☐.

   A. 1   B. 2   C. 3   D. 4

   (b) Write a number in ☐ so that the three-digit number 23☐ is divisible by 5, but not by 2. The number that can be filled in ☐ is (   ).

   A. 0   B. 5   C. 1   D. 2

   (c) In the following statements, the incorrect one is (   ).

   A. A positive integer is either an odd number or an even number.

   B. Any odd number plus 1 gives an even number.

   C. The sum of two odd numbers gives an odd number.

   D. The greatest factor of a number is the least multiple of the number.

2. Fill in the brackets.
   (a) If a number is divisible by 2, then the digit in its ones place must be
   (   ).

   (b) If a number is divisible by 5, then the digit in its ones place must be
   (   ).

   (c) In the two-digit numbers, the least odd number is (   ). The least even number is (   ).

   (d) The greatest two-digit number that is divisible by both 2 and 5 is (   ).

   (e) After 523 is added to by at least (   ), it is divisible by 2. After it is added to by at least (   ), it is divisible by 3. After it is subtracted from by at least (   ), it is divisible by 5.

3. The sum of three consecutive even numbers is 42. What are the three consecutive even numbers?

Factors, multiples and prime numbers

4 The sum of three consecutive odd numbers is 12 greater than the least of the three odd numbers. What are the three consecutive odd numbers?

5 Choose three numbers from 0, 1, 2 and 5 and form a three-digit number to be divisible by 2, 3 and 5. How many such three-digit numbers are there? What are they?

Challenge and extension question

6 Give it a try. Find the feature of the integers that are divisible by 9. Then answer the following question: Given that A is a positive integer and multiple of 45, and the digits in all the value places are either 0 or 3, what is the least possible number of A?

10.5 Prime numbers, composite numbers and prime factorisation (1)

Learning objectives

Recognise and use prime numbers, prime factors and composite numbers

Basic questions

1. Multiple choice questions.
   (a) There are (   ) prime numbers less than 10.
      A. 3   B. 4   C. 5   D. 6
   (b) The product of several prime numbers must be (   ).
      A. a prime number   B. a composite number
      C. an odd number   D. an even number
   (c) In the following statements, the correct one is (   ).
      A. A positive integer is either a prime number or a composite number.
      B. The product of two prime numbers could be an even number.
      C. All even numbers are composite numbers.
      D. The factor of a prime number must be also a prime number.

2. Fill in the brackets.
   (a) 1 has (   ) factor(s). A prime number has (   ) factors. A composite number has at least (   ) factors.
   (b) The lowest prime number is (   ). The lowest composite number is (   ).
   (c) In 1, 5, 18 and 23, the prime numbers are (   ) and the composite numbers are (   ).
   (d) There is a two-digit number. The digit in its tens place is neither a prime number nor a composite number, and the digit in its ones place is the smallest whole number. The number is (   ).
   (e) Write suitable prime numbers in the brackets.
      13 = (   ) + (   )
      16 = (   ) + (   ) = (   ) + (   )
   (f) If both of two consecutive natural numbers are prime numbers, then the two numbers are (   ).

Factors, multiples and prime numbers

3 Write all the prime factors of 66.

4 The product of two prime factors is 91. Find their sum.

5 Two prime factors form a pair of numbers and their sum is 36. Write all such pairs of numbers that satisfy the conditions.

6 Write the positive integers that are less than 10 and satisfy the following conditions.
(a) They are both even numbers and composite numbers: (   ).
(b) They are both even numbers and prime numbers: (   ).
(c) They are both odd numbers and composite numbers: (   ).
(d) They are both odd numbers and prime numbers: (   ).

Challenge and extension questions

7 Of 29, 31, 39, 43, 51, 57, 61, 87, 91 and 97, which are prime numbers?

8 If a two-digit number is not divisible by each of the following four numbers: (   ), then the two-digit number must be a prime number.
Give your reason.

10.6 Prime numbers, composite numbers and prime factorisation (2)

Learning objectives

Recognise and use prime numbers, prime factors and composite numbers

Basic questions

1. Multiple choice questions.
   (a) The correct expression of the prime factorisation of 12 is (   ).
      A. $12 = 2 \times 6$ B. $12 = 3 \times 4$
      C. $12 = 1 \times 2 \times 2 \times 3$ D. $12 = 2 \times 2 \times 3$
   (b) There are (   ) prime factors of 8.
      A. 1   B. 2   C. 3   D. 4
   (c) In the following statements, the incorrect one is (   ).
      A. There are 3 prime factors of 45.
      B. Both 3 and 5 are prime factors of 45.
      C. If A is a composite number and $A = B \times C$, then B and C are both the prime factors of A.
      D. If both B and C are prime numbers and $A = B \times C$, then B and C are both the prime factors of A.
   (d) The product of two different prime numbers has (   ) factors.
      A. 2   B. 3   C. 4   D. 5
   (e) Choose three digits from 0, 1, 2 and 3 to form a three-digit number that is divisible by 2, 3 and 5. There are (   ) such three-digit numbers.
      A. 1   B. 2   C. 3   D. 4

2. Fill in the brackets.
   (a) Each composite number can be written as the multiplication of two or more (   ), and each of them is a prime factor of this composite number.
   (b) Because $m = 2 \times 3 \times 3$, there are (   ) prime factors of m. There are (   ) factors of m.
   (c) The prime factorisation of 20 is (   ).
   (d) The factors of 28 are (   ). The prime factors of 28 are (   ).

Factors, multiples and prime numbers

3 Use the division method to factorise the following numbers into prime numbers. The first one has been done for you.

(a) 18   (b) 21   (c) 60   (d) 100

```
2 | 18
  3 | 9
      3
```

So 18 = 2 × 3 × 3.

4 Given the product of two prime numbers is 143, what is the sum of the two prime numbers?

5 If the product of three consecutive positive integers is 336, what are the three positive integers?

Challenge and extension question

6 Can you evenly divide the eight numbers 40, 44, 45, 63, 65, 78, 99 and 105 into two groups so that the products of the four numbers in each group are equal? Show your working.

Unit test 10

1 Multiple choice questions.

(a) In each of the following pairs of numbers, the pair in which the first number is divisible by the second number is (   ).

    A. 4 and 8   B. 8 and 1   C. 10 and 4   D. 3 and 6

(b) In the following statements about 1, the incorrect one is (   ).

    A. 1 is an odd number.

    B. 1 is a prime number.

    C. There is 1 factor of 1.

    D. 1 is neither a prime number nor a composite number.

(c) If Number $A = 3 \times 3 \times 5$, then there are (   ) factors of Number A.

    A. 3   B. 4   C. 5   D. 6

(d) In $15 = 3 \times 5$, both 3 and 5 are (   ) of 15.

    A. prime numbers   B. composite factors

    C. prime factors   D. prime multiples

(e) The difference of two prime numbers is (   ).

    A. a prime number

    B. a composite number

    C. either a prime number or a composite number

    D. none of the above

(f) In the following statements, the correct one is (   ).

    A. Any positive integer has at least two factors.

    B. 1 is a factor of all positive integers.

    C. The multiples of an integer are always greater than its factors.

    D. The factors of an integer are always less than the integer itself.

2 Fill in the brackets.

(a) The smallest natural number is (   ). The smallest positive integer is (   ).

(b) There are (   ) factors of 9. The least multiple of 9 is (   ).

(c) For the result to be a multiple of 5, the smallest number that should be subtracted from 2012 is (   ).

(d) A number that can be expressed as the product of two equal numbers is known as (   ).

(e) The square numbers from 10 to 50 are (   ), and from 2 to 100,

Factors, multiples and prime numbers

the smallest cube number is ( ), and the largest cube number is ( ).

(f) The odd numbers greater than 20 but less than 25 are ( ). Among them the composite number is ( ).

(g) The prime factorisation of 18 is ( ).

(h) If 12 and 18 are divisible by A, then the greatest possible value of A is ( ).

(i) A two-digit number is a prime number. If the sum of the two digits is 5, then this prime number is ( ).

3 Solve the following questions. Show your working.

(a) Find the prime factorisation of the following integers.
   (i) 34
   (ii) 36

(b) Calculate.
   (i) $3^2 + 5^2$
   (ii) $11^3 - 8^3 + 2^3$

   (iii) $15^2 - 13^2 + 5^3$

(c) There are 40 to 50 apples in the basket. All the apples are taken out exactly either 2 at a time or 3 at a time or 4 at a time without any left over. How many apples are there in the basket?

(d) The length of a wire is between 100 and 110 m. If it is cut into equal pieces of 5 m, there are 4.5 m left over. If it is cut into equal pieces of 6 m, there are 1.5 m left over. How long is the wire?

End of year test

1 Work these out mentally. Write the answers. (12%)

(a) $500 \times 60 =$ (b) $540 \div 60 =$ (c) $12.5 + 12.5 =$ (d) $0.8 - 0.45 =$

(e) $1000 \div 25 =$ (f) $31.07 \times 100 =$ (g) $6.78 + 0.23 =$ (h) $\dfrac{1}{10} - 0.01 =$

(i) $0.78 - 0.6 =$ (j) $1\dfrac{2}{5} + 4\dfrac{3}{5} =$ (k) $1 - \dfrac{3}{10} - \dfrac{13}{20} =$ (l) $4 \times 2\dfrac{3}{13} =$

2 Use the column method to calculate. (Check the answers to the questions marked with *.)(12%)

(a) $90\,800 - 4901 =$ (b) $6.5 + 31.25 =$ (c) $106.23 - 9.8 =$

(d) $7850 \div 27 =$ (e) *$613 \times 604 =$ (f) *$13\,525 \div 45 =$

3 Work these out step by step. (Calculate smartly when possible.)(16%)

(a) $5.56 + (3.68 + 4.44) + 6.32$ (b) $202 \times 55 - 25 \times 55 \times 4$

(c) $10\,000 - (59 + 42) \times 27$ (d) $107.43 - (8.56 - 1.44) - 5.43$

(e) $0.8 + 9.8 + 99.8 + 999.8$ (f) $[500 - (38 + 37) \times 4] \div 25$

End of year test

(g) $1\frac{3}{7} - \frac{2}{7} + \frac{11}{14}$

(h) $8 \times \frac{4}{11} - 4 \times \frac{13}{22} + 3 \times \frac{7}{11}$

4 Fill in the brackets. (20%)

(a) 6 l + 30 ml = (　　　) ml

(b) 4 kg 38 g = (　　　) kg

(c) 12 000 000 m² = (　　　) km²

(d) 0.023 m³ + 56 000 cm³ = (　　　) cm³

(e) 4 lb 8 oz = (　　　) lb

(f) The order of 1, $\frac{4}{7}$ and $\frac{4}{11}$ from the least to the greatest is: (　　　).

(g) In -3, -5.5, $+10$, 0, -7 and 11, the positive numbers are (　　　) and the negative numbers are (　　　). In order starting from the greatest, these are (　　　).

(h) A number consisting of two billions, six hundred thirty seven millions and seven thousands is written in numerals as (　　　). It has (　　　) thousands.

(i) When rounding 56 630 789 to the nearest ten thousand, it is (　　　). When rounding it to the nearest million, it is (　　　).

(j) When the decimal point of the number 0.23 is first moved three places to the right, and then moved two places to the left, the new number is (　　　) times the original number. The difference between the two numbers is (　　　).

(k) The diameter of the Sun is 1 392 000 km, or (　　　) million km. The radius of the Sun is (　　　) km, or (　　　) million km.

(l) In 2, 3, 6, 9, 12, 15 and 24, there are (　　　) factors of 6, and there are (　　　) multiples of 6.

(m) The least two-digit number that is divisible by 2, 3 and 5 is (　　　).

(n) The prime factors of 24 are (　　　).

(o) If $A = 2 \times 3$, $B = 3 \times 5$, then the least multiple of A and B is (　　　).

(p) In 3, 5, 12 and 20, there are (　　　) pairs of numbers that have no common factors except 1.

(q) From 1 to 100, the numbers that are both square numbers and a cube numbers are (　　　).

(r) In a right-angled triangle, if one acute angle is 30°, then the other acute angle is ( ).

(s) Given that the sum of all the angles in a regular pentagon is 540°, the degree of each of the angles is ( ).

(t) The diagram shows two overlapping set squares. ∠3=( ).

5 Find the highest common factor and lowest common multiple in each of the following groups of numbers. (6%)

(a) 9 and 20   (b) 16, 40 and 48

6 Multiple choice questions. (9%)

(a) At the time of ( ), the hour hand and minute hand on a clock face form an acute angle.

A. half past 3   B. 9 o'clock   C. 6 o'clock   D. 12 o'clock

(b) In 3 200 000 mm², 80 000 m², 5 000 000 cm² and 1 km², the greatest area is ( ).

A. 3 200 000 mm²   B. 180 000 m²   C. 5 000 000 cm²   D. 1 km²

(c) In 633 370≈640 000, the method used is ( ).

A. rounding up   B. rounding down
C. round off or rounding up   D. rounding off or rounding down

(d) If the decimal point in 8.76 is removed, this number is increased to ( ) times the original number. It is increased by ( ) times the original number.

A. 99   B. 100   C. 9   D. 10

(e) The year 2017 is written as ( ) in Roman numerals.

A. MM   B. MCMI
C. MMXIIIX   D. MMXVII

(f) If +50 represents that Joe walked 50 m to the east, then -10 represents ( ).

A. Joe walked 10 m further to the east.
B. Joe walked 10 m to the west.
C. Joe walked 10 m less to the east.
D. Joe walked 10 m in a non-easterly direction.

End of year test

(g) 4 is (　　) of 8 and 16.
   A. the lowest common multiple　　B. a common multiple
   C. the highest common factor　　D. a common factor

(h) A bus station offers two bus routes. After two buses, one for each route, depart from the station at the same time in the early morning, a bus for route A departs at an interval of 4 minutes and a bus for route B departs at an interval of 6 minutes. In every (　　) minutes at least, two buses for both routes depart at the same time.
   A. 1　　　　　　B. 2　　　　　　C. 12　　　　　　D. 24

(i) In the following statements, the incorrect one is (　　).
   A. A regular polygon has all angles equal and all sides equal.
   B. There is no reflex angle in a triangle.
   C. A circle is an irregular polygon.
   D. A square is a special regular polygon.

7 Draw the figure step by step. (5%)
Step 1: Draw $\angle AOB = 140°$.
Step 2: Draw OC starting from point O, so that $\angle AOC = \angle COB$.
Step 3: Draw a circle at the vertex of $\angle AOB$ as centre O with a diameter of 2 cm.

8 Application problems. (20%)
(a) A coach is travelling across Europe to London. It has travelled 288 km in 4 hours. If the coach travels at this speed, it will arrive at London in another 12 hours. How many more kilometres does it need to travel to the destination?

(b) A cuboid water tank is 18 cm long, 10 cm wide and 15 cm high. The water level inside the tank is 10 cm high. If an iron block is put entirely into the water tank, the water level will rise to 2 cm below the top of the tank. What is the volume of the iron block?

(c) Read the line graph and answer the questions.

Sales of Supermarket A and Supermarket B in 2012 (in thousand pounds)

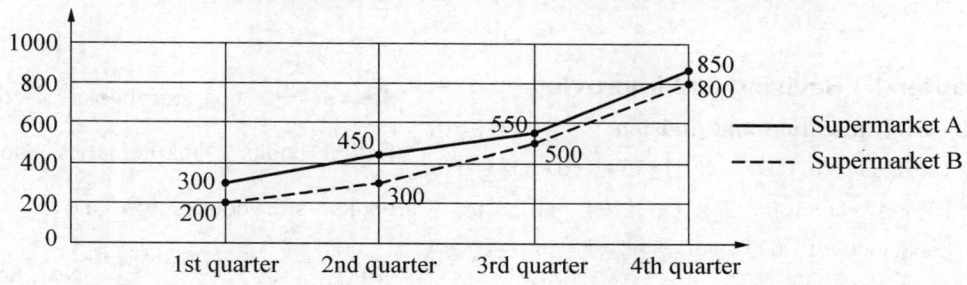

(i) Which supermarket has a faster sales growth from the second quarter to the third quarter?

(ii) What is the difference in sales between the two supermarkets in the whole year?

(d) There are more than 100 but fewer than 140 pupils in Year 5 in a school. If these pupils are divided into groups of 12, there are 3 pupils left over. If they are divided into groups of 8, there are also 3 pupils left over. How many pupils are there in Year 5?

Answers

Chapter 1 Revising and improving

1.1 Multiplication and division

① (a) 1080 (b) 1175 (c) 14 732 (d) 302 600 (e) 106 r 4 (f) 130 **②** (a) 1494 (b) 3800 (c) 2563 (d) 15 609 (e) 34 (f) 20 944 **③** (a) 9900 (b) five 3 (c) 8 116 (d) 1, 2, 3, 4; 5, 6, 7, 8, 9 **④** (a) 52 × 43, 24 × 35; The greatest product is 2236, the least product is 840 (b) 12 346 × 67 889 has the greatest product.

1.2 Addition and subtraction of fractions

① $\frac{5}{6}$ $\frac{3}{8}$ $\frac{4}{12}$ or $\frac{1}{3}$ **②** $\frac{6}{10}$ or $\frac{3}{5}$ $\frac{50}{100}$ or $\frac{5}{10}$ or $\frac{1}{2}$ $\frac{7}{7}$ or 1 **③** (a) $\frac{4}{5}$ (b) $\frac{5}{9}$ (c) $\frac{39}{53}$ (d) $\frac{20}{143}$ (e) $\frac{27}{87}$ (f) $\frac{151}{800}$ (g) $\frac{5}{19}$ (h) $\frac{2}{111}$ **④** (a) $\frac{2}{5}$ (b) $\frac{3}{5} - \frac{2}{5} = \frac{1}{5}$ 6

1.4 Decimals (2)

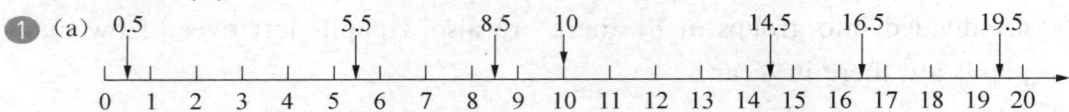

① (a) 0.5 5.5 8.5 10 14.5 16.5 19.5

(number line from 0 to 20 with arrows at 0.5, 5.5, 8.5, 10, 14.5, 16.5, 19.5)

(b) 19.5 0.5 (c) 0.5 5.5 8.5 10 14.5 16.5 19.5 **②** (a) $\frac{1}{10}$ (b) $\frac{1}{100}$ (c) $\frac{23}{100}$ (d) $\frac{1}{5}$ (e) $\frac{1}{2}$ (f) $\frac{99}{100}$ **③** (a) > (b) = (c) > (d) > (e) > (f) > **④** (a) C (b) C (c) B (d) C **⑤** (a) 0.90 0.1 0.01 0.001 (b) 0.91 km 1 km 10 m 1.1 km 1.50 km **⑥** (a) 0.12 0.13 0.21 0.23 0.31 0.32 (b) 2.103 2.130 3.120 3.102 (c) 0.123 0.321 1.023 1.320

1.5 Mathematics plaza — which area is larger?

① (a) 1 cm² (b) 4 cm² (c) 9 cm² (d) 16 cm² 25 cm² Patterns: When the side length of a square is increased to n times its original length (n is a positive integer), its area is increased to n^2 times its original length.

② (a) Example answer:

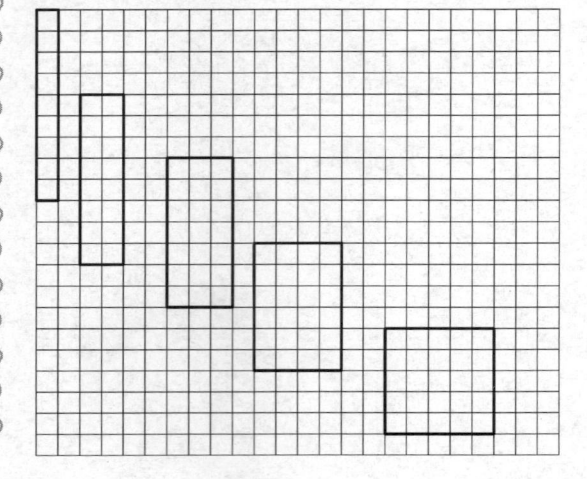

⑤ (a) $\frac{1}{5}$ (b) storybooks fiction books; fiction books mathematics books science books storybooks **⑥** (a) $\frac{3}{16}$ (b) $\frac{49}{100}$ (c) $\frac{16}{22}$ (d) $\frac{13}{100}$ **⑦** No, he cannot. 12 (pages)

1.3 Decimals (1)

① (a) 2 5 7 9 2 (b) 200.304 (c) 5 0.1 0.05 (d) 10 8 0.09 **②** (b) 0.011 (c) 6.06 (d) 120 (e) 80.03 (f) 16.2 **③** (b) 0.560 (c) 3.000 (d) 10.200 (e) 50.100 (f) 120.550 **④** (a) 0.1 (b) 0.2 (c) 0.25 (d) 0.7 (e) 0.29 (f) 0.237 **⑤** (a) 0.01 (b) 0.15 (c) 2.20 (d) 5.05 (e) 0.05 (f) 0.1 (g) 5.5 (h) 3.18 **⑥** 0 1 59 220 **⑦** 14.79, 14.88 or 14.97

Answers

(b) $1 \times 9 = 9$ (cm²) $2 \times 8 = 16$ (cm²) $3 \times 7 = 21$ (cm²) $4 \times 6 = 24$ (cm²) $5 \times 5 = 25$ (cm²)   (c) the same   different   equal

❸ As shown in the table, the areas can be: $10 \times 60 = 600$ (cm²) $20 \times 50 = 1000$ (cm²) $30 \times 40 = 1200$ (cm²)   The area will be the greatest when the length and width are both equal to 35 cm and the window is a square. Therefore the length and width of a rectangular window should be 36 cm and 34 cm respectively.

❹ When the length is 16 m and the width is 8 m, the sheep pen has the maximum area. It is 128 m².   ❺ 288 m²

Unit test 1

❶ (a) 813   (b) 80   (c) 924   (d) 416   (e) 700   (f) 14   (g) 68   (h) 5

❷ (a) 6068   (b) 262 300   (c) 85

❸ (a) 100 000   (b) 6100   (c) 7   (d) 531

❹ (a) $\frac{5}{7}$ (b) $\frac{13}{15}$ (c) $\frac{6}{29}$ (d) $\frac{156}{365}$ (e) $\frac{3}{49}$ (f) $\frac{43}{100}$ ❺ (a) $\frac{3}{10}$ (b) $\frac{3}{100}$ (c) $\frac{33}{100}$ (d) $\frac{71}{100}$ (e) $\frac{7}{10}$ (f) $\frac{87}{100}$ ❻ (a) 2   3   3   5   3   (b) 50   8   0.09   (c) 1.05   0.6   365   (d) 3   (e) 8   112   7   99   4   (f) 0.01   1   0.11   11   (g) 36   (h) 36   (i) 25   51

❼ $\frac{2}{4}$ or $\frac{1}{2}$ $\frac{9}{13}$ $\frac{70}{100}$ or $\frac{7}{10}$ ❽ (a) 46 kg   (b) $\frac{1}{6}$ 10   (c) 225 m²   (d) 196 m²   (e) 42 cm

Chapter 2   Large numbers and measures

2.1 Knowing large numbers (1)

❶ (a)

Group	···	Millions			Thousands			Ones		
Place of value	···	Hundred millions	Ten millions	Millions	Hundred thousands	Ten thousands	Thousands	Hundreds	Tens	Ones

(b) 10   (c) 378   28   867   (d) the thousands   the ones   three hundred and seventy-eight million, twenty-eight thousand, eight hundred and sixty-seven   (e) 21 001 036   ❷ (b)

Ten thousands	Thousands	Hundreds	Tens	Ones
2	5	1	9	8

Twenty-five thousand, one hundred and ninety-eight

$25\,198 = 2 \times 10\,000 + 5 \times 1000 + 1 \times 100 + 9 \times 10 + 8 \times 1$
$= 20\,000 + 5000 + 100 + 90 + 8$

(c)

Hundred thousands	Ten thousands	Thousands	Hundreds	Tens	Ones
4	1	2	7	0	8

Four hundred and twelve thousand, seven hundred and eight

$412\,708 = 4 \times 100\,000 + 1 \times 10\,000 + 2 \times 1000 + 7 \times 100 + 0 \times 10 + 8 \times 1$
$= 400\,000 + 10\,000 + 2000 + 700 + 0 + 8$

(d)

Millions	Hundred thousands	Ten thousands	Thousands	Hundreds	Tens	Ones
2	3	9	5	1	9	8

Two million, three hundred and ninety-five thousand, one hundred and ninety-eight

$2\,395\,198 = 2 \times 1\,000\,000 + 3 \times 100\,000 + 9 \times 10\,000 + 5 \times 1000 + 1 \times 100 + 9 \times 10 + 8 \times 1$
$= 2\,000\,000 + 300\,000 + 90\,000 + 5000 + 100 + 90 + 8$

215

Answers

(e)

Ten millions	Millions	Hundred thousands	Ten thousands	Thousands	Hundreds	Tens	Ones
7	6	2	0	3	0	0	0

Seventy-six million, two hundred and three thousand

76 203 000 = $\underline{7 \times 10\,000\,000} + \underline{6 \times 1\,000\,000} + \underline{2 \times 100\,000} + 0 \times 10\,000 + \underline{3 \times 1000} + \underline{0} \times 100 + \underline{0} \times 10 + \underline{0} \times 1$
= 70 000 000 + 6 000 000 + 200 000 + 0 + 3000 + 0 + 0 + 0

❸ 119 033   70 070 007   961 273 928   500 000 000   ❹ (a) × (b) × (c) √

(b)
69 997 69 998 69 999 70 000 70 001 70 002

❺ 10 976   ❻ (a) 808 000 (b) 200 549 (c) 698 055 (d) 2494 (e) 379 348 (f) 5 087 988   ❼ 50 600, 56 000, 60 500, 65 000, 500 006   500 006, 65 000, 60 500, 56 000, 50 600   ❽ England: 53 012 456; Northern Ireland: 1 810 863; Scotland: 5 295 403; Wales: 3 063 456; Total: 63 182 178 (Source: 2011 UK census; answer may vary if other sources of data are used.)

2.3 Knowing large numbers (3)

❶ (a) eight   ten millions   hundred thousands   thousands   ninety million, three hundred and one thousand (b) 60 054 003 (c) 660 060 006 nine (d) 60 006 080   sixty million, six thousand and eighty (e) 80 43 (f) 7
❷ (a) eight million, two hundred and seventy-one thousand, two hundred and seventy (b) twenty-three thousand, two hundred and fifty (c) four million, seven hundred and ninety-one thousand (d) five billion nine hundred million
❸ (a) × (b) × (c) √ (d) ×
❹ (a) D (b) B (c) A (d) E (e) C
(f) 4 050 000 800 > 400 050 008 > 40 050 008 > 40 000 080 > 405 008   ❺ (5976 − 1432) ÷ 8 = 568   ❻ 100 000   ❼ 790 212   450 212

(d) √   ❺ (a) 6 660 000 (b) 6 606 000   6 066 000 (c) 6 600 600   6 060 600   6 006 600
❻ 975 310 − 103 579 = 871 731

2.2 Knowing large numbers (2)

❶ (a) hundred millions (b) ten thousands   thousands   millions (c) 2   3   500   709
(d) ten billions   10 000 000 000   hundred millions   500 000 000   millions   6 000 000   tens   90 (e) 913   4   913 004 (f) 4000   4   40 (g) 1 000 000   1000   1000   ❷ (a) C (b) B (c) C   ❸ (a) < (b) > (c) <
(d) =   ❹ (a) 69 998   69 999   70 000   70 001   70 002

2.4 Rounding of large numbers (1)

❶ 100   200   500   600   ❷ 10 000   a   20 000, 30 000   b   40 000, 40 000   c   50 000, 70 000   d   80 000, 90 000   e   100 000   ❸ 30 000, 40 000   100 000, 110 000   970 000, 980 000   120 000, 130 000   6 400 000, 6 410 000   390 000, 400 000
❹ (a) 10 000 (b) 56 090 000 (c) 440 000
(d) 1 100 000 (e) 10 000 (f) 9 950 000
❺ (a) 81 (b) 119 (c) 2 (d) 1
❻ (a) One hundred and thirty-six thousand and ninety   Fifty-nine thousand, four hundred   Seventy thousand and twenty   One million, sixty-four thousand, nine hundred and ninety-nine (b) 140 000   60 000   70 000   1 060 000
(c) 1 064 999 > 136 090 > 70 020 > 59 400
❼ (a) 7 777 000   Seven million, seven hundred and seventy-seven thousand   7 780 000
(b) 0~4   4 (c) 5~9   5 (d) 10
❽ 7 000 070   7 000 007

2.5 Rounding of large numbers (2)

❶ 300 000, 400 000   700 000, 800 000   100 000, 200 000   900 000, 1 000 000

500 000, 600 000 ❷ 56 430 000, 56 440 000
56 400 000, 56 500 000 56 000 000, 57 000 000
❸ 5 5 ❹ 5 375 000 9 989 000 1 241 000
1 000 000; 5 380 000 9 990 000 1 240 000
1 000 000; 5 400 000 10 000 000 1 200 000
1 000 000; 5 000 000 10 000 000 1 000 000
1 000 000 ❺ 94 999 85 000 ❻ 604 503
600 000 497

2.6 Square kilometres (1)

❶ (a) 1 cm (b) 1 m (c) 1 km²
❷ 1 000 000 ❸ 12 km² ❹ 108 km²
❺ (a) A (b) A (c) A (d) C (e) A
❻ 0.15 0.33 40 0.49 0.15 22

2.7 Square kilometres (2)

❶ 1 000 000 10 000 ❷ (a) m² (b) cm²
(c) m² (d) m² (e) cm² (f) km²
❸ (a) 26 000 000 (b) 2 080 000 (c) 0.19
(d) 0.013 (e) 8 (f) 50 420 (g) 3 000 000
❹ (a) > (b) < (c) = (d) < (e) <
(f) > ❺ (a) (i) England Northern Ireland
116 584 km² (ii) Wales and Northern Ireland
6935 km² (b) 120×60 = 7200 (cm²) = 0.72 (m²)
❻ (80+15)×(55+15)−80×55 = 2250 (m²)
❼ 12×8−8×8 = 32 (cm²)

2.8 Converting kilograms and grams

❶ 1000 ❷ (a) kg (b) g (c) kg (d) g
(e) kg (f) g ❸ (a) 307 000 (b) 17 000
(c) 6000 (d) 72 025 (e) 43 004 (f) 46 798
❹ (a) > (b) = (c) < (d) > (e) >
(f) > ❺ (a) B (b) B (c) A
❻ (a) 2500×4 = 10 000 (g) = 10 (kg)
(b) 5000−8×620 = 40 (kg) No. (c) 5000÷
25 = 200 (boxes) ❼ (a) × (b) √
(c) × ❽ 46−(46−26)×2 = 6 (kg)

2.9 Litres and millilitres (1)

❶ (a) large litre (b) 1000 ❷ answer may
vary, for example A+B+C or A+D
❸ (a) litres (b) litres (c) millilitres
(d) millilitres (e) millilitres (f) millilitres
(g) millilitres ❹ (a) 2000 (b) 800 000
(c) 82 (d) 50 000 (e) 2600 (f) 30 3
❺ (a) 2000−400 = 1600 (ml) (b) 2000÷
8 = 250 (ml) ❻ (a) B (b) D (c) C
(d) D ❼ (375+11 000)÷25 = 455 (ml)

2.10 Litres and millilitres (2)

❶ (a) E (b) C (c) B (d) A (e) D
❷ (a) millilitres litres (b) 1 (c) 4
(d) 13 000 (e) 12 (f) 10 (g) 5500 (h) 23
(i) 4567 (j) 56 10 (k) 10 700
❸ (a) 70 l > 7 l > 5970 ml > 5900 ml > 600 ml
(b) 200 ml < 260 ml < 2 l < 2060 ml < 20 l
❹ (a) 350×10×16 = 56 000 (ml) = 56 (litres)
(b) 625÷5×8 = 1000 (ml) = 1 (litre)
❺ (a) 1000 (b) 500 (c) 250 750 1500
(d) 200 400 1200

Unit test 2

❶ (a) 4 (b) 36 (c) 30 (d) 910 (e) 200
(f) 210 (g) 560 (h) 40 (i) 724
❷ (a) 6448 (b) 7189 (c) 17 012 (d) 26 r
40 ❸ (a) 4000 (b) 3295 (c) 13 824
(d) 888 ❹ (a) third tens hundreds sixth
ten thousands hundred thousands ninth
millions ten millions hundred millions
(b) nine million, twenty-five thousand 9 25
(c) seventy million, seven hundred thousand
70 700 (d) three million, eighty thousand,
six hundred and four 3080 604 (e) 300 003
three hundred thousand and three
(f) 4 034 020 (g) 1 020 000 (h) 660 000 000
(i) 90 (j) 70 000 000 (k) 20 350
(l) 8300 (m) 5000 (n) 300 000 (o) 3 l 400
ml < 6 l < 7080 ml < 10 l 7 ml ❺ (a) C (b)
A (c) A (d) B A B B (e) C (f) C
❻ (a) 330−98 = 232 (b) Divisor: 98÷(6+
1) = 14 Dividend: 14×6 = 84 (c) (78−31)
×4 = 188 (d) 23×105÷30 = 80 r 15
❼ (a) 18 000÷300 = 60 (bottles) (b) (60+
40)×50 = 5000 (kg) (c) 74 000×3+12 000 =
234 000 (kg) (d) 1 m = 100 cm (30 000×600)
÷(50×50) = 7200 (slates) (e) (300−40)×

Answers

5 = 1300 (ml) 40 × 5 = 200 (ml)

Chapter 3 Dividing by two-digit numbers

3.1 Speed, time and distance (1)

1 (a) √ (b) √ (c) × (d) √ (e) √
2 14 km/h 900 m/min 20 m/s **3** km/h km/min m/min m/min **4** 100 m/min 120 m/min 125 m/min 130 m/min Tom
5 (a) 800 ÷ 8 = 100 (m/min) (b) 800 ÷ 5 = 160 (km/h) **6** 5 m/s

3.2 Speed, time and distance (2)

1 Time = Distance ÷ Speed Speed = Distance ÷ Time **2** (a) Jim faster (b) Joanne faster **3**

Speed	Time	Distance
84 m/min	6 min	504 m
7 km/h	17 h	119 km
118 m/min	8 min	944 m

4 (a) Samantha (b) 700 × 30 = 21 000 (m) = 21 (km) 16 ÷ 2 = 8 (km) (c) (18 + 27) × 8 = 360 (km) (d) (28 − 4 − 2) × 100 = 2200 (m) **5** Linda

3.3 Dividing two-digit or three-digit numbers by a two-digit number (1)

1 (a) 3 (b) 2 (c) 3 (d) 3 (e) 30 (f) 20 (g) 30 (h) 30 (i) 30 (j) 2 (k) 3 (l) 3 (m) 3 (n) 2 (o) 3 (p) 3
2 (a) 23s 4 23s 4 4 92 7 less 4 (b) 63s 8 63s 8 8 504 13 less 8
3 8 r 6 3 r 36 6 5 r 7 4 r 51 7 r 6
4 the goat Its speed, 13 m/s, is the fastest. the cat Its speed, 12 m/s, is the second fastest. the elephant Its speed, 10 m/s, is the slowest. **5** (a) 4 4 × 480 = 1920 (pounds) (b) 11 11 × 200 = 2200 (pounds) (c) 3 × 480 + 2 × 200 = 1840 (pounds) To hire 3 coaches and 2 minibuses.

3.4 Dividing two-digit or three-digit numbers by a two-digit number (2)

1 (a) 3 3 153 just right (b) 8 8 504 too big 7 7 441 39 less 7 (c) 4 4 372 too big 3 3 279 81 less 3 (d) 8 8 344 too big 7 7 301 33 less 7
2 5 r 60 5 r 41 4 r 53 3 r 18 8 r 2 7 r 54 **3** 6 6 7 8 8 9 **4** (a) 192 ÷ 32 = 6 (b) 344 ÷ 43 = 8 (c) 100 000 ÷ 10 = 10 000 (d) 100 000 ÷ 100 = 1000 **5** (855 − 162) ÷ 63 = 11 (days) **6** (760 + 240) ÷ 25 = 40 (seconds)

3.5 Dividing two-digit or three-digit numbers by a two-digit number (3)

1 (a) 4 4 112 too big 3 3 84 5 less 3 (b) 4 4 112 too big 3 3 84 2 2 56 24 less 2 (c) 9 6 7 (d) 8 7 7 (e) 7 6 7 (f) 9 9 9
2 4 2 8 r 21 8 r 12 7 r 20 9 r 28
3 (a) 384 ÷ 48 = 8 (b) 413 ÷ 59 = 7 (c) 960 − 42 × 22 = 36 **4** 1000 − 130 = 870 870 ÷ 130 = 6 (times) r 90 **5** 322 ÷ 63 = 5 r 7 114 ÷ 16 = 7 r 2 213 ÷ 22 = 9 r 15

3.6 Dividing multi-digit numbers by a two-digit number (1)

1 (a) 120 240 120 10 7 17 (b) 1900 2280 1900 50 228 6 56 **2** 25 16 r 20 12 r 20 **3** 76 r 11 43 r 10 30 r 9 23 r 10 18 r 45 12 r 3 **4** (a) 1 3 r 30; 2 6 r 25; 3 9 r 20; 4 12 r 15; 5 15 r 10; 6 18 r 5; 7 21; 8 23 r 30; 9 26 r 25 (b) 1, 2 or 3 and digit from 4 to 9 **5** (a) two tens 10 (b) one 7 (c) 3 (d) 3 **6** 516 ÷ 26 = 19 r 22 990 ÷ 38 = 26 r 2

3.7 Dividing multi-digit numbers by a two-digit number (2)

1 33 r 20 83 r 8 166 r 8 125 **2** 51 r 53 64 r 8 92 r 32 104 r 8 192 r 8 384 r 8
3 3806 580 1000 1212 1000 15 800
4 (a) 84 × 14 ÷ 49 = 24 (b) (999 + 99) ÷

218

Answers

18 = 61 (c) 15×15÷225 = 1 ❺ (a) A
(b) D ❻ 1215÷45 = 27 1789÷38 = 47 r 3

3.8 Practice and exercise (1)

❶ (a) 700 (b) 10 (c) 0 (d) 200 (e) 400
(f) 96 (g) 300 (h) 120 (i) 4 (j) 4
(k) 3 (l) 100 ❷ (a) 266 200 (b) 103
(c) 60 r 31 ❸ (a) 576 (b) 6400
(c) 24 427 (d) 10 (e) 97 (f) 3
❹ (a) 4736−4736÷16 = 4440 (b) (565+
191)÷18 = 42 ❺ (a) 5 50 51 (b) 4
(c) 5 101 0 4 99 90 ❻ 44 hours 11
hours 5 hours and 30 minutes 2 hours and 45
minutes 2 hours 48 minutes

Unit test 3

❶ (a) 12 (b) 780 (c) 90 (d) 40
(e) 1200 (f) 2970 (g) 31 (h) 50 (i) 24
(j) 6 (k) 43 (l) 802 (m) 4 (n) 1200
(o) 76 (p) 8 ❷ (a) 46 828 (b) 170 100
(c) 205 (d) 609 ❸ (a) 96 (b) 12 120
(c) 17 (d) 3026 ❹ (a) 6 000 000 000
(b) 2 610 000 (c) two tens (d) three
hundreds 2 48 (e) any digit from 4 to 9
(f) 3 1 or 2 ❺ (a) B (b) C (c) C
(d) C (e) B ❻ (a) 504÷(84÷3) = 18 (days)
(b) 3×60+310 = 490 (sets) (c) (10+5)×
3 = 45 (km) (d) 4500−125×24 = 1500 (bottles)
❼ 140 km/h 251 km/h 805 km/h

Chapter 4 Comparing fractions, improper fractions and mixed numbers

4.1 Comparing fractions (1)

❶ (a) 3 6 less (b) greater numerator
❷ $\frac{3}{6} > \frac{2}{6}$ $\frac{5}{9} = \frac{5}{9}$ $\frac{7}{10} > \frac{3}{10}$ ❸ Any 3
blocks coloured, any 7 blocks coloured, any 1
block coloured $\frac{1}{8} < \frac{3}{8} < \frac{7}{8}$ ❹ (a) <
(b) > (c) < (d) > (e) < (f) <
(g) > > (h) < < (i) > < ❺ $\frac{1}{9} <$
$\frac{2}{9} < \frac{3}{9} < \frac{5}{9} < \frac{7}{9}$ ❻ $\frac{79}{80} > \frac{50}{80} > \frac{30}{80} > \frac{18}{80} >$

$\frac{1}{80}$ ❼ $1 - \frac{8}{39} - \frac{10}{39} - \frac{11}{39} = \frac{10}{39}$

4.2 Comparing fractions (2)

❶ (a) less (b) less (c) less denominator
❷ (a) $\frac{1}{3}$ $\frac{1}{4}$ $\frac{1}{5}$ $\frac{1}{8}$ (b) $\frac{1}{3} > \frac{1}{4} > \frac{1}{5} >$
$\frac{1}{8}$ (c) smaller less ❸ (a) < (b) >
(c) > (d) > (e) < (f) < (g) < <
(h) > > ❹ $\frac{1}{81} < \frac{1}{36} < \frac{1}{27} < \frac{1}{18} < \frac{1}{9}$
❺ $\frac{1}{10} > \frac{1}{20} > \frac{1}{40} > \frac{1}{70} > \frac{1}{100}$ ❻ 30÷5 =
6 (pieces) 20÷4 = 5 (pieces) Alex takes more.

4.3 Comparing fractions (3)

❶ (a) $\frac{3}{4}$ $\frac{6}{16}$ $\frac{2}{4}$ $\frac{2}{4}$ $\frac{3}{6}$ $\frac{2}{6}$ $\frac{4}{8}$ $\frac{5}{8}$
(b) ④, ⑤, ⑦ (c) more less ❷ (a) <
(b) > (c) < (d) < (e) > (f) >
(g) > > ❸ (a) 7 $\frac{4}{15}$ (b) $\frac{5}{13}$ $\frac{4}{13}$ $\frac{1}{13}$
(c) $\frac{1}{5}$ $\frac{2}{5}$ m $\frac{4}{5}$ $\frac{2}{5}$ m (d) 18 ❹ $\frac{5}{999} <$
$\frac{5}{656} < \frac{5}{123} < \frac{5}{50} < \frac{5}{11}$ ❺ $\frac{4}{7} > \frac{2}{7} > \frac{2}{11}$
❻ $\frac{9}{15}$ m $> \frac{9}{20}$ m The snail climbed higher.
❼ Tom drank more. (Hint: The amount Tom
has left: $1 - \frac{3}{4} = \frac{1}{4}$. The amount Mary has
left: $1 - \frac{2}{3} = \frac{1}{3}$ $\frac{1}{3} > \frac{1}{4}$)

4.4 Comparing fractions (4)

❶ Yes, Ming is right. Each monkey gets $\frac{1}{6}$ of
a basket in each case. ❷ (a) 4 8
(b) 15 6 (c) 2 10 (d) 3 99 (e) 36 3
72 3 6 (f) 33 300 ❸ (a) $\frac{1}{4}$ (b) $\frac{2}{6}$
$\frac{3}{9}$ $\frac{4}{12}$ (answer may vary) (c) 6 (d) $\frac{1}{4}$
❹ (a) $\frac{4}{12} + \frac{6}{12} = \frac{10}{12}$ (m) (b) $1 - \frac{10}{12} = \frac{2}{12}$ (m)
❺ $\frac{3}{7} = \frac{6}{14}$ $\frac{6}{14} > \frac{4}{14}$ Sam walked faster

Answers

6 $\frac{3}{4}$ of the pizzas Two methods of drawing:

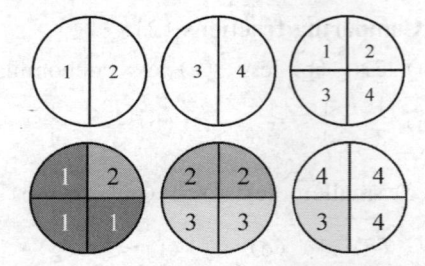

4.5 Improper fractions and mixed numbers

1 $\frac{3}{8}$ $\frac{8}{8}$ or 1 $\frac{9}{8}$ or $1\frac{1}{8}$ **2** Proper fractions: $\frac{7}{12}$ $\frac{79}{100}$ $\frac{181}{365}$ Improper fractions: $\frac{5}{3}$ $\frac{3}{2}$ $\frac{13}{12}$ $\frac{19}{6}$ Mixed numbers: $7\frac{1}{18}$ $1\frac{4}{5}$ $30\frac{1}{2}$ $5\frac{1}{4}$ **3** $\frac{3}{4}$ $2\frac{1}{2}$ 5 $8\frac{2}{3}$ $9\frac{1}{3}$ **4** (a) √ (b) √ (c) × (d) √ (e) × (f) × (g) √ (h) √ **5** (a) $\frac{7}{3}$ (b) $\frac{13}{8}$ (c) $\frac{61}{9}$ (d) $\frac{2377}{39}$ **6** (a) $4\frac{3}{7}$ (b) $6\frac{5}{8}$ (c) 9 (d) $3\frac{7}{30}$ **7**

Quantity	As decimal	As mixed number	As improper fraction
2 m 10 cm	2.1 m	$2\frac{1}{10}$ m	$\frac{21}{10}$ m
90 minutes	1.5 h	$1\frac{1}{2}$ h	$\frac{3}{2}$ h
5 kg 200 g	5.2 kg	$5\frac{1}{5}$ kg	$\frac{26}{5}$ kg
1650 ml	1.65 l	$1\frac{65}{100}$ l	$\frac{165}{100}$ l
30 km 200 m	30.2 km	$30\frac{1}{5}$ km	$\frac{151}{5}$ km
1 m² 900 cm²	1.09 m²	$1\frac{9}{100}$ m²	$\frac{109}{100}$ m²

8 (a) 0, 1, 2, 3 (b) 5, 6, 7, 8

4.6 Adding and subtracting fractions with related denominators (1)

1 $\frac{1}{2}=\frac{3}{6}$ $\frac{2}{5}=\frac{4}{10}$ $\frac{13}{18}=\frac{65}{90}$ $\frac{11}{10}=\frac{110}{100}$ $\frac{17}{20}=\frac{85}{100}$ **2** (a) 2 (b) 4 (c) 20 (d) 26 (e) 75 (f) Any equivalent fraction, for example $\frac{20}{34}$ or $\frac{30}{51}$ **3** (a) $\frac{2}{5}$ (b) $\frac{2}{7}$ (c) 1 (d) $\frac{4}{13}$ (e) $\frac{4}{9}$ (f) $\frac{18}{23}$ **4** (b) $\frac{7}{10}$ (c) $\frac{25}{26}$ (d) $1\frac{1}{5}$ (e) $1\frac{8}{35}$ (f) $2\frac{37}{77}$ **5** (b) $\frac{1}{9}$ (c) $\frac{7}{22}$ (d) $\frac{5}{14}$ (e) $\frac{9}{150}$ (f) $\frac{19}{90}$ **6** (a) $\frac{2}{3}=\frac{6}{9}$ $\frac{6}{9}>\frac{1}{9}$ Jason has more books. (b) $\frac{7}{9}$ (c) $\frac{5}{9}$ (d) 14(books) Method 1: $\left(\frac{2}{3}+\frac{1}{9}\right)\times 18=14$ Method 2: $\frac{2}{3}\times 18+\frac{1}{9}\times 18=14$ **7** (a) $\frac{7}{8}$ (b) $\frac{3}{6}$ or $\frac{1}{2}$ **8** D First express the fractions $\frac{1}{2}$ and $\frac{1}{3}$ with a common denominator, and then add the numerators, i.e., $\frac{1}{2}+\frac{1}{3}=\frac{3}{6}+\frac{2}{6}=\frac{5}{6}$.

4.7 Adding and subtracting fractions with related denominators (2)

1 (a) $\frac{5}{7}$ (b) 0 (c) $\frac{13}{8}$ (d) $\frac{5}{9}$ (e) $\frac{47}{56}$ (f) $\frac{1}{10}$ **2** (a) $1\frac{1}{2}$ (b) $15\frac{3}{7}$ (c) $58\frac{23}{100}$ **3** (a) $\frac{2}{3}$ (b) $\frac{13}{15}$ (c) $4\frac{83}{100}$ **4** (a) $4\frac{4}{7}$ (b) $2\frac{1}{6}$ (c) $\frac{4}{7}$ (d) $\frac{25}{99}$ (e) $\frac{22}{25}$ (f) $1\frac{13}{18}$ **5** (b) $5\frac{7}{13}$ (c) $\frac{1}{6}$ (d) $2\frac{1}{12}$ **6** $\frac{7}{6}$ or $1\frac{1}{6}$ **7** Yes, it would be enough. He would use $7\frac{2}{5}$ m. **8** (a) $9\frac{17}{19}$ (b) $\frac{11}{3}-\frac{25}{9}=\frac{33}{9}-\frac{25}{9}=\frac{8}{9}$

4.8 Multiplying fractions by whole numbers

1 (a) 2 5 10 (b) 2 2 4 (c) 3 3 3 $\frac{9}{10}$ (d) 1 1 1 (e) 5 5 10 $1\frac{1}{9}$

Answers

(f) 4 4 4 2$\frac{2}{5}$ ❷ (b) 4$\frac{1}{6}$ (c) 3$\frac{3}{8}$
❸ (a) × (b) × (c) √ (d) √
❹ (a) $\frac{5}{2}$ (b) $\frac{9}{10}$ (c) 41$\frac{3}{5}$ (d) 146$\frac{2}{5}$
(e) 8$\frac{3}{4}$ (f) $\frac{13}{100}$ ❺ 29 m 49$\frac{1}{2}$ m²
❻ (a) 8$\frac{1}{4}$ (hours) (b) 5$\frac{1}{2}$ (hours)
(c) 11 (hours) ❼ (a) 39$\frac{1}{3}$ (b) 14$\frac{17}{30}$

Unit test 4

❶ (a) 120 (b) 30 (c) 307 (d) $\frac{3}{5}$
(e) $\frac{7}{15}$ (f) $\frac{13}{14}$ (g) 5$\frac{3}{8}$ (h) $\frac{16}{17}$ (i) 20$\frac{1}{5}$
❷ (a) 1$\frac{2}{15}$ (b) $\frac{4}{39}$ (c) 3$\frac{13}{48}$ (d) 4$\frac{2}{3}$
(e) $\frac{1}{2}$ (f) 3$\frac{2}{9}$ (g) 24$\frac{5}{11}$ (h) 5$\frac{13}{18}$
❸ (a) < (b) $\frac{3}{4}=\frac{6}{8}=\frac{9}{12}=\frac{12}{16}$ (c) 3$\frac{1}{4}$
6$\frac{1}{2}$ (d) 3 $\frac{1}{4}$ $\frac{3}{4}$, 1$\frac{1}{2}$ ❹ (a) >
(b) < (c) > (d) = (e) < (f) >
❺ (a) $\frac{8}{12}$ $\frac{4}{12}$ $\frac{4}{14}$ $\frac{1}{14}$ (b) 1 $\frac{3}{4}$ $\frac{1}{2}$ $\frac{2}{8}$
❻ (a) A (b) C ❼ (a) Ben (b) 7 kg
(c) (i) 3$\frac{9}{10}$ (ii) 4$\frac{7}{10}$ (c) 42$\frac{2}{5}$ (d) (i) 17$\frac{7}{10}$
(ii) 11$\frac{4}{5}$ (iii) 47$\frac{1}{5}$

Chapter 5 Consolidation and enhancement

5.1 Large numbers and rounding (1)

❶ (a) 411 000 511 000 900 000 700 000
600 000 (b) 10 10 (c) counting (d) 1 000 000
2 000 000 (e) forty-three million, seven thousand and seventy 43 007 70 (f) 587
❷ (a) four million, two hundred and four thousand, three hundred and twenty-two
(b) ten million, twenty-five thousand and ninety (c) twenty million, two hundred
(d) one billion, ten million, one hundred and one thousand and ten ❸ (a) 59 508 880
(b) 400 854 500 (c) 2 616 329 (d) 110 409 011
❹ (a) C (b) A D (c) B ❺ (a) <
(b) < (c) > (d) < (e) < (f) >
❻ 36 890 000 36 900 000 40 000 000,
98 970 000 99 000 000 100 000 000, 109 830 000
109 800 000 110 000 000 ❼ (a) 853 000
850 000 (b) 300 058 300 000 (c) 853 000,
835 000, 583 000, 538 000, 385 000 and 358 000
(d) 803 050, 805 030, 305 080, 308 050, 508 030
and 503 080 ❽ 5 499 999 4 500 000

5.2 Large numbers and rounding (2)

❶ (a) hundred thousands eleventh
(b) 4 000 444 (c) nine (d) 305 002 001
(e) 206 000 060 (f) 1 000 008 003 (g) eight millions million (h) millions thousands
6 993 000 (i) 258 499 999 257 500 000
❷ (a) A (b) C (c) C (d) B (e) A
❸ (a) 769 010 000 769 000 000 800 000 000
(b) 5 210 180 000 5 211 000 000 5 300 000 000
(c) 1 094 500 000 1 094 000 000 1 000 000 000
❹ (a) any digit from 5 to 9 (b) 4 (c) 5
(d) any digit from 0 to 9 (e) any digit from 0 to 4 ❺ 555 321

5.3 Four operations of numbers

❶ × √ When working on a number sentence involving four operations, perform all the multiplication and division first and then perform the addition and subtraction. ❷ (b) 600
(c) 165 (d) 800 ❸ (a) 42 (b) 26 460
(c) 301 (d) 671 ❹ (a) D (b) D (c) A
❺ (a) (2000÷4−323)×5 = 885 (b) (600÷50+76)×23 = 2024 ❻ (a) Any number except 0 (b) 2 (c) Any number except 0
(d) 4

5.4 Properties of whole number operations (1)

❶ (a) 88 (b) 330 (c) 34 (d) 76 (e) 80
(f) 89 (b)(d)(f) ❷ (b) 132 32 − 21
(c) 89 (d) 19 + 919 (e) a b c +
❸ (a) 400 (b) 303 (c) 245 (d) 4820

Answers

(e) 461　(f) 530　④ Method 1: 1600 − 520 − 480 = 600 (bikes)　Method 2: 1600 − (520 + 480) = 600 (bikes)　⑤ (a) 190　165　−　(b) 42　−　27　⑥ (a) 200　(b) 3073　(c) 450　(d) 590　(e) 144　(f) 4000　(g) 790

5.5 Properties of whole number operations (2)

① (a) 17 ÷ 25　(b) 25 × 4　(c) 128 ×　(d) 17 ÷　Division ×　② (a) 7　(b) 25　(c) 25　(d) 10　(e) 10　(f) 120　③ (a) B　(b) C　(c) A　④ Method 1: 240 ÷ 12 ÷ 2 = 10 (pupils)　Method 2: 240 ÷ (12 × 2) = 10 (pupils)　⑤ 240 ÷ 4 ÷ 6 = 10 (pounds)　⑥ (a) 12　(b) 1008

5.6 Properties of whole number operations (3)

① 3　3　3　3　3　3　multiplied　divided　quotient　division　×　÷　② (b) √　(c) ×　(d) ×　(e) √　③ (a) divided by 8　(b) unchanged　(c) 71　(d) 1150　10　20　④ (a) 20　(b) 16 r 100　(c) 70 r 20　(d) 70 r 200　⑤ (a) 48　(b) 125　(c) 48　(d) 80　(e) 13　(f) 10　⑥ (a) B　(b) D　(c) D　⑦ (a) It is increased by 40　(b) It is decreased by 10　(c) 4800　(d) Yes, it remains unchanged.

5.7 Roman numerals to 1000

①

Roman symbol	Value in digit
I	1
V	5
X	10
L	50
C	100
D	500
M	1000

② 13　56　95　104　400　600　1900　2007

③

Roman numeral	MM	MD	MDLII	MCM	MCMXCV	MMXVI
Year	2000	1500	1552	1900	1995	2016

④

Year	2010	2011	2012	2013	2014	2015	2020	2100
Roman numeral	MMX	MMXI	MMXII	MMXIII	MMXIV	MMXV	MMXX	MMC

5.8 Solving problems in statistics

① Choir　Science and ICT　10　No, because it is not clear if a pupil could participate in one or more than one school club.　② (a) 42 cm　(b) 1st place: Bob, 2nd place: Alvin, 3rd place: Linda, 4th place: Peter, and 5th place: May.　③ (a) 5400　(b)

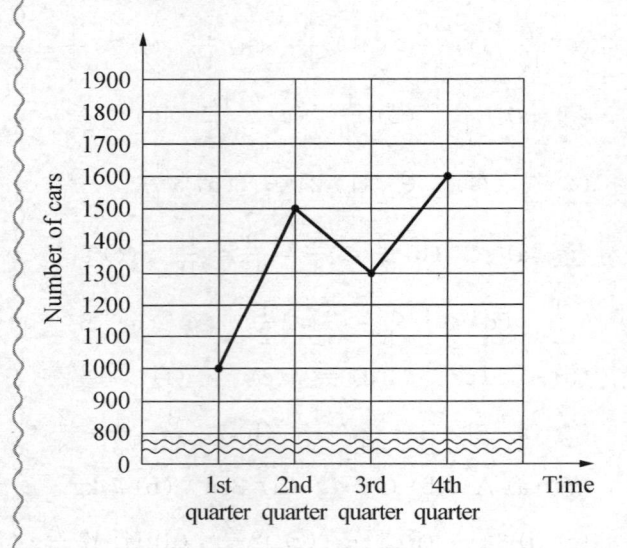

(c) (i) ×　(ii) ×,　(iii) ×　(iv) √　④ (a)

	Usage (m³)	Unit price	Charge
Fresh water used	79	120p	9480p
Used water returned to sewer	73	227p	16 571p
		Total charge	26 051p

(b) 79 m³ or 79 000 litres　(c) £260.51　(d) answer may vary

Unit test 5

① (a) 920　(b) 390　(c) 802　(d) 96　(e) 318　(f) 60　(g) 88　(h) 160　(i) 48　(j) $\frac{19}{30}$　(k) 32　(l) 9100　② (a) $80\frac{4}{7}$

Answers

(b) 37 620   (c) $30\frac{22}{23}$ ❸ (a) 4   (b) 3240
(c) 2240   (d) 750   (e) 40 572   (f) 281 880
(g) $3\frac{8}{35}$ (h) $\frac{2}{9}$ (i) $1\frac{25}{28}$ ❹ (a) 1000s
1000   (b) 120   4   5   6   (c) $\frac{5}{6}$ (d) 6   7
(e) 560 000   (f) 10 700 000   10 800 000
(g) $\frac{6}{100}$ (h) 16   2400   Answer may vary, for
example $240 \div 8$ or $120 \div 4$ (i) 128   (j) 17
1000   (k) 409   999   (l) 15   (m) 6
(n) 3000   ❺ (a) √   (b) ×   (c) ×
(d) ×   (e) ×   ❻ (a) D   (b) C   (c) A
(d) A   (e) B   ❼ (a) $150 \times 2 + 150 = 450$
(b) $(48 - 16) \times 25 \div 8 = 100$ (c) $125 \times 8 + 12 = 1012$ ❽ (a) $780 \times 3 + 66 = 2406$ (books)
(b) (i) $(200 + 180) \div 4 = 95$ (km)
(ii) $315 \div (95 + 10) = 3$ (hours)   (c) $(12 \times 2 + 12) \times 3 + 7 = 115$ (footballs)   (d) Red-ink pens: $(244 + 12) \div (7 + 1) = 32$ (boxes)
Green-ink pens: $32 \times 7 - 12 = 212$ (boxes)
(e) (i) 560   (ii)

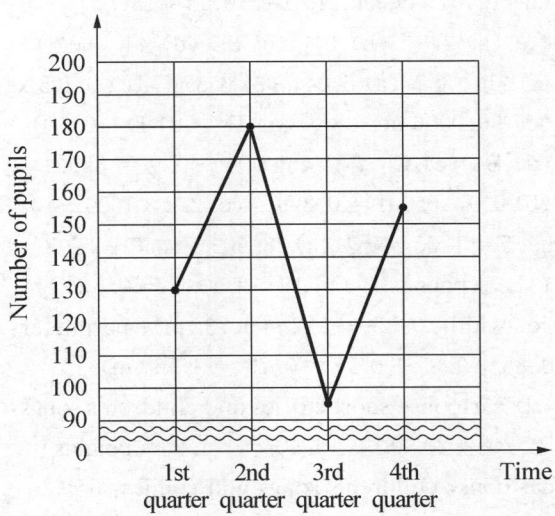

(iii) No. The total number of pupils divided by 6 year groups could be an estimate number of pupils for each year group, which is around or less than 100 pupils. (Answer may vary.)

Chapter 6 Addition and subtraction of decimal numbers

6.1 Moving the decimal point (1)

❶ (a) 1.2   (b) 12   (c) 120   (d) 31.2
(e) 312   (f) 3120   (g) 4.09   (h) 0.409
(i) 0.0409   (j) 0.135   (k) 0.0135   (l) 0.001 35
❷ (a) right   one   two   three   left   0
(b) 10   one   right   (c) two   left   (d) 0.001
420   100   (e) 879   87.9   (f) 100   (g) 103
100   (h) $\frac{1}{100}$ ❸ (a) ×   100   (b) ÷   10
(c) ÷   (d) 10   (e) 3.256   (f) 99 920
❹ (a) C   (b) B   (c) A   (d) C   ❺ $23.80 \times 100 = 2380$ (pounds)   ❻ (a) Simon, James
and Alvin   (b) Her score may be between 9.91~9.95.   ❼ Yes, it does. $12.1 \div 10 = 1.21$.
Moving the decimal point will change the value of the number. The difference between 12.1 and 1.21 is 10.89.   ❽ 1.7

6.2 Moving the decimal point (2)

❶ (a) 25   (b) 90.01   (c) 1.4   (d) 1351
(e) 2.566   (f) 10.01   (g) 0.29   (h) 0.555
(i) 0.8   (j) 60   (k) 630   (l) 20   ❷ (a) 0.9
(b) 0.009   (c) 1510   (d) 0.7   (e) 480
(f) 0.789   (g) 20 200   (h) 9.04   (i) 130
(j) 8   ❸ (a) $1000 \times 0.067 = 67$ (b) $4.6 \times \frac{1}{100} = 0.046$ (c) $1.5 \times 100 - 7.5 \times 10 = 75$
(d) 10   (e) $9.45 \times 10 \div 10 \div 10 \times 100 = 94.5$
❹ (a) 30   660   (b) 50.5   (c) 9.009
(d) 80.04   (e) 10   11 000   ❺ 1st: pony;
2nd: bunny; 3rd: puppy; 4th: baby elephant.
Hint: Method 1: Compare them in m: 0.9 km
= 900 m   1.67 km = 1670 m   1 km 200 m = 1200 m.   400 m < 900 m < 1200 m < 1670 m.
Method 2: Compare them in km: 400 m = 0.4 km   1km 200 m = 1.2 km.   0.4 km < 0.9 km < 1.2 km < 1.67 km.
❻ 569 210   89.7   9010   501 330

6.3 Addition of decimals

❶ (a) 1.2   (b) 3   (c) 8.9   (d) 1.43

223

Answers

(e) 2.3 (f) 7.07 (g) 0.09 (h) 8.5 (i) 4.9
(j) 0.018 (k) 15.63 (l) 1 ❷ (b) 92
(c) 120.97 (d) 97.9 (e) 17.189
(f) 1010.91 ❸ (a) 7.5 pounds (b) 4.55 m
(c) 9.02 l (d) 5.1 km (e) 1 (f) $\frac{585}{1000}$
❹ (a) $8.44+6=14.44$ (b) $100+100\times 0.759 = 175.9$ (c) $0.03 \times 1000 + 69.33 = 99.33$ ❺ $1.3+0.15+1.3+1.05=3.8$ (km)
❻ $80 \times 3 - 0.3 \times 2 = 239.4$ (cm)

6.4 Subtraction of decimals

❶ (a) 0.1 (b) 0.04 (c) 0.004 (d) 5
(e) 0.4 (f) 1.8 (g) 4.8 (h) 0.94 (i) 2.6
(j) 5.5 (k) 0.99 (l) 1.06 ❷ (b) 12.53
(c) 53.93 (d) 9.31 (e) 46.75 (f) 86.49
❸ (a) 7.92 pounds (b) 4.86 km (c) 35.07 m²
(d) $\frac{275}{1000}$ (e) 0.42 l (f) $\frac{52}{100}$ ❹ (a) $0.8 - 0.8 \times \frac{1}{10} = 0.72$ (b) $21.9 \div 10 + (0.58 - 0.25) = 2.52$ ❺ $9.8 - 6.2 + 3.6 = 7.2$
❻ $66.8 \times 2 = 133.6$ (km)

6.5 Addition and subtraction of decimals (1)

❶ (a) 11 (b) 4.72 (c) 0.965 (d) 0.15
(e) 0.506 (f) 1 (g) 0.044 (h) 11.14
(i) 0.901 (j) 5.76 (k) 9 (l) 12.19
❷ (a) 2.06 (b) 24.7 (c) 6.7 (d) 2.13
(e) 10.4 (f) 8 ❸ (a) $63.5 - 24.5 = 39$
(b) $30.52 + (30.52 - 8.8) = 52.24$ (c) $42.62 \div 2 + 2.8 = 24.11$ ❹ $100 - 41.8 - 38.2 = 20$ (pounds) ❺ $(3.4 + 5.6) \times 2 + 1.5 \times 2 = 21$ (cm) ❻ $4.75 + 23.8 + 10.25 + 6.2 = 45$ (pounds) ❼ 16.08 23.54

6.6 Addition and subtraction of decimals (2)

❶ (a) 14.2 (b) 3.07 (c) 0.9 (d) 2.52
(e) 12.1 (f) 12.5 (g) 8.95 (h) 0.001
(i) 6.08 (j) 9.58 (k) 29.17 (l) 0.037
❷ (a) 148.43 (b) 25.47 (c) 38 (d) 5.46
(e) 167.1 (f) 0.985 (g) 64 (h) 550
❸ (a) $90.5 - (7.1 + 12.9) = 70.5$

(b) $(56.04 + 0.99) - (14.6 - 0.26) = 42.69$
(c) $(6.1 - 0.61) \times 100 = 549$ ❹ $8.92 \times 10 + 21.45 = 110.65$ (kg) ❺ (a) 3400
(b) 49.755 ❻ $1 + \frac{3}{10} + \frac{7}{100} = 1.37$ (bags)

6.7 Practice and exercise (2)

❶ (a) 88 (b) 0.5 (c) 910 (d) 7.1
(e) 0.765 (f) 2.7 (g) 231 (h) 5 (i) 1.94
(j) 10.5 (k) 350 (l) 766 ❷ (a) 213.67
(b) 29.636 (c) 81.32 (d) 9.729
❸ (a) 12.904 (b) 0.78 (c) 2250
(d) 3232 (e) 103 (f) 1000 ❹ 2 km 400 m > 2040 m > 0.24 km ❺ (a) 201.5 20.15
(b) one left (c) 501 (d) 100 (e) 71.0006
(f) 132 ❻ pencil box: $(70.5 - 19.5) \div (1 + 2) = 17$ (pounds) schoolbag: $17 \times 2 + 19.5 = 53.5$ (pounds) ❼ $C = 3.01 \times 100 = 301$
$B = 301 \times 1000 = 301\,000$

Unit test 6

❶ (a) 0.006 (b) 1.9 (c) 480 (d) 30.55
(e) 7.08 (f) 20 (g) 0.5 (h) 300.8 (i) 36
❷ (a) 110.108 (b) 258.22 (c) 22.057
(d) 19.01 (check: $19.01 - 0.11 = 18.9$.)
❸ (a) 2.8 (b) 10 (c) 2 (d) 44 (e) 1
(f) 210 ❹ (a) 5.04 (b) 3.856 (c) 0.505 kg
(d) 96.0096 m² ❺ (a) D (b) D (c) B
(d) B (e) C ❻ (a) $900 - 0.9 = 899.1$
(b) $0.9 - 0.001 = 0.899$ (c) $2.2 \times 1000 - 10 \times 99.5 = 1205$ ❼ (a) $28.60 + 74.50 + 28.60 = 131.7$ (pounds) (b) $19 - 9.1 \times 2 = 0.8$ (kg)
(c) width: $0.85 - 0.12 = 0.73$ (m); perimeter: $0.85 + 0.85 + 0.73 + 0.73 = 3.16$ (m)
(d) cartoons, short stories and children's songs: $54.70 + 20.88 + 19.40 = 94.98$ (pounds) cartoons, children's songs and comics: $54.70 + 25.10 + 19.40 = 99.20$ (pounds) short stories, children's songs and comics: $20.88 + 19.40 + 25.10 = 65.38$ (pounds)

Answers

Chapter 7　Introduction to positive and negative numbers

7.1　Positive and negative numbers (1)

❶ 10℃　0℃　−10℃　❷ Positive numbers: 3.2　+20.1　37　Negative numbers: −18　−6.9　−$\frac{9}{10}$　❸ Link Above zero to Below zero, Sell to Buy, Deposit to Withdraw, Receive to Give, Lose to Win　❹ (a) can (b) cannot　❺ ① and C　② and D　③ and B　④ and A　❻ −10　−2　+10　−15　+5　+12　❼ (a) Bills for water, electricity and gas: −270, phone bill: −180　(b) Other expenses: −2850　❽ Place B, Place C

❸

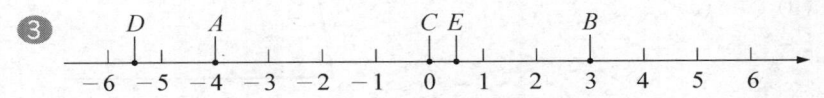

```
       D    A          C E      B
  ├──┼──┼──┼──┼──┼──┼──┼──┼──┼──┼──┼──┤
 −6  −5 −4 −3 −2 −1  0  1  2  3  4  5  6
```

❹ (a) right　2　(b) left　4　(c) −5 (d) +2.5　(e) +3　−3　(f) 6　❺ right

❽

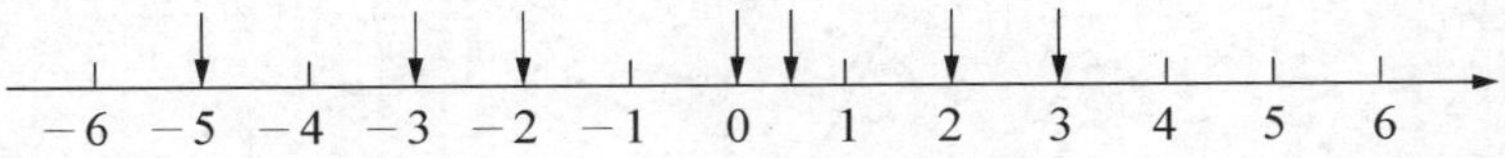

```
        ↓      ↓   ↓    ↓↓↓   ↓
  ├──┼──┼──┼──┼──┼──┼──┼──┼──┼──┼──┼──┤
 −6  −5 −4 −3 −2 −1  0  1  2  3  4  5  6
```

(a) −3 and 3, 2 and −2　(b) 5 units　❾ −3　−21　❿ 2　3　−7.5　−10　2.5　−10　+6　16

7.4　Number lines (2)

❶ (a) <　(b) <　(c) >　(d) >　(e) > (f) >　(g) >　(h) <　(i) <　❷ (a) +6　+5　+4　+3 (answers may vary)　(b) 0　+1　+2　+3 (answers may vary)　(c) 15 (d) right　5　left　8　13　❸ −6.5 < −4 < −3 < 0 < +2 < +7　❹ (a) ×　(b) √ (c) ×　(d) ×　❺ (a) D　(b) B　(c) A (d) B　❻ 19 nautical miles　❼ (a) √ (b) ×　(c) ×　(d) √　(e) ×　(f) × ❽ (a) left　(b) 8 cm　(c) 28 cm

Unit test 7

❶ (a) −200　(b) left　7　(c) +4, 1.7, 3, +2; −3, −5.6, −$\frac{1}{2}$, −1, −8; −5.6,

7.2　Positive and negative numbers (2)

❶ (a) 5 passengers getting off the bus. (b) −£120　(c) −5　+125　−20　105 (d) 505　495　(e) +1.5　75　❷ (a) √ (b) √　(c) ×　(d) ×　❸ (a) D　(b) B (c) D　(d) C　❹ (a) Grace is the tallest. Chloe is the shortest.　(b) 18 cm　❺ (a) −5 +9　(b) 20:00　24:00　7:00　21:00 (c) −8　−13　+4

7.3　Number lines (1)

❶ (a) 30　40　50　60　70　(b) 2　1　0 −1　−2　−3　−4　(c) −5　−10　−15 (d) −200　−100　0　100　❷ A = 2 B = −5　C = −1　D = 3.5

left　❻ positive　less than　greater ❼ (a) D　(b) C　(c) C

−8;　1.7, 0, −$\frac{1}{2}$, −1, +2;　−3, 3 (d) −1　7　(e) −2　(f) 3℃　−1℃ (g) There were 4 fewer people.　(h) right (i) −40　(j) west　−30　(k) 99　85 ❷ (a) ×　(b) ×　(c) ×　(d) ×　(e) × ❸ (a) D　(b) A　(c) B　(d) D　(e) D ❹ (a) (i) Area 2　(ii) Area 5　(iii) Area 7 and Area 3　(b) 3 km to the north (c) (i) right　27 cm　(ii) 6 cm　(iii) 1050 cm (d) (i) Ben's house is 450 m away from the school. Lily's house is 550 m away from the school.　(ii) 90 m per minute　(iii) east of the school; 70 m away from the school; east of the market, 220 m away from it; west of the post office, 280 m away from it.

225

Answers

Chapter 8 Geometry and measurement (1)

8.1 Knowing circles (1)
① (a) circle radius centre (b) centre radius (c) twice (d) 4 m ② (a) C (b) C (c) A ③ 1.5 cm 2.0 cm ④ answers may vary

8.2 Knowing circles (2)
① (a) equal equal (b) $d = r \times 2$ $r = d \div 2$ 10 (c) 3 1.5 ② circles drawn as described. ③ two circles drawn as described.

8.3 Knowing circles (3)
① (a) one infinitely many infinitely many (b) diameter twice centre (c) 5 (d) 72 cm²
② Figure (e) Figure (a) Figure (b)
③ (a) √ (b) × (c) √ (d) √ (e) √
④

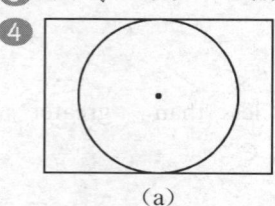

(a)

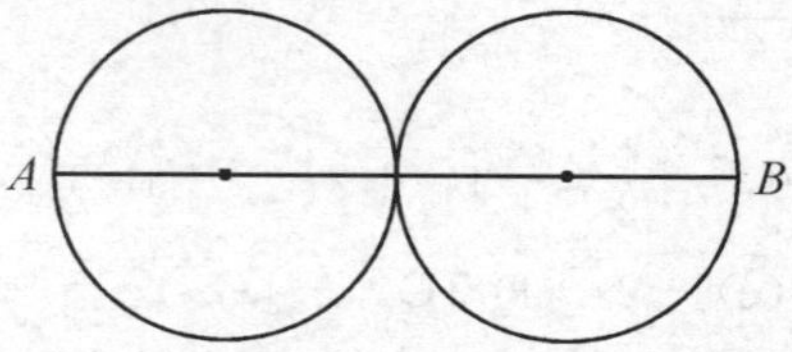

(b)

8.4 Angle concept and notation
① (a) angle vertex sides ∠ (b) A D
② (a) ∠AOB angel AOB (b) ∠1 angle 1 (c) 7 correct markings of the angles from ∠1 to ∠7 ③ (a) ∠3 (b) ∠4 ④ (a) 12 (b) DAG BCI or ECI (c) ∠DAF ∠GBE and so on ⑤ AOF or FOA 4 BAD or DAB or BAO or OAB

8.5 Measurement of angles (1)
① (a) 360 180 90 (b) acute obtuse reflex (c) 2 4 2 (d) 30 acute (e) right (f) straight (g) 22 112 292 (h) 60
② (a) A (b) D (c) C (d) A (e) D
③ (a) × (b) × (c) √ (d) √

④ Acute angles: 76° 2° 45° 89° Obtuse angles: 125° 91° 179° 103° ⑤ Acute angle Full angle Straight angle ⑥ 5 3 2 10

8.6 Measurement of angles (2)
① (a) right full (b) 90 right (c) 90-degree (d) right acute obtuse ② (a) B (b) C D (c) A D (d) D ③ 60° 68° 125° 45° 125° ④ 30° 60° 90° 45° 45° 90° ⑤ All √

8.7 Measurement of angles (3)
① (a) vertex (b) centre (c) O B (d) ∠AOB ②

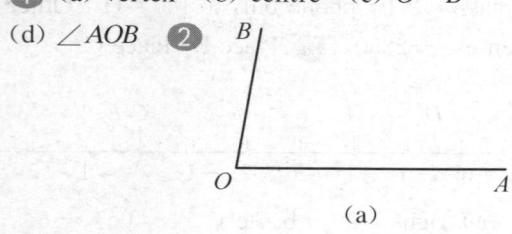

(a)

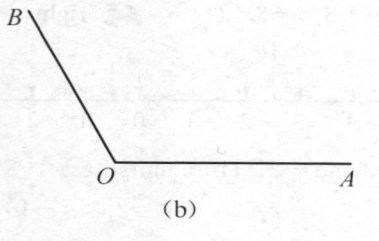

(b)

③

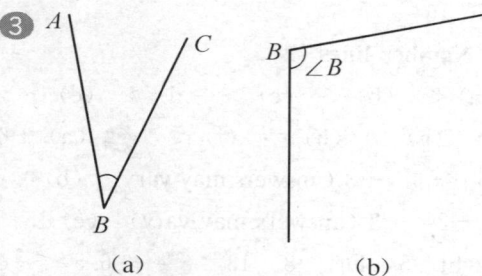

(a)

(b)

(c)

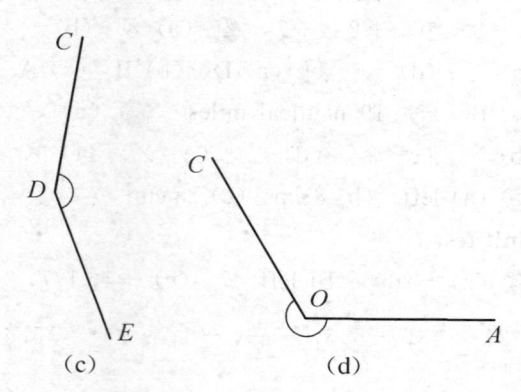

(d)

226

Answers

④ Angles drawn are 35°, 100°, 150°, 240°
⑤ (a) Angle should measure at 80° (d) 50° 50°

8.8 Calculation of angles

① (a) 60° 130° 65° 345° (b) 83°
(c) 80° 36° (d) 40° ② (a) 45° (b) 20°
(c) 75° (d) ∠1 = 50° ∠2 = 140° (e) 150°
(f) ∠2 = 125° ∠3 = 55° ∠4 = 125°
③ 70° ④ ∠BOF = 60° ∠AOE = 30°
∠EOF = 90°

8.9 Angles and sides in polygons

①

Name of polygon	No. of angles	No. of sides	Figure
Triangle	3	3	
Quadrilateral	4	4	
Pentagon	5	5	
Hexagon	6	6	
Octagon	8	8	

② Polygons: squares, equilateral triangles;
Non-polygons: straight lines, cubes, circles, cuboids, prisms ③ (a) √ (b) × (c) ×
(d) √ (e) √ (f) × (g) √ ④ × √
(60° 2.4 cm) √ (between 128° and 129°, 1.1 cm) √ (90°, 2.1 cm) √ (135°, 1 cm)
× N/A √ (108°, 1.5 cm)
⑤ They add up to a straight angle, i.e., 180°;
∠6 = 70° ⑥ All the exterior angles add up to 360°; no; in a regular polygon, they are equal.

Unit test 8

① (a) 26 (b) 125 (c) 111 (d) 81 (e) 0
(f) 1 (g) 280 (h) 3 (i) 4 (j) 90
(k) 1616 (l) 8 ② (a) 1152 (b) 91
(c) 4200 (d) 99 000 (e) 2400 (f) 4388
(g) 7500 (h) 6 ③ (a) 360 full 4
(b) straight right 60° (c) radius
(d) symmetrical diameter 90 centre (e) a straight angle a right angle (f) 79° (g) 150°
(h) 15° (i) isosceles triangles, equilateral triangles, rectangles, squares and circles
④ (a) B (b) B (c) A (d) D (e) D
(f) B ⑤ (a) (b) 135°

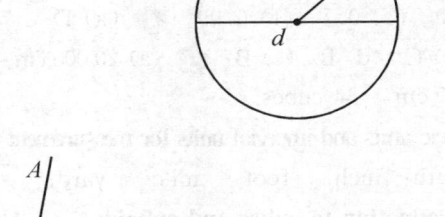

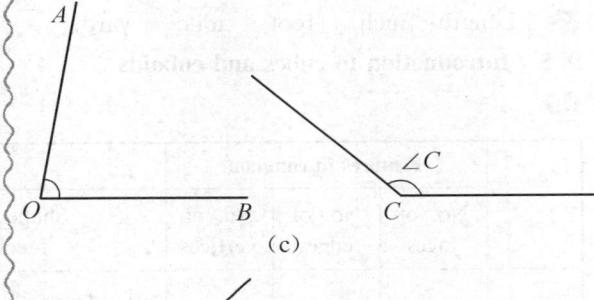

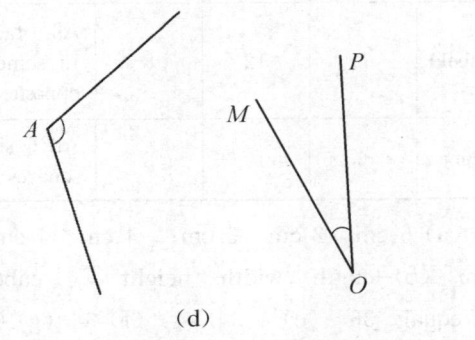

⑥ (a) 28° (b) 50° (c) ∠2 = 50° ∠3 = 130° (d) 120°

Chapter 9 Geometry and measurement (2)

9.1 Volume

① (a) volume (b) 2 3 ② (a) ×
(b) × (c) √ (d) × ③ (a) unchanged

227

Answers

(b) unchanged (c) unchanged
④ (a) unchanged (b) unchanged
(c) unchanged ⑤ The space taken up by the risen water level is the volume of the stone.

9.2 Cubic centimetres and cubic metres (1)

① (a) 1 1 (b) 5 (c) 8 8 ② 24 24 24 24 24 different the same ③ 19 31 5 7 ④ (a) √ (b) × (c) ×
⑤ (a) 30 cm³ (b) 385 cm³

9.3 Cubic centimetres and cubic metres (2)

① (a) 1 1 1 000 000 1 000 000 1 000 000 (b) length area volume
② (a) cm (b) m³ (c) m³ (d) cm³
③ (a) 2 800 000 (b) 8.5 (c) 0.0615 (d) 40 000 (e) 0.7 (f) 6.99 ④ (a) D (b) D (c) C (d) B (e) B ⑤ (a) 20 000 cm³ (b) 64 000 cm³   44 cubes

9.4 Metric units and imperial units for measurement

① Length: inch foot mile yard;

9.5 Introduction to cubes and cuboids

①

	Features in common			Different features		
	No. of faces	No. of edges	No. of vertices	Shape of faces	Area of faces	Length of edges
Cuboid	6	12	8	All 6 faces are rectangles. In some cases, the two opposite sides are squares.	The areas of two opposite sides are equal.	The lengths of the edges of the opposite sides are equal.
Cube	6	12	8	All 6 sides are identical squares	All the areas of the 6 sides are equal.	All the lengths of 12 edges are equal.

② (a) 5 cm 2 cm 3 cm; 4 cm 4 cm 4 cm (b) length width height (c) cube (d) equal 36 (e) 4 4 4 (f) 3 (g) 6 rectangles squares rectangles (h) cube
③ (a) × (b) √ (c) × (d) × (e) × (f) × ④ 34.8 cm ⑤ 45 cm ⑥ The length is 10 cm. The width is 7.5 cm. The height is 5 cm. ⑦ 36 cm

9.6 Volumes of cubes and cuboids (1)

① width height w h length length a

Weight/Mass: ounce pound; Volume/Capacity: gallon pint ② (a) 1760 3 12 (b) 16 16 5 (c) 8 0.5 ③ (a) feet (b) miles (c) gallons (d) acres
④ (a) 3280 (b) 10 758 400 (c) 0.000 001 10.7584 ⑤

	miles per hour (mph)	kilometres per hour (km/h)
Motorway	70	112
Dual carriageway	70	112
Single carriageway	60	96
Built-up area	30	48

⑥ 0.99 × 2.2 × 100 + 12 × 2 × 10 × 2.2 = 745.8 (pounds) ⑦ 1.75 × 4000 = 7000 m²; 7000 ÷ 1 000 000 = 0.007 km² ⑧ 0.22 × 50 × 68 × 1.6 = 1197 (km)

② (a) 18 cm³ (b) 48 cm³ (c) 64 cm³
③ (a) 96 cm³ (b) 729 cm³ ④ (a) 0.45 (b) 3 900 000 (c) 216 (d) 8400 (e) 5 (f) 250 (g) $5bh$ ($abh - 2ab$) ⑤ (a) 24 × 24 ÷ 2 × 5 = 1440 (m³) (b) 480 ÷ 12 × 40 × 40 = 64 000 (cm³) (c) 100 ÷ 10 ÷ 2 = 5 (cm) (d) 4 × 2 × 0.4 = 3.2 (m³) ⑥ 54 cm³

9.7 Volumes of cubes and cuboids (2)

① (a) 24 000 (b) 3375 (c) 64 (d) 91 000 (e) 240 (f) 27 ② (a) × (b) × (c) ×

228

Answers

(d) ✓ ③ (a) $60 \times 60 \times 60 = 216\,000$ (cm³)
(b) $60 \times 60 \times 60 \div 90 \div 40 = 60$ (cm)
(c) 486 cm³ (d) $(8 \times 12 - 10 \times 4 - 7 \times 4) \div 4 = 7$ $10 \times 7 \times 7 = 490$ (cm³) (e) $60 \times 50 \times 0.1 \div 5 = 60$ (times) (f) 8000 cm³ 62.4 kg
④ First combination: Put the 4 cubes into a cuboid: $4 \times 1 \times 1$ $(4+1+1) \times 4 = 24$ The length of the cube edge $= 120 \div 24 = 5$ (cm) The volume $= 500$ (cm³); Second combination: Put the 4 cubes into a cuboid: $2 \times 2 \times 1$ $(2+2+1) \times 4 = 20$ The length of the cube edge $= 120 \div 20 = 6$ (cm) The volume $= 864$ (cm³)

9.8 Volume and capacity (1)

① (a) volume capacity (b) volume capacity litre millilitre (c) 1000 1 1000
② ml 1 m³ 1 1 1 ③ (a) 11 000
(b) 7 (c) 3500 (d) 78.008 (e) 4.4
(f) 0.0202 (g) 230 (h) 4380 (i) 8.012, 8012 (j) 6 80 ④ (a) ml (b) l (c) l
(d) m³ (e) l (f) ml ⑤ $5000 \div 800 = 6.25$; 7 days. ⑥ $330 \div 3 = 110$ (l) The capacity of the freezer is 110 litres; $110 \times 2 = 220$ (l) The capacity of the fridge is 220 litres
⑦ Bucket A: 6.6 litres, Bucket B: 4.4 litres

9.9 Volume and capacity (2)

① (a) 180 (b) 40 (c) 216 (d) 8000
② (a) ✓ (b) ✗ (c) ✗ ③ $95 \times 64 \times 40 = 243\,200$ cm³ ④ 850 litres ⑤ 61.2 litres
⑥ 16 200 cm³ 16.2 litres ⑦ $22\,500 \div 1000 = 22.5$ m³ $22.5 \div 4.5 \div 2.5 = 2$ (m)
⑧ (a) $30 \times 25 \times 24 = 18\,000$ cm³ $= 18$ litres
(b) $3000 \div 30 \div 25 = 4$ (cm) ⑨ 0.5 m

Unit test 9

① (a) 216 cm³ (b) 56 cm³ ② (a) 2 000 050
(b) 27 000 (c) 4 (d) length ③ (a) ✗
(b) ✗ (c) ✗ (d) ✗ ④ (a) C (b) B
(c) B ⑤ The capacity of the fridge: 145.53 litres; The capacity of the freezer: 107.73 litres. ⑥ 468 kg. ⑦ 13 cm ⑧ 22.5 cm
⑨ (a) 40 cm³ (b) Yes, it will; 400 millilitres

Chapter 10 Factors, multiples and prime numbers

10.1 Meaning of integers and divisibility

① whole numbers natural numbers integers
② (a) D (b) B (c) C ③ (a) Positive 0
(b) dividend divisor; a dividend a divisor integer zero (c) 1 5 (d) 2 (e) 3 or 6 or 12 ④ Natural numbers: 15 0 100 Integers: 15 -1 0 100 Positive integers: 15 100 ⑤ ①⑤ ②③④⑥ ⑥ $6 \div 2$ $8 \div 2$ $10 \div 2$ $12 \div 2$ $20 \div 2$ $6 \div 3$ $9 \div 3$ $12 \div 3$ $15 \div 3$ $10 \div 5$ $15 \div 5$ $20 \div 5$ $20 \div 10$
⑦ Yes. Let $a \div c = m$ and $b \div c = n$. If a and b are both divisible by c, then both m and n are integers. Therefore, $m+n$, $m-n$ and $m \times n$ are also integers, that is, the sum, difference and product of a and b are also divisible by c.

10.2 Factors and multiples

① (a) B (b) C (c) D ② (a) multiple factor of a (b) 4 3 (c) 1, 2, 3, 6 (d) 5 or 15 (e) 3 (f) 5 ③ 1, 3, 9 ④ With 1 factor: 1 With 2 factors: 2 31 61 With more than 2 factors: 9 39 57 91 ⑤ 4 combinations (1×24 2×12 3×8 4×6)
⑥ 3 factors: 4 9; 4 factors: 6 8 10 14 15; 5 factors: 16 6 factors: 12 18

10.3 Square numbers and cube numbers

① (a) D (b) B (c) D (d) C (e) D
② (a) square number (b) cube number
(c) 4 100 (d) 8 64 (e) 1 and 64
(f) 13 824 ③ 110; 44 100 ④ Square numbers: 1 64 100 121 144; Cube numbers: 1 8 64 1000; Numbers that are neither square numbers nor cube numbers: 5 99 ⑤ (a) 13 (b) 999 (c) 9097 ⑥ 1 64 729 4096

10.4 Numbers divisible by 2 and 5

① (a) D (b) B (c) C ② (a) 0 or 2 or 4 or 6 or 8 (b) 0 or 5 (c) 11 10 (d) 90
(e) 1 2 3 ③ 12 14 16 ④ 3 5 7

Answers

5 4. They are: 120 210 150 510
6 The sum of all the digits in the value places is a multiple of 9.   3330

10.5 Prime numbers, composite numbers and prime factorisation (1)

1 (a) B (b) B (c) B   **2** (a) 1 2 3
(b) 2 4   (c) 5, 23 18   (d) 10   (e) $13 = 2+11$ $16 = 3+13 = 5+11$ (f) 2 and 3
3 2 3 11   **4** 20   **5** 5 and 31   7 and 29   13 and 23   17 and 19   **6** (a) 4 6 8
(b) 2   (c) 9   (d) 3 5 7   **7** 29 31 43 61 97   **8** 2, 3, 5 and 7   If a two-digit number is a composite number, then it can be expressed as a product of two numbers, which cannot be both greater than 9 (otherwise it will be 100 or greater). In other words, one of the factors must be equal to or less than 9, which must be a multiple of 2, 3, 5 or 7. Therefore, if it is not divisible by 2, 3, 5 and 7, it must be a prime number.

10.6 Prime numbers, composite numbers and prime factorisation (2)

1 (a) D (b) C (c) C (d) C (e) B
2 (a) prime numbers   (b) 3 6   (c) $20 = 2 \times 2 \times 5$ (d) 1 2 4 7 14 28; 2 2 7
3 (b) $21 = 3 \times 7$ (c) $60 = 2 \times 2 \times 3 \times 5$
(d) $100 = 2 \times 2 \times 5 \times 5$ **4** 24 (Hint: $143 = 11 \times 13$)   **5** 6 7 8 (Hint: $336 = 2^4 \times 3 \times 7$)
6 Yes. Group 1: 44 45 78 105; Group 2: 40 63 65 99 (Hint: The factorisation of the eight numbers is: $40 = 2 \times 2 \times 2 \times 5$ $44 = 2 \times 2 \times 11$ $45 = 3 \times 3 \times 5$ $63 = 3 \times 3 \times 7$ $65 = 5 \times 13$ $78 = 2 \times 3 \times 13$ $99 = 3 \times 3 \times 11$ $105 = 3 \times 5 \times 7$)

Unit test 10

1 (a) B (b) B (c) D (d) C (e) D
(f) B   **2** (a) 1 1   (b) 3 9   (c) 2
(d) square mumber   (e) 16 25 36 49; 8; 64   (f) 21 23; 21   (g) $18 = 2 \times 3 \times 3$
(h) 6   (i) 23 or 41   **3** (a) (i) $34 = 2 \times 17$
(ii) $36 = 2 \times 2 \times 3 \times 3$ (b) (i) 34   (ii) 827
(iii) 181   (c) 48   (d) 109.5 m

End of year test

1 (a) 30 000   (b) 9   (c) 25   (d) 0.35
(e) 40   (f) 3107   (g) 7.01   (h) 0.09
(i) 0.18   (j) 6   (k) $\frac{1}{20}$ (l) $8\frac{12}{13}$
2 (a) 85 899   (b) 37.75   (c) 96.43
(d) 290 r 20   (e) 370 252   check: $370\,252 \div 604 = 613$ or $370\,252 \div 613 = 604$ (f) 300 r 25   check: $300 \times 45 + 25 = 135\,25$
3 (a) 20   (b) 5610   (c) 7273   (d) 94.88
(e) 1110.2   (f) 8   (g) $1\frac{13}{14}$ (h) $2\frac{5}{11}$
4 (a) 6030   (b) 4.038   (c) 12   (d) 79 000
(e) 4.5   (f) $\frac{4}{11}$ $\frac{4}{7}$ 1   (g) 10   11; −3   −5.5   −7; 11   10   0   −3   −5.5   −7
(h) 2 637 007 000   2 637 007   (i) 56 630 000   57 000 000   (j) 10   2.07   (k) 1.392   696 000   0.696   (l) 3   3   (m) 30   (n) 2   2   2   3
(o) 30   (p) 3   (q) 1   64   (r) 60°   (s) 108°
(t) 15°   **5** (a) 1   180   (b) 8   240
6 (a) A   (b) D   (c) A   (d) B   A   (e) D
(f) B   (g) D   (h) C   (i) C
7

Angles drawn are $\angle AOC = 70°$, $\angle COB = 70°$; circle radius 1 cm   **8** (a) 864 km
(b) 540 cm³   (c) (i) Supermarket B   (ii) 350 (thousand pounds)   (d) 123

Notes

Notes

Notes

Notes